THE ANALYTIC FIELD AND
ITS TRANSFORMATIONS

THE ANALYTIC FIELD AND ITS TRANSFORMATIONS

*Antonino Ferro and
Giuseppe Civitarese*

KARNAC

First published in 2015 by
Karnac Books Ltd
118 Finchley Road
London NW3 5HT

British Library Cataloguing in Publication Data

A C.I.P. for this book is available from the British Library

ISBN-13: 978-1-78220-182-3

Typeset by V Publishing Solutions Pvt Ltd., Chennai, India

www.karnacbooks.com

To our patients

CONTENTS

vii

ACKNOWLEDGEMENTS

Chapter One is based on Civitarese, G., & Ferro, A. (2013). The meaning and use of metaphor in analytic field theory. *Psychoanalytic Inquiry, 33*: 190–209.

Chapter Three is based on Civitarese, G., & Ferro, F. (2013). Mourning and the empty couch: A conversation between psychoanalysts. In: G. Junkers (Ed.), *The Empty Couch: Reflections on Giving up Analytic Work*, (pp. XV–XXV). Routledge: London.

Chapter Four is based on Civitarese, G., & Ferro, A. (2012). The secret of faces. Commentary on "Ways of hearing: Getting inside psychoanalysis" by Rachael Peltz. *Psychoanalytic Dialogues, 22*: 296–304.

Chapter Five is based on Ferro, A., & Civitarese, G. (2013). Espacements, *Filigrane, 22*: 55–74.

Chapter Six is based on Ferro, A., & Civitarese, G. (2013). Analysts in search of an author: Voltaire or Artemisia Gentileschi? Commentary on "Field theory in psychoanalysis, part II: Bionian field theory and contemporary interpersonal/relational psychoanalysis" by Donnel B. Stern. *Psychoanalytic Dialogues, 23*: 646–653.

Chapter Seven is based on Ferro, A., & Civitarese, G. (2014). Confrontation in the Bionian model of the analytic field. *Psychoanalytic Inquiry* in press.

Chapter Eight is based on Ferro, A. (2008). A beam of intense darkness by James Grotstein, Karnac Books, London, 2007, 382 pp. *International Journal of Psycho-Analysis, 89*: 867–884.

Chapter Nine is based on Civitarese, G. (2014). Between "other" and "other": Merleau-Ponty as a precursor of the analytic field. *Fort Da, 20*: 9–29.

Chapter Ten is based on Ferro, A. (1996). Carla's panic attacks: Insight and transformation. *International Journal of Psycho-Analysis, 77*: 997–1011.

ABOUT THE AUTHORS

Antonino Ferro is a training and supervising analyst in the Italian Psychoanalytic Society, the American Psychoanalytic Association and the International Psychoanalytical Association. He has been a visiting professor of psychoanalysis in various institutions in Europe, North America, South America and Australia. He received the Sigourney Award in 2007.

Giuseppe Civitarese, psychiatrist, Ph.D. in psychiatry and relational sciences, is a training and supervising analyst in the Italian Psychoanalytic Society (SPI) and a member of the American Psychoanalytic Association (APsaA) and of the International Psychoanalytical Association (IPA). He lives and is in private practice in Pavia, Italy. Currently, he is the editor of the *Rivista di Psicoanalisi*, the official journal of the Italian Psychoanalytic Society. He has published several books, which include: *The Intimate Room: Theory and Technique of the Analytic Field*, London 2010; *The Violence of Emotions: Bion and Post-Bionian Psychoanalysis*, London 2012; *Perdere la testa: Abiezione, conflitto estetico e critica psico-analitica* [*Losing Your Head: Abjection, Aesthetic Conflict and Psychoanalytic*

Criticism], Firenze 2012; *I sensi e L'inconscio* [*Senses and the Unconscious*], Rome 2014. He has also co-edited *L'ipocondria e il dubbio: L'approccio psicoanalitico* [*Hypochondria and Doubt: The Psychoanalytic Approach*], FrancoAngeli, Milano 2011 and (with H. Levine) *The Bion Tradition*, London, 2015.

PREFACE

In this book we present a collection of articles written jointly by its two authors over the last few years.[1] All revolve around the post-Bionian theory of the analytic field (BFT). The reason we have brought them together in a new publication is to make them readily accessible to a wider audience than the readership of the individual journals in which they were published and to meet the growing interest that this model is arousing in the world of psychoanalysis. Indeed, analytic field theory is emerging as a new paradigm in psychoanalysis. Going hand in hand with this is an ever-growing interest in Bion in general. One need only look at the sharp increase in citations in *Psychoanalytic Electronic Publishing* in recent years. A further boost is likely to come from the forthcoming publication of Bion's complete works edited by Chris Mawson and published by Karnac.

The influence of Bion has been profound not only in the United Kingdom (Donald Meltzer, Meg Harris Williams), but also in Brazil and Italy, to which he travelled several times to hold seminars, as well as in Los Angeles, where he spent the last ten years of his life. In South America, prominent Bion scholars are Paulo C. Sandler and Rafael López-Corvo. The contributions of Joan and Neville Symington in Australia and of León Grinberg in Argentina can also not go unmentioned. In Italy, there are Claudio Neri, in Rome; Roberto Basile, in Milan; Fulvio Mazzacane, Maurizio Collovà, Giovanni Foresti, Elena Molinari, and Pierluigi Politi in Pavia (co-authors with Antonino Ferro and Giuseppe Civitarese of *Sognare l'analisi; Psicoanalisi in giallo; Psicoanalisi oggi*); in Boston, Howard Levine and Lawrence Brown, editors of *Growth and Turbulence in the Container/Contained: Bion's Continuing Legacy*; in New York, Montana Katz, who has edited two *Psychoanalytic Inquiry* monographs on the field concept, as well as the volume *Metaphor and Fields: Common Ground, Common Language, and the Future of Psychoanalysis*; in San Francisco, among others, Rachael Peltz, Peter Carnochan, Peter Goldberg and, of course, Thomas Ogden; in Los Angeles, James Grotstein and Joseph Aguayo; in Paris, Monica Horovitz; and in Cape Town, Duncan Cartwright (*Containing States of Mind: Exploring Bion's Container Model in Psychoanalytic Psychotherapy*). This is only to name a few.

BFT, understood as one of the possible models of psychoanalysis that takes its inspiration from Bion, is also meeting with increasing recognition and dissemination. For example, in an article in *Psychoanalytic Review* Kernberg mentions it as one of the main theoretical currents of contemporary psychoanalysis. In a recent review of four books by Italian authors in *Contemporary Psychoanalysis*, Wendy Katz speaks of the growing attention being paid to Bion in the United States. Routledge's *Handbook of Psychoanalysis*, edited by Jeff Prager and Anthony Elliott, dedicates a specific chapter to BFT, and so on.

Bion mounts a systematic deconstruction of the principles of classical psychoanalysis. His aim, however, is not to destroy it, but rather to bring out its untapped potential and to develop ideas that have remained on its margins. In his close critical engagement with Freud he not only prescribes, but also shows, how essential it is to have a mental attitude of openness to the new and the importance of not locking oneself up inside a "religious" vision.

In its Italian version, the analytic field theory embraces Bion's both rigorous and radical spirit. BFT is a field of inquiry that refuses *a priori*, at least from its own specific perspective, to immobilise the facts of the analysis within a rigid historical or intrapsychic framework. Its intention is rather to bring out the historicity of the present, the way in which the relationship is formed instant by instant from a subtle interplay of identity and differentiation, proximity and distance. This principle resonates with the need (which Bion at some point felt) not to speak of the unconscious but of "unconscioused", replacing the noun with the verb to better reflect processuality and becoming.

The focus shifts from content to function, from *what* to *how*. The investigation looks more at the formation of meanings than meanings themselves. Investigating in depth the determinations of the shared unconscious field that is structured at every encounter between bodies and minds means investigating a horizon of meaning that is ever present. For brevity's sake we sometimes call this model intersubjective. This term is useful but potentially misleading if the stress is placed on the second part of the compound expression—which emphasises the fact that there are two interacting subjects that are exchanging things—and not on *inter* (*between*), the place where the analysis occurs. The same applies to the term "relational". In actual fact, the analyst no longer looks at the patient, but at the patient *with* himself; he lives as if involved in a shared journey.

The field is seen as that which has always been there; once the meeting has taken place, it presents itself as preliminary to the relationship with the other. Between the ego that knows, even if it is not master in his own house, and the other, also not master in its own house, a third term insinuates itself. Subject and object are not opposed, but are considered as components of a single system. The unconscious common field is accepted as an unobjectifiable assumption which cannot be taken directly as the theme of the analysis. Indirectly, however, and based on some theoretical postulates, we can see its derivatives.

So, if we adopt this principle seriously, the portrait of psychoanalysis BFT paints depicts a way of proceeding that can never take its tools for granted and consider them definitive; it is forced to engage in continual self-reflection. It can understand the other only through self-understanding, only through a radical contextualisation of the construction of meaning. What it seeks to do is to grasp the making of meaning in the mutuality of conscious and unconscious experience.

A special kind of circularity characterises the interpretive activity of the analyst, which consists in coming back each time to question the unconscious assumptions of his understanding. In this sense analysis is more like a research activity than striving to achieve a goal. I do not presume to come up with something originary. The truth of the analysis is no longer something one arrives at, it cannot be fixed or possessed; it lies rather in the experience, it *is* the experience. The answer lies in the question—or, rather, asking the question is the feature of this model that most closely corresponds to the idea that what feeds and grows the mind is the weaving of a sustainable meaning, or dreaming reality, just as in the nurturing relationship between mother and child.

It has been our constant effort in this book to refine these concepts. Not only for this reason, but also because it was not designed from the outset as a single book, it is inevitable that there are repetitions here and there and the same points are touched on several times. Our hope, however, is that instead of boring or even irritating the reader, it can be productive for the reader to go back to the same things but each time with a slightly "different" perspective, seeing a different facet each time. The pleasure will then not only be reading but also "writing" a new book along with the authors and also continuing their research work. For us ideally the consulting room should be an atelier filled with as much creative mess as we are able to tolerate.

Let us now run quickly through the various chapters of the book.

Each of the principal psychoanalytic models is underlain by certain key metaphors. For example, the archaeological and surgical metaphors, as well as that of the analyst-as-screen, all throw light on some of Freud's basic concepts. In classical psychoanalysis, however, metaphor still tends to be an illegitimate or secondary element. Analytic field theory, on the other hand, reserves a completely different place for it, both as an instrument of technique in clinical work and as a conceptual device in theoretical activity. Metaphor and the field are linked in a chiasm: the field metaphor transforms Kleinian relational theory into a radically intersubjective theory, which, in turn, places metaphor at a point along the spectrum of dreaming—to paraphrase Bion, it is the stuff of analysis. For the sake of illustration, in the first chapter we examine first the origins and meaning of the field metaphor in analytic field theory; we then consider the mutual implications of this particular development of post-Bion psychoanalysis and the modern linguistic theory of metaphor; and, finally, we put the theoretical hypotheses discussed in the first part of this contribution to work in the clinical situation.

In the second chapter we comment on a seminar Bion held in Paris in 1978. The focus here is on the "artistic" side of analysis. Theory and practice are carried out not only through concepts but also through the style of each author/analyst: style of living, thinking, and writing. Style expresses that which cannot become a theme; it is the result of a kind of pre-theoretical understanding. We do not, however, just read Bion but we also introduce some clinical vignettes into the text so that we in turn are read by the text and thereby help to create a third area of creative exchanges between different generations of analysts and between theory and clinical practice.

The creative, stylistic or narrative aspect is also evident in the third chapter, where we have chosen the form of a conversation to address some of the essential themes of psychoanalytic thought: mourning, ageing, our passion for psychoanalysis, and psychoanalysis as a profession.

The aesthetic dimension of analysis comes back in the fourth chapter, which is about a text by Rachael Peltz: "Ways of hearing: Getting inside psychoanalysis". In fact the aesthetic experience can serve as a model for all that is deepest and truest in our lives and in the analytic encounter. We all have an "inner painter" who transforms primitive sensoriality into images or pictograms and then ties them up into oneiric thoughts, dreaming and thinking in order to give a personal meaning to experience. This model gives us the possibility in the clinical work to be more attentive to the musical, rhythmic, or semiotic aspects of the interaction between patient and analyst. In the text we comment on, Rachael Peltz shows in a beautiful vignette how, by equating analysis to the aesthetic experience, it is possible to help the patient to reach a fuller sense of consonance and contact between mind and body.

The fifth chapter is dedicated to the metaphor of the text. "Spacings" are the gaps printers place between words, which help determine the meaning of each sentence. Accordingly, spacing is the term we have chosen to address the issue of the inextricable interweaving of space and time, concepts that cannot be seen as separate but as implying each other. So we emphasise how subjectivity arises from skilful punctuation work that organises the text of the relationship. Meaning is born in the space created by the tolerable absence of the object: where else can this come from if not from a continuous activity of spacing? Introducing the right spacing means keeping time with each other and finding the right distance.

We emphasise this same point in the next two chapters. In the sixth chapter we take spacing into account by highlighting the importance of being closely guided by the compass of the unconscious, and contrasting this method with interpersonalism. We comment on Stern's characterisation of differences between interpersonal and relational psychoanalysis and Bionian field theory. The critical points on which a consensus is not, for the time being, readily possible concern the relationship between the external and internal worlds and the various conceptions of unconscious experience. Interpersonalists believe that, before forging a link with the external world (whose role we would be foolish to deny), it is clinically more useful to apprehend this internal world as rigorously and over as wide a range as possible—which they do by radically transforming the external world into a dream of the field. Conversely, in their view we may be reassured but partly misled by the concept of a dialectic between the external and internal worlds that fails to take account of the utter pervasiveness of the unconscious and the fact that it speaks even when seemingly silent—not only *negatively* in micro- and macroenactments but also *positively* in waking dream thought, which is an expression of its poetic activity that unceasingly confers meaning on experience.

In the seventh chapter we deal with the same principle in a revisitation of the classical concept of confrontation. On the basis of some clinical examples we try to show how confrontation should be subordinated to the principle of the patient's emotional sustainability. Confrontation can also be carried out in an indirect way, by using the "characters" of the analytic dialogue, and certainly by responding to the signals coming from the emotional LED that light up continuously in the field.

Among the authors who have contributed most to raising awareness of and creatively developing Bion's thinking is James Grotstein. The eighth chapter takes the form of a long review-essay about one of his best books. We believe that knowledge of the work of this author is essential to an understanding of Bion and the BFT model.

On the philosophical side, the same could be said for Merleau-Ponty—the subject of the penultimate chapter. We are convinced that the study of his ideas gives depth and complexity to the concept of the analytic field, because it provides a radical critique of any psychology of the isolated subject. For Merleau-Ponty what the subject encounters in the world is generated in the encounter itself; it does not come into being as an agent that causes a reaction in him, nor as a projection that the subject directs towards and attributes to the thing. We repeat here that it is essential to operate from the point of view of the field, going beyond the perspective of two isolated individuals interacting with each other. Even when, for brevity's sake, we use a descriptive language that seems to reintroduce the vision of analyst and patient as two separate entities, in reality we always imply that they are places in the field. By convention we will focus more on the functionality (or lack of it) of this system and its transformations, and less to bring the various components back to the original source. The qualities of the field cannot be reduced to the simple sum of its original parts. If this were so, we would not need to use the metaphor of the field.

The book closes with a chapter that emphasises in its very title the key concept of transformation. Unlike most of the short vignettes scattered throughout the text, here a single clinical situation is examined at greater length. An account is given of the analysis of a young woman suffering from severe panic attacks. The initial problems of the setting are described and how they are progressively overcome, the emergence of highly structured psychotic nuclei and the gradual approach to the patient's splits. Whereas the panic attacks were originally attributed to the shattering of the symbiotic link, the chapter shows how they increasingly prove to be bound up with the activation of uncontainable emotions of hate, jealousy, and anger, by which the patient feels flooded and overwhelmed, and which are evacuated in the panic attacks until it becomes possible to metabolise them, transform them and make them thinkable, at first in the here and now of the sessions and later through the discovery of the infantile roots both of their virulence and of the deficiency of the parental capacity for containment. These primitive emotions often appear in the form of "characters" that represent split-off parts of the patient. For example a significant dream about monsters emerging from cracks actually ushers in the ability to think.

Note

1. With the exception of Chapters Eight and Ten, written by Antonino Ferro, and Chapter Nine, written by Giuseppe Civitarese.

CHAPTER ONE

The meaning and use of metaphor in analytic field theory

As I lay in bed, with my eyes shut, I said to myself that
everything is capable of transposition.

—Marcel Proust, *The Prisoner*

Each of the principal psychoanalytic models is underlain by certain key metaphors. For example, the archaeological and surgical metaphors, as well as that of the analyst-as-screen, all throw light on some of Freud's basic concepts. In classical psychoanalysis, however, metaphor still tends to be an illegitimate or secondary element. Analytic field theory, on the other hand, reserves a completely different place for it, both as an instrument of technique in clinical work and as a conceptual device in theoretical activity.

Metaphor and the field are linked in a chiasm: The field metaphor transforms Kleinian relational theory into a radically intersubjective theory, which in turn places metaphor at a point along the spectrum of dreaming—to paraphrase Bion, it is the stuff of analysis.

For the sake of illustration, we examine first the origins and meaning of the field metaphor in analytic field theory; we then consider the mutual implications of this particular development of post-Bion psychoanalysis and the modern linguistic theory of metaphor; and, finally, we put the theoretical hypotheses discussed in the first part of this contribution to work in the clinical situation.

Origins of the analytic field metaphor

Madeleine and Willy Baranger developed the notion of the analytic field on the basis of Gestalt theory, the ontology of Merleau-Ponty (1945; in turn influenced by the dialectic of Hegel and by Kojève's reading of it), Klein's concepts of projective and introjective identification, Isaacs's (1948) concept of unconscious fantasy, and Grinberg's (1957)[1] notion of projective counteridentification (Etchegoyen, 1991). The Barangers' basic idea was that patient and analyst generate unconscious field fantasies, or couple fantasies, which may even become actual obstacles (*bastions* or *bulwarks*) to the psychoanalytic process. These are bipersonal fantasies "which cannot be reduced to [their] habitual formulation— as, for example, in Isaacs—that is, as an expression of the individual's instinctual life" (Bezoari & Ferro, 1991, p. 48).

Among the non-psychoanalytic sources, let us briefly consider Merleau-Ponty, because he furnished a philosophical foundation for the field concept, which he emphasised to such an extent as to make it the cornerstone of his own theory, and because his conception of corporeality is extraordinarily modern. By the metaphor of the field, Merleau-Ponty (1945) conceptualised the rigorously interdependent relationship that comes into being between subject and context, the reciprocal and constant influence of self and other, and the dynamic continuity arising between consciousness and the spatiotemporal parameters of experience of the world (time and space not being containers within which the individual moves, but instead being born together with him[2])—the intersubjective determinants of identity.[3] The subject is formed on the basis of a substrate of anonymous, pre-reflective, and pre-personal intersensoriality/intercorporeality even before any actual self-reflective capacity exists. An albeit still obscure pre-categorial background which, however, does not lack meaning, paves the way for the entry of the transcendental ego on to the world stage.

In this phase (which then remains, as it were, one of the constant dimensions of experience, given that the ego will never be able to free itself from the environmental context and from the contingency of a certain life situation), subject and object are not distinguished from each other—that is to say, they are dialectically correlated. Rather than existing as positive entities, pure presences-in-themselves, except in an abstract sense, they mold each other in an incessant, fluid to-and-fro traffic of sensations regulated by the "porosity of the flesh". Subject and object *co-originate* in a primordial medium to which both belong. Touching something is, at the same time, being touched. Our sense of the world is not only an intellectual content, and cannot dispense with our experience of our bodies; it stems from our *fleshly* existence and is present even before a consciousness of self forms. Hence Merleau-Ponty's assertion: "I am a field, an experience" (Merleau-Ponty, 1945, p. 473)—that is, *a system of relationships*.

The Barangers' essay in which the French philosopher's vision is subsumed, "The analytic situation as a dynamic field", dates from 1961–1962. Significantly, in the same years Winnicott and Bion were laying the foundations of a radically intersubjective psycho-analytic theory of the birth of the psyche. The dialectic that underlies subjectivity—which could in Bion's sense be formulated in terms of the binary couple *narcissism/socialism*—seen as an ongoing process, is the same as that which Winnicott sought to apprehend by his famous gerunds, such as *coming-into-being, a going concern, holding, handling, object-presenting* or *indwelling*. In this way, as Ogden explained:

> Winnicott captures something of the experience of the paradoxical simultaneity of at-one-ment and separateness. (A related concep-tion of intersubjectivity was suggested by Bion's [1962a] notion of the container-contained dialectic. However, Winnicott was the first to place the psychological state of the mother on an equal footing with that of infant in the constitution of the mother–infant [relation-ship]. This is fully articulated in Winnicott's statement that "There is no such thing as an infant [apart from the maternal provision]") [Winnicott, 1960]. (Ogden, 1992, p. 620)

For an ideal genealogy of the field metaphor in psychoanalysis, Bion is an unavoidable reference. Although the Barangers did not quote him in their now classical paper, Madeleine Baranger[4] (2005; Churcher, 2008) acknowledged his influence on her from the early 1950s on. At that time, Bion was already developing a highly original theory of the analytic field, although he did not use that metaphor.[5] In his contributions on the "basic assumptions" (Bion, 1948, p. 65), which date precisely from those years (Ferro & Basile, 2009), he developed the concept of unconscious fantasy within the group. The analytic couple is, in fact, already a group. In Bion's view, individuals are endowed with *valences*—the term, borrowed from chemistry, denotes the propensity of atoms to bind together into molecules—that is, the spontaneous and instinctive (unconscious, automatic, and inevitable) capacity to establish mutual emotional bonds, "for sharing and acting on a basic assumption" (Bion, 1948, p. 153), "behaviour in the human being that is more analogous to tropism in plants than to purposive behaviour" (ibid, p. 116f). The basic assumption, whether pair, fight–flight, or dependent, gives rise to "other mental activities that have in common the attribute of powerful emotional drives" (ibid, p. 146). It is "the 'cement' that keeps the group assembled" (López-Corvo, 2002, p. 39).

Valences and basic assumptions express the psychological function of an individual as dictated by the "proto-mental system". The proto-mental system is one of Bion's more speculative concepts, in that it "transcends experience" (Bion, 1948, p. 101). He coined it to explain the tenacity of the emotional bonds that keep the group together, linking its members in a common psychological situation, and to denote a dimension of the psyche in which the basic assumptions that are for the time being inactive can be accommodated. The proto-mental system is "one in which physical and psychological or mental are undifferentiated. It is a matrix from which spring the *phenomena which at first appear*—on a psychological level and in the light of psychological investigation—*to be discrete feelings* only loosely associated with one another. It is from this matrix that emotions proper to the basic assumption flow to reinforce, pervade, and, on occasion, to dominate the mental life of the group. Since it is a level in which physical and mental are undifferentiated, it stands to reason that, when distress from this source manifests itself, it can manifest itself just as well in physical forms as in psychological" (ibid, pp. 101–102, our emphasis).

The absence of a distinction between the physical and the mental in the proto-mental system is, of course, reminiscent of the ambiguous status of the drives in Freud, as a "concept on the frontier between the somatic and the mental", just as the valences call to mind the concept of libido (Fornaro, 1990, p. 55); the point here, however, is that "proto-mental phenomena are a function of the group" (Bion, 1948, p. 103). The individual's proto-mental system is merely a part of a larger whole, namely the proto-mental matrix of the group, and cannot therefore be studied in isolation from it.

It will be seen that, already for Bion—who was here absolutely in unison with Merleau-Ponty—the subject cannot be thought of except on the basis of the intrinsic intersubjective dimension of the proto-mental system, of the area of "initial biopsychic emergence" (Fornaro, 1990, p. 20, translated). Mental life extends beyond the physical boundaries of the individual; it is "transindividual" (ibid, p. 20, translated). Hence the (relative) absence of a distinction between mind and soma in the individual is in some way correlated with the background of a substantial (relative) absence of distinction between individuals.

With regard to Merleau-Ponty's postulate of the ego-as-field and Bion's of the proto-mental area, the concept of projective identification now assumes powerful explanatory force, because it, so to speak, confers *tangibility* on the communication channels through which this common, unconscious psychological area can establish itself, as well as on the *way* in which it can do so. It imparts *visibility*—in Greek, *theorein* means to see or contemplate—to the concrete and indispensable points of contiguity whereby the processes of inter-individual mental influencing take place.

These theoretical foundations show that, already with Bion, and even more with the developments that came after him and the transition to an analytic field theory, psychoanalysis underwent a change of paradigm of the kind described by Kuhn (1962). For example, it may be misleading to define the characteristics of the analytic field in terms of the use of the classical concepts of transference and countertransference, because these presuppose a configuration in which analysand and analyst "face each other" as two positive, pure, complete, and separate subjectivities, each somehow totally "external" to the other. Ogden commented:

> I believe the use of the term *countertransference* to refer to everything the analyst thinks and feels and experiences sensorially obscures the simultaneity of the dialectic of oneness and twoness, of individual subjectivity and intersubjectivity that is the foundation of the psychoanalytic relationship. (Ogden, 1994a, p. 8, n.).

In a theoretical framework inspired by a one-person psychoanalysis, the concept of projective identification, too, would assume an a-dialectic and substantially solipsistic meaning. If, however, subject and object are thought of as places in an intersubjective field, it will be realised, as Ogden (2008) wrote, that when a patient goes into analysis, he, so to speak, *loses his own mind*. He reconnects with the re-established proto-mental area. He initiates a communication that involves him in depth and can be channeled in such a way as to repair dysfunctional places in his internal group configuration, to restart the conversation that the various parts of the mind incessantly carry on among themselves, while always seeking better ways of thinking about his current emotional problem (however, terms such as unconscious thought, dreaming, thinking, and the like must be seen as virtually equivalent).

Elements of the analytic field theory

Analytic field theory fruitfully combines the contribution of the Barangers with the developments of post-Bion thought and certain ideas derived from modern narrativity known in the English-speaking world by the labels of *critical theory* and *reader-response criticism*, and developed in Italy by, in particular, Umberto Eco (Ferro, 1999). Another important component, on the other hand, stems, via Luciana Nissim Momigliano (2001), from Robert Langs and his original conception of the spiralling progression of the unconscious dialogue between patient and analyst. Other significant notions are the emphasis by Ogden (1979) on the concept of projective identification in a strongly relational sense, and that author's more recent idea, avowedly inspired by Kojève's[6] lectures on Hegel, of the "intersubjective analytic third" (Ogden, 1994b). Nor must one disregard the fundamental contribution of Bleger (1967) on the "institutional" nature of the setting and on everything involved in the formation of the individual's so-called *meta-ego* (Civitarese, 2008a).

These initial remarks already point to the reason for the central position of the metaphor—and with it the philosophy—of the field, perhaps because no other lends itself better to the construction of a radically intersubjective psychoanalytic model, which we consider to be most suited to a psychoanalysis for our time. By virtue of a whole set of theoretical increments, the metaphor of the field has succeeded in expressing all its theoretical and clinical potentialities, such as grasping/casting, characters of the session, narrative derivatives of waking dream thought, transformations in dream, weak or unsaturated interpretation, and the like (Ferro, 1992).

The field metaphor is, of course, borrowed from electromagnetic or gravitational field theory. Its essential properties are that it represents a *dynamic* totality, and that it is *inclusive, invisible* (but deducible from its effects on its constitutive elements), and *delimited* (even if constantly in the throes of contraction or expansion).

The field is intrinsically unstable and subjected to continuous displacements of energy. The forces concentrated at a given point in the field can have effects on other forces in locations remote from that point. Hence, all the elements in a field are structured as a differential system in which each term is defined in relation to the others in a process of constant, mutual cross-reference. This is not very different from de Saussure's conception of the structure of language, Lacan's (1947) of the system of signifiers in the unconscious, or Derrida's of the text. Perhaps only chaos theory could offer an effective representation of the dynamism of the field, because it can model the complex vectorial manifestations that give rise to turbulence, catastrophic points, and ultimately changes of state.

Furthermore, the field is delimited. It is a container. This does not, of course, mean that it is a closed system; instead, by causing itself to be contained, it is, itself, in a dialectical relationship with what is outside it—that is, with other, broader containers (social groups, institutions, ideologies, etc.). However, the fact that the field is relatively closed permits account to be taken of what may be defined as *inclusiveness*. This is an aspect given an original interpretation by Antonino Ferro, who radicalised the model of the field already outlined by the authors mentioned previously, and invites one to see any element within the fictional frame of the setting as (virtually) a function of the analytic field.

In clinical psychoanalytic work, the field concept effectively supports the extension of the dream paradigm of the session, to which it imparts rigour, because it puts to work in the couple Klein's concept of projective identification (albeit as revised and corrected by Bion and Ogden) and Bion's (1992) of "waking dream thought" (we dream not only at night but also during the day). There is no point in the field (whether an event, a memory, a dream, an enactment, a reverie, an association, an emotion, a sensation, or whatever) that is not touched by the "electromagnetic waves" of the intersecting projective identifications of patient and analyst, and that does not correspond to the recordings made of it by their respective alpha functions; it might, in fact, be better to invoke the alpha function of the field (or its *gamma function*, as

Francesco Corrao called it). This function represents the capacity of the couple, outside the rigid framework of a subject/object dichotomy, to narrate, dream, think, and construct metaphors or myths to attribute a specific meaning to their joint experience. The field takes the form of:

> a system dedicated to the transformation of sensory and emotional experiences into thoughts and meanings, [and confers life on a] theory of treatment centered on the transformations and developments of the psychoanalytic field (which includes the analyst, the patient, and theories) rather than on individuals and contents. (Neri & Selvaggi, 2006, p. 182, translated)

A limitation of the field metaphor is that it might suggest a two-dimensional situation. This may, indeed, be the case when a quasi-autistic type of mental functioning arises. Instead of actual characters, there are only flat, emotionless picture cards. The patient draws the analyst into an exclusively concrete world. Play is impossible. There are no metaphors, no dreams, and no reveries. If, however, these possibilities can gradually be introduced, that will be tantamount to adding new dimensions or worlds to the field. Moreover, except in these situations the, field is, as a rule, multidimensional—it is a *pluriverse*.

Each of the characters in the analytic dialogue, including those called the analyst and the patient (Ferro, 2010), and their internal worlds (!), represents a specific place in the analytic field. However, the following can also be places in the field: its scenic component (the ongoing formation and transformation of the characters); the analyst's mind; the countertransference; the place of formation of images (waking dream thought) and its derivatives; the analyst's actual countertransference dreams; his reveries; the internal worlds of the analyst and the patient; their histories; their relationship; enactments; projective identifications and all their vicissitudes; and the transgenerational elements of both protagonists (Bezoari & Ferro, 1991; Ferro, 2006). The art of the analyst is to apprehend the patient's point of view, using the restrictions imposed from time to time on the field by the viewpoint that can be assumed by dwelling in one of its many different places.

It would, of course, be misleading to think of this situation in terms of a process of constant, hyperwakeful monitoring of the field, which would be mechanical and unproductive. The metaphor of virtual reality (Civitarese, 2008a), which is basically an extreme form of the concept of the transference neurosis, can be used to show how a clinical and theoretical field model aims to keep two aspects in balance—namely, the usefulness for the actors in, and authors of, the analytic dialogue of losing themselves in the fiction established by the setting (which means intimacy, closeness, spontaneity, emotional intensity, and authenticity), and the need to re-emerge from it to gain access to the plurality of the possible worlds in which they are simultaneously living.

In this way, it is possible to satisfy, on the one hand, a poetics and an aesthetics of emotional involvement (how to allow oneself to be captured by the text of the analysis, and why), and, on the other, a poetics and an aesthetics of disenchantment (how to achieve the insight that the text is a fiction, and in view of what effects). The analytic field might then, perhaps, be definable as a medium—a means of communication—in which the analyst seeks to achieve the best possible balance between immersion and interactivity, between semiotic transparency and self-referential demystification (like dreaming and waking from a dream, both of which are necessary for the definition of a dream). Unless the oscillations between these poles are made explicit, the result will be narrative interpretations or, in other words, transference interpretations (which are, in fact, nothing but metanarrations).

When Ferro (1992) attributed an innate transformative capacity to the field and to the narrativities it expresses, he was on no account invoking some kind of magical virtue inherent in it, but rigorously articulating the intersubjective implications of the field metaphor and of analytic field theory. The mere fact of being in a room already modifies the chemical composition of the air breathed by its occupants. Likewise, any change in the medium in which they are immersed influences both patient and analyst, even if the change is coincidental and peripheral to the points of concentration of the system of forces in the field that correspond to the two subjectivities involved. If a cellphone rings, the field is modified. The modification is even greater after a significant exchange in the analytic dialogue. Between the two places represented by the patient and the analyst, there occur interactions that are, to a greater or lesser extent, direct and of variable intensity and, to a greater or lesser extent, differentiated in terms of the continuum from metonymy to metaphor, from sensoriality/intercorporeality to the exchange of concepts or to the vicissitudes of the unconscious projective and introjective processes.

The field, seen as a dynamic system that identifies with the analytic couple and interweaves narrations that tell, instant by instant, of its own functioning, is a viewpoint very different from that of an analyst acting as a screen for the patient's projections. If three negative characters appear in the first analytic session after the summer break, they may be regarded as three areas of emotional congestion, lumps of non-thinkability waiting to be narrated and broken up (like the crime featuring at the beginning of a traditional thriller)—but without any need to be made explicit by interpretation, unless the actual psychoanalytic game of interpretation itself becomes a place in the field, or a character in the text of the analysis. If one of the three baddies were an incompetent lifeguard or a rude barman, the narration could develop along the lines of understanding why he behaves in this way, of making hypotheses, of getting to know them, of considering them from a number of different possible points of view, and of trying to guess the reasons for them—in a word, with a view to seeing if it is possible to bring about a transformation that can rid the field of the initial atmosphere of persecution. Of course, the patient could perfectly well signal the change in the plot by allowing a new character to take the stage. Beneath the new mask, however, the analyst would have no difficulty in recognising the same tangled ball of emotions in the process of transformation.

Metaphor as a rhetorical figure and as a basic cognitive mechanism

Metaphor, in the sense of a rhetorical figure, is a schema (a "configuration" according to Mortara Garavelli, 2010) that serves to model the expression of thought. A synonym of a rhetorical figure is a "trope", which means "turn", denoting an effect of "deviation and transposition of meaning". When the "deviated use" becomes habitual, the metaphor turns into *catachresis* (this Greek coinage means "misuse"). The irregularity receives the sanction of law and even becomes the norm. A catachresis, like certain state pardons granted for especially common offenses, is the fruit of a "necessity": it provides a name for an object that did not previously have one. The institution of a catachresis is therefore governed by a principle of economy which is applied at the cost of a certain imprecision, while also involving an effect of polysemy, or expansion of meaning. It is only when a catachresis is awakened from its sleep—as often occurs in analysis by virtue of the attention devoted to the play of the signifier, for example in the case of a parapraxis or a joke—that its primal nature as a metaphor is revealed. The memory of the underlying abuse then comes to the surface. A catachresis is usually seen as different from *extinct* or lexicalised metaphors, which are now completely unrecognisable as such except by exploring the derivation of the word concerned (for example, the Italian word *testa* [head] comes from the identical Latin word, which originally denoted the shell of a tortoise; Mortara Garavelli, 2010).

Metaphor is deemed the queen of tropes, "the easiest to recognize and the most difficult to define … a mechanism that is so universal and so within everyone's reach has resisted every attempt to explain it completely and homogeneously" (Mortara Garavelli, 2010, p. 9, translated). After all, metaphor is not always the contraction of a comparison or a simile that is abbreviated or described as such. The analogy is, in fact, often not recorded, but created. Metaphor is the invention of an intelligence that is "sympathetic" (de Beistegui, 2010, p. 35, translated) to the matter of the world, a way of assigning a personal meaning to it, and of impressing one's own style on it. It is not the fruit of an analysis of the similarities and differences between two terms/objects thought of as always identical with themselves, but itself generates the relationship. Establishing a metaphor is tantamount to the use of a kind of violence, to causing a slight shock; in this respect, it is more consonant with a psychoanalysis understood as a development of narrations or opening up of possible worlds, and less with a psychoanalysis that translates the unconscious into the conscious and is inspired by a cold, distant, and objective intelligence, as, for example, Freud's surgical metaphor might suggest.

It is, at any rate, clear that, on the one hand, language is composed of a gradient of abusive acts (cf. de Saussure's notion of the arbitrary nature of the link that joins the signifier to the signified, the word to the thing, or separates them from each other, or Aulagnier's idea of the "violence" of interpretation, 1975); on the other, it is nothing but a "cemetery of tropes" (Mortara Garavelli, 2010, p. 11, translated): Violence and mourning would appear to lie at the origin of language and culture. Be that as it may, metaphor's constant transportation of heterogeneous terms remote from each other, like the subterranean cars of a subway train between stations, serves the purpose of seeing reality—of seeing it for the first time, as children do; and children of course produce highly original metaphors. They also make it possible to see again with new eyes, a capacity possessed by poets in greater measure than anyone else. For this reason, it is indeed the case that "metaphors can be the ghosts of ideas waiting to be born" (Bion, 1977, p. 418). They are ultimately the royal road to reality, because they express the functioning of what we sense to be a basic cognitive mechanism of the psyche—an actual "principle of knowledge rather than of recognition" (de Beistegui, 2010, p. 44, translated).

In a famous passage from *Totem and Taboo*, Freud discussed the way in which magic thought treats past situations as if they were present:

> It is further to be noticed that the two principles of association—similarity [*Ähnlichkeit*] and contiguity [*Kontiguität*]—are both included in the more comprehensive concept of "contact" [*Berührung*]. Association by contiguity is contact in the literal sense; association by similarity is contact in the metaphorical sense. The use of the same word for the two kinds of relation is no doubt accounted for by *some identity* [*Eine ... Identität*] in the psychical processes concerned which we have not yet grasped. (Freud, 1912–1913, p. 85, our emphasis)

Freud here identified an essential, albeit problematic, quality of the mind that makes the creation of meaning possible. He postulated the existence on the infralinguistic level of a central psychic mechanism, albeit as yet indeterminate, and does so by invoking linguistics and rhetoric. He thus subordinates similarity (metaphor, from the Greek *metapherein*, "to transport") and contiguity (metonymy, from the Greek *metonymia*, "exchange of name"—although what is involved here is not so much the classical definition of the figure as the type of semantic relationship, based on its implication of coexistence/proximity) to contact. But when we say "contact," are we not, in fact, still referring to an idea of contiguity? In other words, are we not stating that the second of the modes of relating, contact in the direct sense, is primary? It is no coincidence that the English words, as well as their Italian equivalents, have a common root in the Latin *contingere*.

Freud here seemed to be alluding precisely to the relationship between metaphor and metonymy, a figure (of "contiguity"—Mortara Garavelli, 2010, p. 23, translated) that is no less important and no less difficult to define. The debate is ongoing in the linguistic field: some hold that metaphor can be reduced to metonymy because it is the fruit of a twofold metonymy ("'two metonymies short-circuited,' or, as it were, the product of two synecdoches;" ibid, p. 24, translated). From this point of view, metonymy is the only transformational device, or trope, that can be thought of both as a general function of semiosis, and as something that entails a strategy of thought that cannot be further broken down.[7]

Ordinary usage of course relies on traditional definitions and customary practical distinctions. However, this hypothesis will facilitate the tracing of thought, and the huge gulf it can bridge in joining even the most diverse of objects in metaphor, back to their bodily and sensory roots (as Merleau-Ponty taught); to the cheek-breast interface (a relationship of contiguity), an "area of sensations of a soothing sort" that is the first nucleus of subjectivity (Ogden, 1994b, p. 174); and to the first (the most elementary) "translation," which Freud may have had in mind in 1895 when he wrote in the 'Project' (Freud, 1950 [1895]) that, for an infant at the beginning of life, the object is his own cry. Metonymy would then, in effect, be metaphor in its ground state, and thought an extension (virtualisation) of the concrete and direct inter-body contact that acts as a matrix for a child's nascent psyche (or for the development of the rudimentary subjectivity/alpha function with which a child might already be endowed at birth). *Transferred contact* (i.e., contact at a distance) would then be referred to *direct contact*, the intellect to its sensory and bodily roots, and the isolated subject to the intersubjective field.

However, as (mostly verbal) rhetorical figures, do metaphor and metonymy not correspond, as Lacan maintained, to the two key dream mechanisms discovered by Freud, namely condensation and displacement? So in trying to define metaphor and metonymy, are we not actually referring to the meaning of dreaming? After all, did Bion (1992) not say that we dream not only at night but also during the day, and that to dream is to think? Here, then, linguistic theory and psychoanalysis, although starting from different vertices, are seen to converge in formulating the idea that to name things (to think), it is necessary to construct metaphors or to dream (to displace/to condense), and that these are two modes of expression, albeit on different levels of abstraction, of one and the same basic psychological process.

This meeting between a new theory of dreams (and of reverie) and narratology (and the modern theory of metaphor) underlies the model of the mind that serves as a framework for analytic field theory. Let us, therefore, briefly consider this model before turning to clinical examples.

A model of the mind

In psychoanalysis, the realm of the image is the dream. Perhaps we should say "was" rather than "is", at least since Bion provided us with a model of the mind involving the continuous production of images (that could be called pictograms) by a function (described as the alpha function) on the basis of the sensoriality that pervades us from whatever source. The sequence of images somehow soothes and pacifies the mind whenever the transformation is successful. The result is a sequence of such images or pictograms, called dream thought of the waking state. These images are normally unknowable in themselves. Given, for example, a sequence of powerful sense impressions, such as relatively undefined proto-emotional states of rage → relief → longing, a possible sequence of pictograms might be as shown in Figure 1.

Of course, the choice and construction of an individual pictogram and of sequences of pictograms are extremely subjective. It is like one and the same subject painted by Degas, and then by Caravaggio, Monet, Chagall, Picasso, etc.

This, then, is the mind's first locus of creativity. In Bion's terms, it would be the transformation beta (via the alpha function) → alpha.

There is also a second locus of creativity in the mind. In a manner that is again extremely subjective, the sequence of pictograms (waking dream thought) is narrated—that is, put into words. Here, too, an infinite number of narrative genres can be used to perform this transformation. In any case, *narrative derivatives* of the pictograms (or of the alpha elements, or of waking dream thought) are the outcome.

The sequence in the previous example could generate a set of stories differing in style but all characterised by one constant—namely, the succession rage–relief–longing. A memory of infancy leads to a diary entry, a chronicled event, a fantasy, and so on.

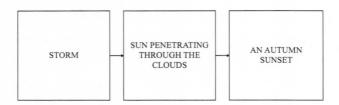

Figure 1. Example of a Pictogram.

We can also come into contact with a pictogram of the sequence that forms in our mind in (and outside) an analytic session, by the phenomenon we call reverie. Reverie enables us to make contact with the image synthesised by the alpha function—for example, that of a storm.

Another situation in which a pictogram of the sequence originating in waking dream thought is seen is when the patient projects one of these images to the outside, thus endowing it with a strongly sensory character; this is not a true hallucination, because the meaning it conveys can easily be guessed. A telling example is that of the patient who responded to a request by one of the present authors for an increase in fees by exclaiming: "Good heavens, I can see a chicken being plucked on the wall opposite!"

According to this model of psychic life, throughout the day an enormous number of pictograms (alpha elements) are constantly forming and being transferred to memory. These are acted upon by an "alpha-megafunction" (Grotstein, 2007, p. 271)—a mental device that performs a kind of second pressing or weaving of this material, eventually giving rise to dream images. These are the most digested elements which our apparatus for thinking thoughts is capable of producing.

It is no coincidence that Ogden (2008) held that a psychoanalyst's work consists of dreaming—that is, of undertaking the transformations of sensory storms into images that the patient cannot perform by himself. It follows, too, that the aim of analysis is to develop in the patient the capacity to generate images, to create dreams out of the forms of concrete thought represented by symptoms.

O'Shaughnessy (2005) distinguished Bion's notion of waking dream thought from Klein's conception that the infant mind possesses from the beginning a rich unconscious fantasy life manifested in sensations and affects. Both of these processes confer meaning on experience, even if waking dream thought entails something new—namely, the idea of a primary process (situated upstream of unconscious fantasy) of transformation/alphabetisation of the crude data of experience.

Let us try to describe what happens in the analyst's consulting room. The patient arrives with a variously sized bottle of ink (his anxieties and proto-emotions—in the jargon, his *beta elements*), which he keeps pouring on to the special kind of blotting paper represented by the field. The field absorbs the ink and becomes thoroughly soaked in it. Analyst and patient dip their pens into this ink to write down the text of the session.

What was previously a mere formless blot is transformed into stories, narrations, and constructions. In this way, what at first had a soiling effect becomes susceptible to thought, narration, and sharing.

Another image of the patient's problem might be that of a big horse, with *"ferri"*(!)[8] on its hoofs, which, as it gallops, clip-clop back and forth like the types of an old-fashioned typewriter. However, eventually the horse finds a groom to take care of it, and as its hoofs flail back and forth, it begins to write at first fragments of stories, and then complete stories. Moreover, in the process of writing it calms down, grows ever smaller, and ultimately ceases to be a problem.

The aesthetic metaphor and the analytic field

So far, we have considered the significance of the field metaphor as the organising schema of a particular psychoanalytic model.[9] Examples include the use of the archaeological, military, and chess metaphors in Freud's theories; Bion's digestive and sexual metaphors; or the gastronomic or cinematographic metaphors employed by Ferro (1992, 1996). We then proceeded to examine metaphor as a rhetorical figure and an elementary psychological mechanism (cf. also the now classical studies of Lakoff & Johnson, 1980); and, on the basis of a passage from Freud and certain cues from the linguistic theory of metaphor, we postulated the substantial identity of metaphors and dreams (and visual images). Last, we come now to the meaning and use of metaphor in both the broad sense (referring to the level of discourse) and the specific sense (of an image or rhetorical figure involved in discourse), as a technical device in clinical psychoanalytic work within a field model.

Playing with metaphors: not just herbivores

Paolo begins his analysis as the good boy that he is. In his first session, he tells me about his attempts to fix his Vespa, which has been lying about forgotten for years. After a number of sessions devoted to this subject, I venture to suggest that "sometimes a *vespa* [Italian for wasp] will sting." A prolonged silence ensues.

In the next session Paolo, who has hitherto always come along with a laptop, tells me: "My computer has been struck by lightning and it is literally completely burnt out". So I mitigate the pressure of my interpretations, which was intended to demechanise certain aspects of the patient, but when I later return to a more pungent interpretative regime, there appears "the neighbour who collects weapons and who seemed to be aiming a threatening submachine gun". When I return to a more playful style of interpretation, Paolo mentions the neighbour again, saying that his gun—now he has had a clear view of it!—has a red plug on top of it. It is manifestly a toy weapon, so there is no reason to be worried.

As the analysis proceeds, he tells me about his grandmother's farm, which is populated by a whole menagerie of chickens, ducks, hens, sheep, cows, and so on—until one day I ask him if he is not fed up with all these herbivores (!). Paolo at first reacts as if struck by a wave of persecution, but in the final session before the summer holidays, I am surprised to be given a present of little toy wild animals. On returning from the summer holidays, he discovers, carved into the beams of the ceiling of my consulting room, a five-pointed star, the symbol of the Red Brigades—which neither I nor the patients on the couch had ever noticed in thirty or more years.

I now realise that rage and revolution have entered the room. However, when I try to find the carving again, I cannot focus on it: these aspects of Paolo tend to disappear. On another occasion when he shows me the five-pointed star and the mark of the Red Brigades, I take the opportunity of telling him that he has the eyes of a hawk. In this way, I am substituting the hawk for the lost little sparrow he kept in a cage, about which he had told me at length.

These more intensely passionate aspects make their entry into the sessions, albeit in bleached-white form, when he receives a letter from his girlfriend, from whom he has heard nothing for a long time; after a prolonged silence on my part, he comments: "I didn't know whether to tear it up or to open it with the letter opener".

It can thus be seen that metaphor in the strict sense of the term (as a word-related fact) belongs to the order of the narrative derivatives of waking dream thought, but also that the process whereby it comes into being is the same as that of unconscious thought. The transformations from sensoriality into narrative derivatives are "metaphorical", and conversely the metaphors are narrative derivatives.

Metaphors living or dead? The check

Andrea tells me of the climate of anxiety into which he was plunged by a friend who made him fear that he would no longer receive his monthly pay cheque for his new job. In fact, it would not be very serious even if he did not receive this cheque, as that would enable him to look for a more satisfying, better paying job. However, his friend has succeeded in making him feel persecuted and threatened, as well as open to the envy of others.

The friend, of course, represents a kind of functioning in the patient himself which, in the absence of analysis at the weekend, manages to undermine his (wavering) basic level of confidence, plunging him into a climate of discomfort and distrust, and causing him to lose sight of the progress he has made.

I now make a metaphorical intervention. I tell him that he reminds me of a competent swimmer who is told that his lifejacket might be removed or that he will not be given one, because he doesn't need it and it would get in his way. My point is that this image, however, is not a pre-constituted metaphor, because it arises in me, with him, there, in real time, for the first time and simultaneously with his communications. It is a reverie produced on the spot, or rather, one whose discursive formulation arises out of a reverie—which is not directly communicable in itself, in its visual form, just as a dream is not communicable except by a kind of intersemiotic transmutation/translation; that is, after being transferred from one system of signs to another, different system of signs.

Introducing the patient to the world of metaphors, or the resumption of dreaming: Lucio's grease gun

I tell Lucio that I shall be away for a couple of weeks (for professional reasons). He begins the next session by saying that *he has not had any dreams*. He then tells me that he took the cat along to be neutered and that he feels quite calm. He adds that he has met with one of the leaders of a pacifist association, who has been abandoned by his wife and weeps inconsolably. His wife cheated on him, taking up again with a female fellow student with whom she had already had a relationship.

I tell him that, if we were to look at these two communications as if they were two dreams (that is always one of my listening vertices when a patient speaks to me), we might think that he was worried that, if the cat had not been neutered, it might perhaps scratch me. What is more, who knows what might happen if the member of the pacifist organisation who cried because of *my* cheating on him, even if the cheating was in a way "justified" (for a congress, as he tells me he has discovered on the Internet), was actually the Mexican revolutionary Pancho Villa or simply the Italian national hero, Garibaldi.

Lucio immediately gets my drift, and says that he has, nevertheless, begun to make some progress. He has not yet become Garibaldi, but has at least taken on some of that worthy's boldness of character. He has, for example, plucked up the courage to go to the pharmacy to buy a vaginal lubricant for his girlfriend, who suffers from dryness in that region. In the past, he would never have exposed himself in this way, but this time he felt no shame. He asked for a "non-spermicidal vaginal lubricant". He then remembers the film *Kill Bill*, in which a male nurse gave a jar of Vaseline to someone about to have sex with a woman whose vagina was so dry that "without the Vaseline it would have been like sticking his penis into a can of sand".

I tell him he has been quite Garibaldi-like in managing to show his needs to the pharmacist, but at the same time, it seems to me that he feels the need to lubricate his relationships, because he wants to avoid any friction with others. Yet he is still leaving something "alive"; he is not eliminating everything. Lucio confirms my interpretation, telling me of some episodes from his childhood in which, so as not to upset his parents, he always avoided any "friction" with his classmates, in what was, in fact, a pretty turbulent class. In the same session, he makes a slip, when he tells me of his "fear of not being able to stop" (he meant to say the opposite), and then wonders whether he should see himself as a bull dressed up as an ox or an ox dressed up as a bull. We then work on these themes of containment/non-containment, referring also to the Michael Douglas movie *Falling Down*, and Lucio returns to the subject of lubrication as the end of the session approaches. As a boy, he tells me, he already enjoyed using a grease gun to lubricate the gears of his bicycle; it was a sort of elongated contraption with a nozzle that made a very good job of lubricating. I now tell him that it seems obvious to me that a bull likes making women grow fat,[10] and what better way could there be of making them pregnant (referring to a wish to have children that cannot be made fully explicit).

We thus observe an entire spectrum of shades of defence concerning the "bulls", the feared and uncontainable proto-emotions that extend from the production of autism to that of a bonsai, of a mechanism, and of lethargy. In particular, however, we see how, little by little, a space for dreaming is regained by a series of metaphorical openings—in fact amounting to a kind of ongoing metaphor.

Negative reverie

The analyst's mind should be receptive and capable of absorbing and containing the patient's emotions—that is, of transforming proto-sensory and proto-emotional states into images, and hence into thought, and then of imparting the method to the patient. Any narration, however seemingly realistic, always tells us as analysts (and only as analysts) of something else: of the patient's internal world and, in particular, if we are able to listen, of the appropriateness or otherwise of his instruments (for feeling, dreaming, and thinking). In substance, analysis has to do with all the methods whereby these instruments (and apparatuses) can be developed (and sometimes created).

A symptom often takes the form of a stopper to prevent the emergence of something unknown both to the patient and to ourselves, but about which we ought sooner or later to become capable of dreaming together. At the beginning of an analysis, and at the beginning of each session, we should deploy our *negative capability* (a PS without persecution), and be able to wait for a meaning to slowly take shape. Every hypothesis of meaning that we formulate, and every misused metaphor that we employ, should be rapidly set aside, so as to put ourselves into a mental state open to the new and unpredictable.

Things do not always turn out that way. Our functioning is sometimes affected by various degrees of negative reverie (–R), partially or totally blocked reverie—perhaps even a situation of reversed functioning, in which the mind that is supposed to receive and transform projects things into the mind that wants and needs to evacuate and find a space and method to manage proto-emotions. These forms of mental functioning—these traumatic facts (trauma is basically exposure to more beta elements than one can receive and transform, either by oneself or with the other's help)—are then, as always, narrated in an infinite number of scripts.

Gino

In one of his sessions, Gino takes out a Barbie Doll and says: "How's the dancer today?"

The therapist interprets the question as directed to herself and answers: "Very well, and how are you?"

"I'm at the cemetery", he answers (this seems to be something that has actually happened; it is the only way Gino can deal with the despair he has felt in the interval between sessions). He says the girl he likes most was not in class and the teacher was not listening. Gino is immediately noticing that the therapist has failed to pick up his depression, and adds that he would like to touch the long, bushy hair of his female classmates. Disorientated by the concreteness of the communication, the therapist (whose hair is cut short almost to her scalp) fails to grasp his wish for a gentle, soft touch, and says: "Does it turn you on?" Now also disorientated, Gino mentions a girl in his class who removed the hand he had placed on her hair, and then tells the therapist that he saw a boy blowing on a girl's hair. The feeling of being repelled makes Gino puff, but the warm, emotional component of puffing is lost in the blowing.

He goes on: "Our teacher came to school wearing an undershirt, so can the boys wear a T-shirt on top of their sweaters?" He adds: "They're speaking German". There is a coded message here; restoring the freeze-dried emotion that has been sucked away, the communication becomes: "You told me something about yourself (being turned on), so can I reveal intimate things too instead of covering them up?"

Gino is, in effect, constantly sucking in the emotional sap of metaphor, and what the therapist ought to be doing (but cannot because she is in –R) is to restore sap and emotional and affective solidity to what (seemingly) has to remain totally neutral in order to be expressed.

Gino begins another session as follows: "Do you have a short-sleeved T-shirt? Take off your sweater!" His meaning seems to be: "Uncover yourself, show the emotions you have underneath!" He then adds: "Is my hair clean?" He is afraid the therapist might think there is something dirty in his communication (the "turning on" mentioned by the therapist), whereas Gino's communication is innocent! He adds: "I want to grow a pigtail; I also like people with a crest on their heads". Although this, too, could be seen as a sensualisation or erotisation of the communication, I do not think that is correct. Until not long ago, in his sessions Gino used to lean over the desk with his face as close as possible to the therapist's. It was like the tropism of a plant toward the light, a kind of vegetable behaviour (but previously, locked up in his mute amimia, his behaviour had been mineral in nature for years on end!). Unable to say "I feel attracted by you", he moves toward the other, like a climbing plant. He now feels that the next stage in his evolution is the leap from the plant world of concrete metaphor to the animal world of proto-emotions, the pigtail, and the crest as representatives of a no-longer-vegetable world. This development could also be seen as possessing a sexual element, as a transition from pollination to a more sexual form of functioning of minds. An emotional thread is, indeed, beginning to form, binding the two minds together, even if it is still wrapped in thick layers of sweater/insulation/German.

Metaphor, reverie and free association

The dichotomy of living versus dead metaphor is reflected in that of reverie versus free association. There are differences between a free association and a reverie. The latter is characterised by direct contact with the pictogram that constitutes the waking dream thought. It comes into being upstream of interpretation, and in some way inspires or suggests it. It is an image (which is usually communicable to the patient only in exceptional cases, but would then come under the heading of self-disclosure) that is created in the mind—spontaneously and not to order—whose difficulty lies in organising it in a pertinent, explanatory communication. Rather than, in effect, being taken from an encyclopedia (that is, from the harvesting of preformed metaphors present in language), this communication should be created there, in that place, for the first time, like a small fragment of a dream triggered by situations permeated with projective identifications or, if you will, beta elements. The only possible approach for bringing out this stratum of thought processes is a negative one (Bion's "negative capability", 1970, p. 125).

Any reverie could also be said to be a free association, but the opposite is not the case, even though the boundary is sometimes blurred. An association may share the nature of reverie if it is spontaneous and is received in a state of passivity. Mostly, however, it emerges among the entities that can be described as "narrative derivatives" (Ferro, 2002a, p. 598) of waking dream thought. Unlike reverie, a free association can also be forced. A free association—which may be a metaphor already recorded in language, either because it is banal or because it has become a catachresis—arises at a less early stage of thought, downstream of waking dream thought, when the level of narrative derivatives has already been reached. It is, rather, a widening of narration.

Giovanna's analysis has reached an impasse with no obvious way out, when I come into contact with—I actually SEE—a sailboat in a bottle, which provides me with a visual description of what is happening in the analytic field: The sailboat of the analysis is bottled up. Hence the interpretation: "It seems to me that we are stalled, and I find myself imagining a sailboat in a bottle—a boat made like the analysis for sailing ...," and so on.

The corresponding metaphor, on the other hand, would be if I were to use an example taken from one of Conrad's typical tales in which a sailboat is "becalmed". I could then more readily describe a situation of which I am already aware, to which the image of the sailboat in the bottle belongs; indeed, it suggests, triggers, and inspires the interpretation.

Trasformations of the field and narration

As these vignettes show, in an analytic field theory, the analyst's reveries and affective and visual transformations based on the patient's narration, together with any metaphors that stem from these, are the actual factors of growth. The analyst transforms anxieties and persecution feelings into affective images; he has a dream about the patient's communication. He shapes the alpha elements and passes them on to the patient—but, in particular, he puts the patient in touch with his own functioning (his alpha function), which governs these transformations. It is not so much metaphor in itself, as a living metaphor, arising there and specific to that patient at that time, that bears witness to the oneiric functioning of the analyst's mind and supplies him with the method for performing this act (paradoxically, in some cases, even if he does not say or do anything). The same can be said of the situation in which the analyst reawakens one of the now lexicalised or extinct metaphors used by the patient or by himself.

With patients who are more seriously ill (or with the more seriously ill parts of all patients), only this level can permit the development of the alpha function—that is to say, of the patient's own capacity to dream, both while awake and while asleep, because a more explicit offer of meaning might arouse a sense of persecution.

The session proceeds by a kind of oneiric reciprocity, both when the patient dreams (if he can) the analyst's intervention and mental state, and when the analyst dreams the response to give to the patient (Civitarese, 2006, 2014; Ferro et al., 2007). The more this response is dreamed—that is, the fruit of unconscious thought—the more it will be a factor in shaping the patient's alpha function or in mending any defects in it.

However, what we have described for the sake of simplicity as belonging to the analyst and the patient actually takes place in a dimension that transcends both, which is that of the field. This situation could, therefore, be re-described from this other complex viewpoint in terms of turbulences and the alpha function of the field. The idea is that, if we creatively transform the field constituted by the two subjectivities, each will benefit—in particular, the patient, because, by definition, he comes along with less capacity to dream experience, or, in other words, to assign a personal meaning to it, and hence to contain emotions.

If the drama undergone by a character in the tale comprising the analytic dialogue is resolved, the positive turn of the plot is a narrative form that reflects profound emotional transformations occurring in the common psychological area of the analytic field, which are therefore bound to be relevant to both members of the analytic couple, albeit as a rule asymmetrically (because, after all, the analyst should also be capable of a certain detachment). Of course, whereas this situation is in our view more correctly described in intersubjective or field terms, there is no reason why it could not be portrayed more abstractly or with its complexity simplified, for example by the fiction of two completely separate subjectivities, or indeed using less radical relational models.

The vignettes show that, from a field vertex, rather than "giving interpretations" or "making interventions" *directed to* the patient, the need is to *attune oneself to* the emotions that are not yet thinkable for the patient and to help him to give shape to them. Attention will then be paid more to the development of the container—that is, to facilitating the growth of the capacity to think—than to its contents. In order to be in unison with the patient, the guiding principle is to reach him at the point where he is, and to take account of the degree of truth about himself that proves *tolerable* to him—that is, as Eco (1984) says in connection with metaphors, of his *limit of acceptability*. For this reason, the analyst must pay attention to the derivatives of waking dream thought, as a basis for constantly attempting to apprehend the signals addressed to him by the patient about where he is and how he reacts to what he says (or does not say) to him. The essential aim is to weave together the emotional threads making for growth of the patient's capacity to dream/think/symbolise. To this end, the conversation often proceeds on a twofold level, in which the manifest text *metaphorises* the latent text of the unconscious/field dimension of the relationship—the invisible "electromagnetic waves" that establish it, exactly as in the case of play in the therapy of children.

As rhetorical figures involved in the text of the analysis, metaphors appear to us as *transformations* (A becomes B; the real appears to us, on the phenomenal level, as a given reality) which are *narrative*—that is, expressed in words: there is a temporality, a becoming. Felicitous metaphors have a containing effect (the frightening and unknowable "O" is "cooked"). By virtue of their metonymic basis, they represent a point of equilibrium between emotions and thought, because they are pervaded with sensoriality (i.e., they retain the mark of things), while at the same time distancing themselves from things (which they symbolise). They are *sensible ideas* (Carbone, 2008)—that is to say, they combine emotion and thought. They therefore restore a bodily element to the mind; they reunite psyche and soma; they reforge the "psychosomatic collusion" (Winnicott, 1974, p. 104) that is the foundation of subjectivity; they are dreams that *create* reality and give it a personal meaning.

It will therefore be understood that, in order to live, rather than knowing how the mechanisms of the unconscious work or receiving logical or rational types of explanations, patients need good metaphors. As in the case of aesthetic experience in art, there is nothing like a good metaphor to give someone a feeling of truth about his existence. An apt metaphor is an image of which we can never have too much; it is an inexhaustible source of meaning. To be apt, however, in analysis a narration must be attuned to the patient; it must contain his most anxiety-inducing emotions at their point of urgency. The analyst must be capable of reverie, have a well developed alpha function, and be in a receptive state. Reveries give birth to living metaphors, while, conversely, metaphors are an excellent, if not the only, way of using reverie.

In the dialogue, priority is given to the clear text furnished by the patient, because the metaphorical discourse as a whole is open and unsaturated, conveys emotions, and creates meaning. In our view, analytic field theory is the approach that places the greatest possible emphasis on metaphors and on metaphorical discourse, because, by virtue of its strict inclusiveness (at least in principle), there is nothing that cannot refer to the field and to the transference, and hence nothing that is present only for itself, like a lexicalised or extinct metaphor. As Proust writes in "The captive", and as quoted in the epigraph to this contribution, "everything is capable of transposition". There is no fact, event, memory, account of a dream, and the like, that cannot stand for something else. If we accept the suggestion of one of us (Ferro, 2009) that we should precede everything the patient says (as well as everything that we say) with the words "I dreamt that ...," in order to recover an "internal setting" (Civitarese, 2011a), the frame of reference is immediately shifted, thus saving his (or our) words from running aground on a realism lacking in personal significance, reopening the way to the play of meaning, and revealing to the patient (and to ourselves) the path toward the resumption of dreaming one's interrupted or undreamt dreams—that is, one's very existence (Ogden, 2005).

Notes

1. The Barangers also took inspiration from Kurt Lewin, Heinrich Racker, and Enrique Pichon Rivière (de León de Bernardi, 2008). Churcher (2008) pointed out that Lewin's name is replaced by that of Merleau-Ponty in the second, revised version of the Barangers' 1961–1962 paper as republished in 1969.

2. Translator's note: For convenience, the masculine form is used for both sexes throughout this translation.

3. The lectures delivered at the Sorbonne in the 1950–1951 academic year, "The child's relation with others" (published in English in 1964), demonstrated Merleau-Ponty's familiarity with Klein's works. Klein used the concept of projective identification as the basis of an intersubjective theory of the psyche that was both extraordinarily advanced and in some respects complementary to that of Merleau-Ponty. According to Angelino, Melanie Klein fascinated Merleau-Ponty "because her writings are rich in highly concrete, indeed brutal, and quite shocking descriptions of our relations with others and with things, which bear out what he thought about the role of corporeality and the drives (libido and aggression) in our relationship with the world" (Angelino, 2005, p. 374, translated). Klein studied in detail, to a degree bordering on obsession, the mechanisms of the first introjections/projections and identifications of a child when still immersed in a state of partial non-distinction from the object. Klein, admittedly, accepted the existence of a primitive ego from birth, but, as Kristeva noted, "The fragile ego is not truly separated in the sense of a 'subject' separated from an 'object,' but it incessantly consumes the breast from within and ejects the breast into the outside world by constructing-vacating itself while constructing-vacating the Other" (Kristeva, 2000, p. 62f.). The point,

however, is that Klein's model proves valuable not only for representing the relationship between the subject and his environment at the stage described by Freud as that of primary narcissism, but also when the subject is no longer in such an elementary phase of constitution of the ego. Like Klein, Merleau-Ponty considered that identity can be thought of only in terms of difference, of the intersection between the subject's body and the world of things and other people. A person can be himself only by projecting himself outside his own self into the other, and vice versa. The subject (S) constructs himself only by transferring himself into the object (O), which is thereby transformed (O'), and by then re-introjecting from the object what he had deposited in it, thereby in turn being modified (S'); the structure of the chiasm—the resulting notation seems to allude ironically to a kind of appeal to the other—would be SOO'S . Hence, the approaches of Klein and Merleau-Ponty can be seen as complementary. Oddly enough, because Klein was interested mainly in the unconscious and in psychic reality, she in effect disregarded the *carnal*—feeling and felt—aspect of the body (even though the body is absolutely the protagonist of the subject's unconscious fantasies). Merleau-Ponty's concentration on the experience of the body, on the other hand, lead him to develop theories very close to current notions of the unrepressed, or *sensory*, unconscious and of procedural, rather than declarative, memories.

4. Cf. Baranger M: "It was when we reviewed Bion's studies on small groups that we modified and added precision to our thinking in a direction different from transference–countertransference interaction. ... We then understood that the field is much more than interaction and intersubjective relations. ... Translating what is described as the group's 'basic assumption' to the individual analytic situation, we spoke of the 'basic unconscious phantasy' that emerges in the analytic situation, created by the same field situation. ... This phantasy is not the sum or combination of the individual fantasies of the two members of the analytic couple, but an original set of fantasies created by the field situation itself. It emerges in the process of the analytic situation and has no existence outside the field situation, although it is rooted in the unconscious of the members" (M. Baranger, 2005, p. 62f.).

5. However, consider the following passage from Bion's letter to Rickman of March 7, 1943: "The more I look at it the more it seems to me that some very serious work needs to be done along analytical and field theory lines to elucidate". (Conci, 2011). The article published in *The Lancet* in 1943 and signed by both, "Intra-group tensions in therapy—Their study as the task of the group" (which subsequently became the first chapter of *Experiences in Groups* (Bion, 1948), contains what is clearly a

field theory. Lacan (1947) had no hesitation in describing this article as miraculous!

6. Kojève concisely summed up Hegel's conception of the subject as follows: "If they are to be *human*, they must be at least *two* in number" (Kojève, 1947, p. 43).

7. Cf. Eco: metaphor "A trope that seems to be the most primary will appear instead as the most derivative, as the result of a semantic calculus that presupposes other preliminary semiotic operations. A curious situation for a figure of speech that has been recognised by many to be the basis of every other" (Eco, 1984, p. 87).

8. Translator's note: Literally horseshoes, but the Italian word is also the plural of *ferro*, the name of the analyst and one of the authors of this article.

9. New metaphors are among the "mutations" that cause a scientific paradigm to evolve (Kuhn, 1962).

10. Translator's note: The Italian word *grasso* can mean either grease or fat.

CHAPTER TWO

Stone got eyes: on Bion's seminar in Paris

Get out your colours!

The seminar Bion held in Paris in 1978[1] inspires in the reader a growing
sense of gratitude the deeper into the text he goes. The voice is unmis-
takably his: simple, direct, highly communicative, and charismatic all at
the same time. Its vigour comes from its conciseness and use of verbs. As
usual, the language this voice embodies introduces us to a world where
everything seems at one and at the same time strange, fascinating, and
true. The originality of the perspectives Bion proposes and the way he
does so ignites in the reader emotions of many different colours. We are
spectators at a show that is both surprising and enchanting. Sudden
flashes of insight shine for an instant like fireworks against the darkness of our ignorance. Thus it is that the reader feels gratitude—but also
envy, happiness, and a sense of calm and safety.

We experience relief when we hear Bion declare himself in favour of
a certain kind of insanity. It would be easy for the analyst to agree with
the patient if he were suffering from the same disorders, but "it is supposed" he remains in touch with reality. But no matter how consciously
we admit it, deep down we rebel against the idea of having a certain
share of madness inside us.

We also feel a great sense of relief when we hear him speak of the analyst as someone who has to discover the artist in himself and who should not worry about being "non-scientific" (of course, from another more general perspective he does worry about it, but that's not the point here). At times we find it difficult to renounce the so-called scientific nature of psychoanalysis, because we need certainty and faith, and we are unwilling to recognise that we are much closer to artists and that we should be able to explore the analytic situations we live through from every possible vertex.

We deal with things that the senses do not see and that we can only intuit. To make them visible, we can talk about them, but then we are forced to acknowledge the dramatic inadequacy of our language. How can we speak of emotions? How can we touch others with words?

Laura and negation

Back from the summer holidays Laura mentions her two daughters, one five and the other twelve, each with their own difficulties. She explains that they had suffered a lot because of the distance from the father; they were angry with him, jealous of the other people he was with. Laura then speaks of her husband as someone who denies all emotion and who opposed her idea of taking at least the younger child to a "psychologist" because he does not believe in psychology in the slightest, and if anything thinks that psychologists have an adverse effect on people's minds.

It is clear what is happening: on the one hand, Laura is seething with emotions of anger and jealousy that have to do with the analysis and holidays; on the other, she denies it.

How can I tell her all this without her rejecting it right away? For some time now I have been using a particular mode of interpretation. I express my thoughts about interpretation along these lines: "I have a problem; I have things I want to tell you, but I know that they would make you angry and that you would tell me they are not true. What should I do? What I would like to say to you is ..."

If we were artists, it would be easier. Artists are not limited to abstract verbal communication. But we are artists, Bion suggests, or, at least, we should have the courage to use our skills as artists—after all, don't we all dream at night and during the day? Don't we all compose the poetry of the mind that Freud (1891) talks about in his book *On Aphasia*? Don't we all constantly transform "sensoriality" into images, sounds, colours, all possible kinds of pictograms, audiograms, etc. olfactograms, and then assemble these fragments into narratives, paintings, olfactory melodies, musical odours, and so on. Then our "atelier" must be in creative disorder to the maximum degree we are able to bear, certain that the shadows and shapes will then come to life. If we discovered that we are just not capable of it, then that would be sad. We should infer from this—Bion explains with his typical calm, peremptory tone, which leaves us convinced and baffled—that we are in the wrong job.

The whole Paris seminar focuses on the problem of how to transform invisible emotions into emotions that can be painted, smelt, tasted, touched. Colours, senses, emotions, desires: this is the lexicon of experience that is alive. A patient comes to analysis either because they do not feel anything, which cuts them off from the lifeblood of life, or because they are too upset by violent emotions, which leave them stunned at every occasion. In both cases, they are unable to give a personal meaning to what happens to them. The truth of their existence eludes them: not a "scientific" or rational truth but an emotional one. But the truth about himself that the analyst can offer will give a sense of joy and fullness of life only if it is the result of sharing, only if it springs from heartfelt agreement. How to achieve this truth and how to say it, which is in fact the same thing, is the problem with which the analyst is continually confronted.

For this reason, if we are trying to say something true and to find "a language [...] of the soul for the soul" (Rimbaud, 1871, p. 364[2]), like the poet, the analyst must be a clairvoyant. After all, even stone has eyes, as Bion reminds us by quoting from *Vitrail*, a poem by José-Maria de Hereida, and sees the light that spreads over it ("the effigies on the tombs: they cannot see, they cannot hear, but with their eyes of stone they see these colours spread out on the floor"). Artists are masters of these transformations. Every genuine artist tells the truth, albeit in his own way, in his own unmistakable style. How does Cézanne do it, for example (since Bion refers to the painting of Mont Sainte-Victoire)? It's a mystery. Recently while visiting the Cézanne exhibition at Milan's Royal Palace, at some point I had a kind of epiphany: that's how he does it! His apples are not motionless on the canvas but they move! Seeing is believing. They move! This was a way of understanding Cézanne and containing the anxiety of not understanding.

But even in analysis, and when we write about analysis, the characters must move (and must move us), they must live, they must impress us as if they were not made of paper but of flesh. "Does the last scientific article that you read in the *International Journal of Psychoanalysis* remind you of real people, or doesn't it?" Bion asks rhetorically. How many articles, books (how many analyses) were born dead or struggle to find the barest shred of vitality? It is thus evident that the problem of language, expression, and writing runs through the whole of psychoanalysis and that it is wrong to imagine it as a hiatus between clinical and theoretical activity.

The problem, during the session as on the page, is how to transform "O" into something that has the flavour of real experience and is thus rich in personal meaning.

Manuela

Manuela is an extremely obliging ten-year-old girl in analysis. She sees her twelve-year-old sister as a rival. The sister has recently recovered from a serious illness and now her parents have given her the Alsatian puppy she always dreamt of. Manuela's analyst is very annoyed by what he believes to be an unwise purchase and parental intrusion into Manuela's analysis, because the girl has a "phobia of dogs". He decides to take it up with the parents and reproaches them for having disturbed Manuela's analysis without even stopping to think for a moment.

By doing this, however, Manuela's analyst leaves "a fact" (buying the dog) as a mere "fact", that is, within the therapy, an "O", without directing this "O" towards its subjectivisation within the analysis itself. He does not allow it as a "fact in itself"—if you will—to transform itself from being a β element, into K, α, meaning, narrative. Indeed, in analysis any "O" can only take the path of column 2 in Bion's Grid (precisely where we find lies), to be transformed into the subjective truth of that analysis. It would still be a misrepresentation/travesty/transformation of "O", as Grotstein constantly reminds us (2007).

After all, from this perspective the puppy could be dreamt of as the hooligan Manuela is afraid of, something alive and new that comes into her psychic life and into the analysis, and the parents who have bought it as a description of the analyst's work, who has managed to bring something new and alive into the analysis. Of course other vertices are needed, too, but are not so cogently psychoanalytic.

Basically, starting off a transformation means dreaming "the facts" into narremes that form part of a complete narrative. This involves having the courage to consider dreams not as a way of getting in touch with the emotional or psychological truth, but as a lie capable of bending "O" to our need for meanings and narratives that organise emotions, affects, contingencies, and events.

Dreaming impossible worlds

Bion orchestrates the seminar with the consummate skill of an accomplished speaker. He does not describe the subject of the talk but dramatises it immediately. How should I talk?, he asks himself. In English? And if I were speaking in French, would you understand? But this is no trivial question of courtesy towards his audience, because the language one really speaks is not so easy to determine. It is crucial that one speak one's own language, not school French (or school psychoanalysis). There are the senses, what we can see directly, and there is intuition, what we can see but not with the senses. A patient comes to the session, is of a certain age, but we think he is of a different age. It is not obvious how old he is and when he was actually born. We do not care much what his birth certificate says because that is not the reason he has come for analysis. Perhaps he is actually much younger or older than he feels he is. For the analyst what is important is putting himself in a position where he knows what age the patient thinks he is.

Jane

In a wonderful story by Somerset Maugham, "Jane", the protagonist, a widow of about sixty years of age, listless and lacking any real charm, is sought in marriage by a young man in his early twenties. The enthusiasm and dedication he shows "transforms" her. Jane regains her youth and fascination. I imagine it is as if she had lost twenty years. Jane then leaves the young man to marry someone of the same age as her with whom she thinks she has many more things in common. Her sister-in-law—herself a widow—witnesses these changes and as she does so experiences a series of emotions: anger, resentment, jealousy, envy.

We care nothing about the patient's age. We are interested in the stories that we manage to kindle with her and, what is no less important, those we fail to kindle.

Carlotta

There was a time I was working in the front line service for people who turned for advice to the Centre of Psychoanalysis of which I was a member. One day I opened the appointments diary and saw the name "XY" together with a professional title (Engineer), so I went into the waiting room and invited the only person there to come into my office, addressing him with typical Italian respect for titles as *Ingegnere*. With an offended and resentful air he said in a tone of the utmost seriousness: "I am not an engineer, I am a seven-year-old girl and my name is Carlotta".

At the time I had been unable to "see Carlotta"; now many years have passed and I am used to accepting all the possible identities of the patient in front of me and all the possible stories we can generate, all the possible worlds (from the point of view of psychic reality) and all the impossible worlds (in terms of material reality); the only thing that limits me is the patient's occasional comment that I am "off course". Then there are the stories we are not able to "open up" out of self-defence. Our identity, which is also made up of occluded stories, is still the central part of the creative work we share with the patient. But when this creative work is accessible, that is, when we have a sense of inner security that allows us to see everything as if for the first time, it is not wrong to speak of pleasure.

Pleasure is one of the key questions that Bion addresses in his Paris seminar: do you like the music you play? Are you passionate about the story of the book you're writing? Do you want to know how it's going to end? Are you curious to know why someone has a certain face, with certain wrinkles? Are you fascinated by the shapes and figures formed by the play of light in the room? What artistic genre (vertex) do you find most appropriate to express yourself? If we were painters, what colours would we use to depict the encounter? If we were musicians, what kind of music would we play? What fantasies would we have together with this patient and what would they be about? Do we want to see him again the next day? And will he want to come again? This is the tone of the questions that Bion addresses to the reader. He does this to make us understand that it is essential to apprehend how we feel. These things are far from being obvious.

The essential point Bion is insisting on here is the importance of forgetting about psychoanalysis and psychiatry, diagnosis, and other things, and leaving the mind as open as possible to feelings, fantasies and emotions as they are triggered in the encounter. In particular, we must not ward off the most erratic assumptions that we make and the most improbable fantasies that run through our minds, as they may be much more relevant to the only "facts" that count in the analysis (feelings) than everything we can remember of the past and the future. But to do this one needs a great soul, a soul which, like that of the artists we admire, embraces all that is human.

A game we often play with small groups of analysts is to ask them to think up short stories starting only from a title and then get them to try writing the same story in a different narrative genre, as Queneau does in his *Exercises in Style*. We ask them to tell the same story each time with a different storyline: say, a detective story, a film noir, a romantic comedy, or erotic fiction. We ask them to rewrite the same story as if, for example, the protagonist were a seven-year-old child or a fifty-seven-year-old housewife. A colleague has dubbed this "Operation Svitol", after a popular product that is used in Italy to lubricate rusty locks.

In Ogden's view, helping the patient to dream dreams that he would be incapable of dreaming alone, is the goal of psychoanalysis. The curiosity we, and the patient, feel towards occluded stories must be at its maximum and we need to give ourselves and our patients sufficient reasons for wanting to develop the "dream that we are creating together".

What Bion is also suggesting, between the lines, is that it is not only important to take pleasure in doing analysis and the disciplined use of intuition, but that we also need to develop a personal style. The analyst is himself in his style, not in the theories he learns from books. In this way he can try to bring to life the artist he has in itself (or to put it another way, to make his unconscious and his dream-thought work). It is no coincidence that the seminar closes on the theme of how important it is to experience the beauty of interpretation or also how patients can turn to us with very beautiful words. Beauty, concludes Bion, is what makes bearable that which we fear. Just as we want the analysis to help the patient to become what he is, so too we should allow ourselves the freedom to become the analysts we are.

Bion's last writings and seminars have something phenomenal about them. As a consummate artist Bion brings about in the participants at the seminar and in his readers the transformation he is talking about. Quite naturally he says things that we have inside us but which we never dared to think. If we did not have them inside us, if we did not feel them to be true, we would not recognise them. Instead, we feel with a sense of wonder that we are understood, our anxieties feel accepted, the rules that weigh us down become less burdensome.

It is sometimes said that Bion's writings contain very few clinical illustrations. This is true but equally it is not true. Bion could never be any different from what he is in his seminars. He creates a situation in which one is aware of some disturbance in the air. Gradually, this disorder is made visible, then absorbed and transformed. In this sense, reading the seminar is an aesthetic experience. What is expressed and the way it is expressed are inextricably intertwined. The same thing said in different words would be less true (or *truer*). Many writers feel this way; a case in point is Cormac McCarthy (2010):[3] "I'm not interested in writing short stories. Anything that doesn't take years of your life and drive you to suicide hardly seems worth doing". This is something we sense very forcefully in Bion.

Surely this something that it is so worth engaging ourselves for to the point of risking madness is in fact life itself. Bion lived psychoanalysis with the same passion with which he lived his life. It could not be any different. Otherwise we would be looking at a strange split personality. This means that the lesson of the seminar is not only a lesson in psychoanalysis but a life lesson—as Winnicott pointed out regarding the importance of staying "alive". An analyst who is not "alive" would not be able to help anyone; at most he might make boring, cerebral interventions and use some algorithm to help him understand the suffering of others—but without any true humanity. He would certainly not be able to rekindle a flame of life in the patient (in himself).

There can be no doubt, however, that the seminar is also a true lesson in theory and psychoanalytic technique. Bion's enigmatic style might be confusing, because it takes us to familiar places and makes us look at them as if they were not familiar. But in actual fact everything he says can be translated into precise and effective technical principles and recommendations: analysis is therapy that serves to enhance people's ability to find a meaning in existence; the facts of the analysis are intangible, namely emotions and feelings; to apprehend these facts we need to develop intuition, in other words, to put the unconscious to work; analyst and patient are part of a field in which it is difficult to say what belongs to one and what to the other; we must transcend the boundaries between body and mind, and between subject and object; the analyst should be in a particular state of hallucinosis that helps him see things as the patient sees them; in this way he can tell the patient something true, which he, like the reader, acknowledges as having within himself, but which he had never thought of that way; the experience of sharing is the model of anything that sounds true, and so on.

"Get out your colours!", Bion suggests. The invitation is also to read this text (in fact, to listen to the verbal text of the seminar) not so as to know what Bion really means or meant, but *to be read* by the text and to expand one's awareness of one's own experience and sense of the fullness of life (Ogden, 2012). What matters to Bion is that the reader write his own text while reading it (think his thoughts as he listens), that he become its author on a par with the actual author. For this reason, not only as a way of reading Bion's text but as a way for us to be read by his text, we have decided to insert some of our own clinical material, as a kind of indirect or performative comment.

Defences against knowledge

In the Paris seminar we find hardly any of the strange terms Bion deployed to revamp the entire lexicon of psychoanalysis. Nor do we sense the rarefied atmosphere of his most abstract writings, for example, in *Transformations*. There is a beautiful passage where one of the seminar participants tries to bring things back onto the known territory of psychoanalytic theory. Bion has just finished talking about the need to see what is not there, which is truer than what can be perceived through the senses. He gives the example of the painting of a tree and how the artist is also able to show the beholder roots that are invisible because they are underground. A colleague then asks if this metaphor has anything to do with the unconscious. Remaining just about desolately patient or (patiently desolate), Bion says that "unconscious" is one of those words invented by Freud to draw attention to something that really exists, but then, as usual, one gets caught up in endless disputes between Kleinians and Freudians and all sorts of theories, and that eventually one loses sight of the simple fact that what is at stake is a human being and a mind.

Often the limitations to the creativity of the analysis are a question of how far down the analyst, and consequently the analytic couple, is willing to go, bearing in mind that their relationship is in many ways asymmetric, with responsibility for the depth of the immersion lying with the analyst.

What means or defences can the analyst use to avoid diving into waters that are too deep for him?

One much used means is to fail to provide the humus suitable for the development of the characters the patient has brought into play. The easiest, most naive and, at the same time, most subtle of these means is to situate the "characters" as people in history.

For example, if a patient talks about an uncle suspected of uxoricide, this criminal aspect that he is trying to place in the field can be "bonsaized" and crystallised by placing it inside the patient's history rather than providing him with all the seeds of growth and development that would enable the criminal aspects of the patient (and perhaps of the analyst, or both) to find a script and an appropriate setting.

Another ploy that likewise extinguishes stories that it would be possible to develop is to turn to the comfort of a supposed External Reality, which can then be doubly chained when it becomes Historical Reality.

The criminal cousin

A patient talks of a cousin of his grandfather who had been a member of the Salvatore Mesina gang, a gang responsible for a number of kidnappings, some of which had ended fatally for the victims. Logically, this character, "the grandfather's criminal cousin", can be put to sleep, or be lethargised or it can become a "seed" that will germinate any number of possible stories if it finds suitable terrain and is given adequate irrigation; and this will put on the playbill split-off and previously never thought psychic operations.

Essentially each story is the possible progeny of sequences of pictograms that may be faced with a censor, like the priest in the *Cinema Paradiso* who cut out all the kisses or also the unforgettable Peppino De Filippo in *The Temptation of Dr. Antonio* by Fellini (1962), who was outraged by the advertising billboard of Anita Ekberg that had been placed in front of his house and wanted it removed at all costs. He then dreamt that she "descended" from the billboard and, like some huge King Kong in New York, invaded night-time Rome. At the end a procession of prigs led by a priest advanced though the dark. Like zombies out of *Thriller* they sang the praises of Dr. Mazzuolo who had delivered them from the devil. But by now he had repented, or rather had fallen into a swoon that could only herald the arrival of psychiatrists.

Essentially each analyst at work often resorts to "blacklisting" potential characters who are likely to cause disturbance, disorder, and fear during the analytical work, becoming encysted in the patient, like dangerous war remnants that are sometimes defused by bomb disposal experts and that sometimes explode unexpectedly, catching everyone by surprise.

At all events, the responsibility for an analysis, whether it be at 45°, 90°, 180° or 360°, rests mainly on the shoulders of the analyst. Analyses can be like a closed fan where the slats are still positioned on top of each other, and where many stories will never see the light of day, or they can be "fans with gradually opening slats" that will tell growing numbers of possible stories. But fans can be opened more and more, so there's never an end.

It is often the case that theories, even those that have proved most useful—like the Oedipus complex or the Unconscious—(and in saying this we are simply paraphrasing what Bion says in his *Tavistock Seminars*, 2005a), insofar as they are already known, function as barriers, as light pollution obscuring what we do not know. Moreover, this is the only really interesting work to be done in analysis: going in search of the unknown and learning to tolerate knowing less and less but having learnt the method for trying to learn more.

We are in no doubt that many analyses are in fact conducted by analysts who behave like ostriches with their heads in the sand of theory—so as not to risk seeing things that might frighten and hurt them. What we are trying to say is that the analyst often stands as the great anaesthetist or narcotiser of "possible stories", all of whose subversive power remains embryonic compared to often more normopathic, adequate, and orthodox aspects.

Perhaps the question of orthodoxy (and hence of adaptation to what is known and shared) is also connected to this as a phobia of possible subversion, and if psychoanalysis has historically had an incredible subversive power, many now call upon it as a way of tranquillising with maps of pseudo-normality.

The imperative often seems to be to defend ourselves from the "present". This is what happened in the case of posters for an exhibition by Maurizio Cattelan in Milan that featured Hitler kneeling in prayer. The posters were immediately banned on the grounds that they offended the memory of the victims of Nazism. Few realised that this particular Hitler might not be the Hitler of the past, but a memento of the Hitler who inhabits the human community, and that metaphorical and concrete deportations may still be continuing in the indifference of all.[4]

Again, there was the scandal of puppets of children hanging in trees, another work by Cattelan some years ago, also stigmatised for their supposed bad taste, whereas in fact they were perhaps a comment about a truth of today, for example, lack of respect for "children" in all possible forms.[5] Everything that makes us think is branded as bad taste and not seen as a way of shaking up slumbering minds.

Religions receive different treatment. Every religion represents a different attempt to use orthodox rules to deal with all the emotions that seethe inside us. Even a different religion, which calls into question one's own, is seen as a source of disturbance. Just imagine the absence of religions, and to repeat the point, the need for orthodoxy is no different in psychoanalysis.

Liliana and abuse

Liliana has a dream in which she is in a doctor's waiting room, when she sees a middle-aged woman arrive holding in her hand a syringe which is full of a liquid that turns people red. The woman wants to inject this liquid into a teenager in the room, but Liliana fights to stop her, and the woman only manages to inject half of the vial.

Liliana is suffering a crisis of shame that causes her a variety of inhibitions. It seems that now she can fight, at least in part, against the injection that causes red flushes and embarrassment.

I do not interpret the dream in a decodifying way but comment on the events.

The following day Liliana tells me about a relative of hers who is married to a girl who is very respectable but rather stiff and inhibited. He has now met a young girl from the south of Italy, who has eyes that burn with passion and who comes across as "feisty".

The relative does not know what to do; maybe he is falling in love with this girl, but what would effect would this have on family peace? This "story", if one listens to it as if it were a dream, seems to me to continue the story of the day before: the teenager, if not inhibited by injections of shame and embarrassment, turns into this "passionate girl from the south" who introduces intense emotions into the field.

Without being aware of it, I am pleased to welcome the casting of this "new character"—a real step towards symbolisation—and perhaps show my fondness for living emotions rather than the tranquillity that comes from the emotional quiet of a bland diet.

The next day the patient changes the setting and starts to speak of her daughter, a high school student who would like to change schools because she has a teacher who wants her pupils to think exactly like her, something her daughter can't stand because she sees it as abuse and oppression. At the time I fall into the trap of a story that comes from an "external event" Liliana is facing until I realise that it is simply continuing our common dream. Liliana is speaking to me of my coming down in favour of the girl from the south the day before and how she experienced my "preference" as mistreatment and abuse of power, whereas what I should be doing is giving her time and the freedom to take up a position of her own.

Our need not to know anything new, to confirm the idea that we have of ourselves as individuals and as analysts, has a strength and a tenacity that surprise us on every occasion. We feel so fragile that we are ready to dress ourselves up in any lie we think will protect us from that which we fear. No wonder then if in the Paris seminar, to move our feelings, Bion also attributed eyes to stone and described analytical work as both hard and exciting.

Notes

1. www.psychoanalysis.org.uk/bion78.htm last accessed 8 July 2014.
2. Rimbaud, A. (2002). *Rimbaud Complete*. New York: Modern Library Inc. (First published 1871).
3. http://ricerca.repubblica.it/repubblica/archivio/repubblica/2010/01/10/mccarthy-vi-racconto-la-strada-amore.html?ref=search last accessed 8 July 2014.
4. Hitler prega al ghetto di Varsavia, l'ultima provocazione di Cattelan. *La Repubblica*, 28/December 2012.
5. Berizzi, P. (2004). Bimbi impiccati, arte scandalosa. Bufera sull'opera di Cattelan. *La Repubblica*, 6 May 2004.

CHAPTER THREE

Mourning and the empty couch: a conversation between analysts

The "empty couch" accompanies us in our job as analysts no less than the "occupied couch".[1]

At the beginning there is an empty corner to be filled in the room selected to host it.

There isn't an analyst who wouldn't remember when he acquired his first couch.

I remember it perfectly.

I imagine that you too had to choose from different styles and wanted to satisfy different needs. It would be interesting to find out if different theoretical tendencies have as much influence as aesthetics.

Couches searching for patients

I chose mine on the base of two impulses. It was a day couch similar to my own analyst's (who had Sicilian-Austrian origins). On top of which, it looked like the one that my Sicilian grandparents had in their bedroom. As a child I spent so many hours on it!

Where did you find it?

I bought mine through a second-hand goods magazine, *Seconda Mano*. At the time I owned a Citroen Diane and I loaded it on the car roof to take it from Milan to Pavia. I had it restored so it acquired the look of a proper day couch. It laid there empty for a few months until I was registered by the Board and I was able to take my first patient. I had not wanted to corrupt its status of sacred object with patients in psychotherapy. Therefore for one full year I only used it four hours a week. The hours became eight with my second patient and, once I was registered, multiplied quickly.

A couch by now fully occupied.

Yes, but every now and then I had the experience of the "empty couch" again—when a patient would skip a session and each time the "emptiness" would be pregnant with meaning.

It would remain empty on weekends and holidays ...

But I did not take any notice.

And what has changed?

Now, it's a little bit like it is with children. It's like when we start thinking that they will be leaving home. We begin to look at their rooms as something very precious that we did not notice for a long time until we discover that it's going to be over!

The famous "empty nest" syndrome!

But let us go back to the couch. It has been empty also in the case of some seriously ill patients who couldn't accept to use it until the magic moment when they decided to "move in".

No, not the couch!

Of course, there are patients who aren't trusting enough to lie down. Your couch is different from mine. I have a *chaise longue*, one of those designed by Le Corbusier (but bought only because, as the patent had expired, it was dirt cheap). It's special because it is a reclining couch. For this reason it is also suitable as "half-empty" couch. Year after year S., at the beginning of each session, insisted in raising the back so that her bust would be practically as straight as if she was sitting on the chair opposite her. I don't need to tell you that I tried to interpret this in a million ways. Without any success. Today, having concluded the therapy by mutual agreement, and with very mixed results, sometimes I feel that I only treated "half" a patient.

Maybe the distance between Dr. Jekyll and Mr. Hyde was so great that it defeated all the effort invested in the case. Perhaps she couldn't afford to overcome a split, however deep, that provided her with a sense of security.

This is also what I tell myself. In the end, among the last things I told her, I think I said to her rather fondly about her having defied her father.

And what was her reply?

She smiled.

The supervisions empty couch

She had only "half- moved" into the couch. I could even expect a "low-intensity" transference …

However, on the topic of removals, my couch moved with me when I moved houses and when I opened my professional rooms out of them. Altogether, three times. Throughout the years, it was always occupied many hours each day. Then, without me even taking notice, it began to be lighter. Once I became a specialist in training, I very slowly began to increase the supervision hours and to decrease the hours of work behind the couch.

The emptiness again.

Not only that but the rhythm of the empty/full couch also marked the happy and sad moments of my life when I had to cancel a session because of one of the many events that can occur. Now, as I find myself working more and more as a supervisor, the couch is even emptier and lighter. At this stage I am inclined to think that, totally irresponsibly,[2] I must have used some defence mechanisms.

Or do you mean "unconsciously"?

Ah, I would like to know that!

Anyway, as you know better than I, Ogden, our Californian friend—I don't know how but he always manages to surprise me—emphasised that, like analysis, supervision is a new and unprecedented form of relationship invented by Freud. He also added that, as when analysing a patient, it's a matter of dreaming his dream never dreamt—it is the same for the analyst's interrupted dream while supervising him.

You mean to say that ultimately it's a case of making an effort to see the couch occupied, only *apparently* empty, which means to interpret also the supervision session as a dream.

Even where you think you should be only adopting effective teaching or good "pedagogy".

I can see that you are starting to learn the lesson!

Where did the analyst go?

On the topic of defences sometimes it is not the couch that is empty but the analyst's chair. In fact you could see this as a particular example of the previous one, which means that in both situations what goes missing is the relationship. There are many studies on *burn out* of psychiatrists when they have to deal with serious pathologies, with chronic cases, with lack of resources or conflict with the institution in which they operate, but I believe there is not enough research on *burn out* of analysts, especially in its most insidious forms.

Of what kind?

The symptoms are lack of enthusiasm for a job that he had originally chosen with passion, the feeling of living a not gratifying routine, the tendency to drag along at the expense[3] of patients, an emotional withdrawal that is dangerous for him and for the others.

Would you say that another aspect of these problems is the rivalry among groups and individuals due to power issues within the institutional organs of psychoanalytic societies?

You read my mind. The status of the analyst is precarious. He feels that he has little social recognition even if he has gained a good reputation for his scientific achievements. He regrets not having followed other careers and he simply needs to be able to put a feather on his cap or to pin a medal on the lapel of his coat every now and then.

At that stage he ends up confusing a scientific society with a convent (with all its consequences: see what happens in Eco's *In the name of the Rose!*) or with a political party.

I agree. An analyst's career does not offer many possibilities. It's kind of stuck. Year after year one is forced to always do the same things, and with time, a feeling of fragility takes over and the horizons of one's life begins to close. One can clearly see it in the puerile narcissism of many colleagues. Freud got that right as well: we should follow his advice more and every now and then go back to analysis.

And don't you dare to tell me now that Freud understood it all!!

Why?!? Isn't it true?!

The multiplication of couches

Anyway, you make me reflect … I realise only now that we are talking about it that the multiplication of couches is a defence mechanism that

I have unconsciously put into practice. I added one at home. I justified it by telling myself that, should I become ill, I could continue to work from home without going out (I NEVER DID IT!). I also put a second one in my rooms in Milan where I work on weekends and where I only hold supervision groups.

And there, you don't know what to do with it.

Yet, even there, where I don't need it, I convinced myself that it was necessary to have a couch. It helps to prove that I am an analyst.

After all, if I am allowed to say it, what analysts "invest" in a piece of furniture is comic! Even more so as we said that what really matters is the internal setting of the analyst, not the material one.

To tell you the truth I believe that, both in my life at home or in the professional rooms where I meet my groups, it was a way to make it more a daily presence, not strictly connected to my job, but with a domestic usage, disconnected from the patient, as it was in my grandparents' house: the day-couch for the afternoon nap. Maybe it's a trick to prevent the grief of the empty couch by restoring its function as a piece of daily furniture.

An overcrowded couch

Of course, we should know it well, we sometimes use defences against depression that become manic. Think of when one works too much. Unfortunately this only produces one result: when one sees too many patients, the couch appears to be empty because one ends up not seeing anybody.

You mean: one really doesn't see them, even if they are there?

That is exactly what I mean. The same happens if, in between patients, one does not make a long enough pause. He loses himself maybe because he is chased by the ghosts of age and of financial crisis, by the needs of growing children, by the need to be reassured of his own worth through the dependence of his patients. Subtle forms of perversion can then creep into the relationship. It's easy to become distracted, restless, bored.

Let the one who is guiltless be the first to throw a stone … as the Gospel says. It must be for this reason that some time ago I happened to book two appointments at the same time, a new consultation and a catch-up session that had been decided a longtime before.

It's a possibility, for sure. However, even in this case every cloud has a silver lining. The key is finding an analytical perspective to the event.

Accidents of this kind, although embarrassing, push us to exercise a little auto-analysis and, if possible, to straighten the situation. Furthermore, if it is coincidental, it's also useful for analysis.

In fact, so it was. The two patients who arrived at the same time—I realised later on—from a certain point of view were the same person or, even better, carried different aspects of the same patient. As always, one must never give too much credit to the senses, and instead must rely on intuition. The famous, should I say infamous, Bion's "Faith"!

By saying so, you make me realise that there are many ways to do that. For instance, as the couch becomes lighter the configuration of the "chairs set in a circle" becomes more important; the chairs make the activity of supervision more relevant and at the same time they fill the room with many "patients". Two birds with one stone.

The supervision group

Yes, and you shouldn't delude yourself. It's not really that the groups work so well to deny grief. I find myself playing the role of "grandfather" and uncle to these people on supervision who come like grandchildren to fill a space.

Do you mean that it's like the feeling of rheumatic pain when the weather changes?

More or less. On the other hand, it is reasonable for the analyst to gradually lighten the couch weight. In the years, I arrived at an extreme when I had thirteen patients four times a week instead of the five sittings that I have now. I also know that in my future there are four or five new patients who are waiting for analysis but that after these I have decided to take no more.

At some stage one realises they are too old to have another child because there wouldn't be enough time to reasonably expect to bring it up to the age in which it is independent.

But since I am one of those people who think that for them to be an analyst there has to be both a *"setting"* and a patient—I ask myself WHAT WILL I be when I do not have any more patients on my couch.

The empty chair

The problem brings another question: what will become of my analyst's chair'??? When, gradually, I will leave my seat vacant and I will begin the exile from my ex-kingdom, even if it is a voluntary one, what will I call myself? Ex-analyst? I could say: Member of the Psycho-Analytical Society. And I could add: with old lost functions (the couch and the chair) and with new acquired functions (groups, teaching, writing). But how will I define myself, what will I call myself? My father was a surgeon ... Let see ... How did he introduce himself when he stopped operating? Maybe "retired doctor" ... Maybe we, too, could call ourselves ...

Don't say it!

I will not say it.

My father, instead, is a farmer. At seventy-seven he does not want to hear about retiring. On the contrary, he just bought vineyards that belonged to his father, a very Freudian choice!

Turning seventy

Be careful, turning seventy is a daunting finishing line!

As you always say, a "pivotal moment".

Like turning sixty.

Why not also fifty?

And forty then???

Don't exaggerate!

True.

I have a confession. When I printed the notes you sent me for this work and I saw the words "seventies"[4] written on it, I actually read "170s"!!! I wish!!! When one talks about the unconscious ...

Analysis as a practice for mourning

It is something worth wishing for ourselves! The point is that, for the analyst, analysis implies a sort of "continuous mourning", from abstinence to non-acting in the context of *setting* and time; the time of sessions, holidays, mourning for the end of analysis and for letting the patient go his own way. Then other kinds of mourning come with the end of our own analysis.

We could also add to this list the mourning implicit in changing one's institutional status, the mourning of not-understanding and the mourning related to the different stages in life that continuously end.

Who is afraid of the empty couch?

Let's go back to our story. Why do analysts find it so hard to age? In all psychoanalytical societies the powerful roles are in the hands of the most senior members, the gerontocracy, who put their brain to rest a few decades ago. Airline pilots retire and so do academics, bus drivers, surgeons, teachers, hairdressers, and bank employees.

Not the analysts.

Not the analysts.

Does this mean that they feel they belong to a church or a political party more than to a scientific society? Or do they nurture a subtle and very insidious lack of faith in the method? As if their role was more important than their function?

You would need a totally secular psychoanalysis.

Yes.

But you well know that politics is not foreign to the struggle of ideas within the scientific community.

It goes without saying, but isn't it possible to see the victory of a kind of politics that aims for quality of research, for originality and creativity less than for the principle of authority?

Trips

I wonder if the trips made on invitations by psychoanalytical societies might not carry the same meaning. In fact they are an instrument of politics because of the net of relationships that they allow you to establish but they also constitute a further defence mechanism. Also the famous administrative "offices" may well have a consolatory value. Even those give you the chance to escape the claustrophobic climate that can subtly surround you when you have such a solitary job.

Interruptions

This topic brings us back to the theme of mourning. Is it the case that we have a job that from its beginning confronts us with the theme of mourning? We establish a strong bond with somebody who eventually will leave us. Obsessively, analysts refer in all they do to the mother–child relationship model or anyway to the oedipal family model. Loewald goes to the extreme and say that curing with analysis means ending up loving a patient as you would love your own child.

But there are different types of children … Some never want to leave home. Others go when we feel they are still too fragile to venture into the real world. Others again abandon us suddenly and these are the most painful situations. Moreover, often they were the ones whom we loved the most … May be this is exactly the reason …

Looking at an empty couch in the time slot of a patient who has stopped analysis is one of the hardest things to accept. We feel guilty and angry. Sometimes this all remains an unconscious feeling.

The analyst is forced to come to terms with his own limits.

Bion affirms that it is a miracle after all that a patient continues to come back day after day.

It's important for me to say this, not because it's necessarily true, but because it tears us away from the psychosis of everyday banalities, when the thing has already taken its own course.

What one feels is not very different from when a romantic relationship is severed. Even the steadiness of personal professional identity starts shaking.

Sometimes our patients make us understand through the smallest clues how hard it is to deal with separation. Did it never happen to you, for example, to notice that a patient, leaving at the end of a session, left something on the couch?

Lost objects

Let me think … You just took a patient to the door. You go back to the room and you realise at a glance that there is something on the couch: a key, a mobile phone, a handkerchief, a few coins or a match.

That happened with A.: a few days after the death of his beloved mother, when the sitting ends, I see on the empty couch the red and black beads of a bracelet from a not-for-profit shop that he used to wear on his wrist. The sight immediately gives me the idea of what he is going through. The thread that kept together the life of an almost home-bound person, wrapped in a very tight bond with his mother, has been cut. His emotions roll on the floor with nothing that keeps them together. But also, from a point of view closer to us, may be a session that, because of his uncontainable pain, didn't console him at all.

This also appears to allude to the critical moment of departure.

Those beads remained for me the symbol of good and bad, black and red emotions: those emotions we can feel only if we meet somebody with whom we share an experience.

Some patients are so afraid to become alone that, in order not to be in the difficult situation of having to separate, they never come to therapy. I mean: they come, but aren't really there.

The invisible patient

What do you mean? "Invisible" patients?!

Exactly.

Bion writes somewhere that if the analyst thinks that the patient who is coming is not married, even if he in reality is, he must take this very seriously and should not trust his senses. As you can see, it's the opposite of a medical treatment which is based on evidence. The point is that our evidence is different and is related to subjectivity, with events that one can know or grasp by intuition or feeling only, with things that one does not smell or see, even if, when one talks about them, it should be as if they were really seen, touched, smelled, suffered, tasted.

And the "invisible patients"?

It is an example of empty couch. The invisible patient comes regularly to sessions. He speaks. He never asks anything. He appears not to notice the presence of the analyst. Just as he came, he gets up and goes away. He is hard to see because he does neither bring nor stir emotions. What he needs instead is to transmit the sentiment that he carries inside that the world is ending. May be in *bonsai* scale.

I find myself pretty well in your description. I noticed E. only after I upset her by cancelling a few sessions in a row at the last minute. In this way I managed to tease a lioness that was asleep in the corner. Her roars made me fear awful consequences but in the meantime her analysis became more pleasant. E. came out of the cage in which she was imprisoned and in which she had unfortunately locked herself again at times and she made me see that it was possible to have lively sessions with her also.

Skipped sessions

Sometimes the patient is only temporarily invisible. Some patients need to skip many sessions. But it isn't a way *not* to be analysed. It's *their* way. They make you understand in the clearest possible way that even when they are there, it is as if they were not there or that they don't feel "seen" by the analyst. The analyst goes through the session with the patient's phantom. It can also happen that he is the one who chases the patient away. It sometimes happened to me that I mistook the ending time of a session. By asking my too "good" patient S. to finish before time, I was making time, in her hour, even if for only a few minutes, for M., another much "naughtier" patient. But here again, was she another patient or a hidden aspect of the first one that I unconsciously was trying to provoke?

Is Freud dead?

On the topic of phantoms, lately the "empty couch phantom" wonders around in psychoanalytical societies. How many times have we been told that Freud is dead, that psychoanalysis is a superstition from last century, that Wittgenstein tore it to bits and that Popper had it dead and buried! The list of writers that occasionally try to emerge from anonymity by attacking Freud supposed misbehaviour ("He betrayed his wife to sleep with his sister in law!"), and usually in bad faith, grows continuously and gets the attention of the more superficial newspapers and audience. Cognitive sciences are aggressive (although they are themselves in a critical stage, maybe more than psychoanalysis itself), the world of academics locks itself in its caste privileges. The analyst, who already needs to deal with what is left of the ideals that led him to follow such an uncertain career (at least in regard to his conscious reasons for choosing it), endures a chronic sense of frustration. It may be not be a big worry but, in the long run, the constant dripping wears away the stone.

If this picture is also accompanied by the not-very-rosy perspective of seeing the number of patients drop, the feeling grows dramatically. The empty couch becomes then the ghost that hovers about in informal meetings, in conventions and also when he is alone with the patient.

It is the usual refrain. "Are you going through a critical stage?" is the distressed question that everybody asks you.

I would say that there is something else. It is the feeling of having devoted all your life to something that, after all, didn't deserve it and that is destined to disappear from the list of things that matter.

May be in this way one could explain the faith based inflexibility and the cult of authority that underline statements such as : "Freud said that!", with variations such as "Freud already said that", "Freud would have loved it", up to comical effects, when one finds, let's say, in Freud in 1908 something that anticipates Freud in 1923. Of the kind: not only that Freud said that, but also that he said it before he even said it (if you want I will send you the bibliography).

I agree, but I believe that there does not exist a deeper theory of the function of the mind nor any better cure for some disorders that most other theories would give up as untreatable. Therefore it's unlikely that psychoanalysis will die or that it's already dead without us even noticing. I would like to suggest banning certain little words that grow like weeds in our theoretical fields: "drift", for example, or "specificity", "risk", "Babel" etc. It would be nice if we were not scared to use our brain without fearing at every step disastrous drifts, losing the specificity of something or run God knows what risk. If you take notice, they are diabolical little words.

I agree. They almost always express moralistic attitudes, really anti-Freudian. The point is that this situation results in wide anxiety, due to the fear that the object (the couch) in which we have strongly invested might disappear. I repeat, the phantom of the empty couch hovers about the psychoanalytical societies.

One may think that this is a sort of trick of destiny or rather of necessity: it is as if people who, as a job, practice mourning and teach other people to practice with mourning, find it hard to identify in a discipline that requires them to stay in uncertainty and doubt.

The psychoanalyst with no couch

It appears that one of the signs of this crisis is the reduction of vocations for this job among psychiatrists in training.

It's like this, and not only in Italy. The crisis of psychoanalysis coincides with the crisis of Freudian psychiatry.

We could call it psychoanalysis (or the psychoanalyst) without a couch.

It is a species that is becoming progressively rare. Biological psychiatry dominates.

The password for the National Health Service is *"manage or perish"*.

Following the same logic, also cognitive therapies become victim of this efficient mercantilism.

Or of the pharmaceutical industry.

A praise for the "siesta"

I must tell you something. It happens occasionally, when I am too tired and a patient has cancelled a session, that I lie on the couch and have a *siesta*. I had never thought about it. But couldn't it be a good way to chase the phantom away from the empty couch? To exorcise the sudden hole? In this manner the patient becomes his own therapist's therapist, his best colleague, by inviting him, in a sort of way, to have a little extra analysis. The analyst who allows himself to have a siesta on the vacant couch, prepares to concretely dream the interrupted dream of his patient's accidental absence.

Lately, during one of these pauses, I dreamt that I was at the beach on a cliff and that I had to dive. Somebody, a friend, was loudly inviting me to do it, but I was afraid that below, in the waves, there may be a shark. But I dived ... Mmmm ... I am one who shakes only at the thought of swimming where there is only the reef to protect me from sharks. Even in the swimming pool I use the ladder ... Could it be a way of telling myself that somewhere there was some aggression that it couldn't enter the room? That it was the only way to reach me? That the empty couch represents the shark which we all have to face? Could it simply represent nothing else but death? What does it all mean? HOW WOULD YOU INTERPRET IT?

Empty paragraph

Notes

1. We chose not to mark the turns of speaking, even if the respective "voices" are easy to guess. A small amount of ambiguity serves the purpose to also imagine the dialogue as an interior one.
2. There is a word play here. In Italian, "irresponsibly" is "incoscientemente", "unconsciously" is "inconsciamente".
3. In Italian: "alle spalle", literally: "behind his back".
4. In Italian: "I 70".

CHAPTER FOUR

The secret of faces

"I've never seen anywhere such a precise observation of the way time makes its mark on foreheads, eyelids, jaws or chins", wrote John and Katya Berger (2010, p. 23) about the faces painted by Mantegna in the Bridal Chamber of Mantua's Ducal Palace, which the same authors call "the most beautiful room in the world" (ibid, p. 11). The Bergers' keen vision helps us to see Mantegna's lines and colours; himself painting with words, he opens our senses to the perception of beauty. Like Berger with words and Mantegna with his brush, the analyst paints his faces—that is, his patients' minds—and seeks to depict their most subtle shades, the traces of time, "the signs of appointments not kept, of decisions not taken" (Benjamin, as cited in Berger, 2004, p. 12, translated).

On the left-hand side of the fresco mural in Mantua, Mantegna portrays the meeting between Ludovico Gonzaga and his son, who has brought him a letter. Each patient, too, comes along with his[1] letters—sometimes literally so—which convey his despair, hate, and love, as well as the inhuman, dehumanised, or not-yet-human and lifeless parts of himself, and asks to be helped to become what he is. However, in order to provide this help, one must be capable, precisely, of discerning the signs left by time on his face, and of showing them to him: "Look at the faces everywhere on these painted walls. Have your seen wrinkles, lines on faces better rendered? Have you ever seen painted wrinkles which are so alive?—or, rather, which have been so lived?" (Berger & Berger, 2010, p. 23).

In drawing a parallel between Berger, on one hand, and Bion, Ferro, and Ogden, on the other, Dr. Rachael Peltz (2012) stresses the creative, or "artistic", dimension of analysis: she is implicitly suggesting that the aesthetic experience can serve as a model for all that is deepest and truest in the vicissitudes of our lives. The aesthetic experience coincides with the discovery (or perhaps the rediscovery) of a felicitous form that contains our anxieties. By virtue of his creativity, as the expression of an exceptional capacity for reverie, the artist enables us to discover something that is at once already known and new—something we already had in ourselves but as yet in a raw, unprocessed state, a clod of emotions both attractive and disquieting that are but dimly sensed. A work of art, it may be asserted, is the fruit of the artist's dreaming—a form of dreaming which, like Ogden (2005), we regard as the deepest psychological labour of which we as human beings are capable for the purpose of assigning a personal meaning to experience. Our minds continually transform primitive sensory input into images (alpha-elements), which they then compose into sequences of dreamlike thoughts ready to be stored in memory and to be thought and dreamed; in other words, we each make up our own "fiction" of reality (in the sense of imagining, molding, and shaping it).

In analysis, dreaming signifies "painting" emotions with images and reveries, because these are halfway between bodily sensations and the abstractions of reason; it signifies restoring body to mind (or mind to body); and equates to regaining the ideal state, which is never acquired once and for all, that Winnicott calls "psychosomatic collusion". If the images required for re-establishing this ideal condition of equilibrium are to be rediscovered, however, another person's mind is needed; re-immersion in a kind of proto-mental area (Bion) is necessary. After all, there is no such thing as a primal or pure image which is not immediately captured within the symbolic order—that is, which, to be endowed with meaning, can dispense with the encounter and collaboration with the Other and his recognition. The *human* capacity to dream lived experience has always belonged to the sphere of language, culture, and social life—to the intermediate space, which Freud called the *Zwischenreich*, or in-between realm. Thus for Bion the focus of analysis is not the patient, and still less the analyst, but the something *between* that happens between them. Light is cast on this *between* by the interstices emphasised by Berger (and, following in his footsteps, by Dr. Peltz)—the unexpected spaces that suddenly appear and surprise us.

Why then is it so important to perceive and know how to paint the signs left on faces by time? The reason is that acceptance of the limits of the human condition, feeling the passage of time, and being able to be moved when confronted with beauty are closely connected. Truly experiencing beauty, both in art and in the analyst's office (which then also actually becomes "the most beautiful room in the world") is possible only if one accepts the transience of all things—only if one is prepared to endure the *rhythm* of the visible and the invisible, of the (not necessarily physical) presence and absence of the Other. That is what Meltzer subsumes in the concept of the aesthetic conflict: being simultaneously aware of the passion for the mother's face and the torment of not knowing what that face conceals in her mind. For this reason, one never tires of admiring great pictures, just as one never tires of contemplating the loved face.

It is no coincidence that the word "face", in turn borrowed from Berger, occurs so often in Dr. Peltz's text. This (quite appropriate) insistence can be interpreted as an indication—or symptom—of the fact that all contemplation of an art work is ultimately equivalent to scrutinising the mother's face. Whether it be Morandi's bottles or Cézanne's apples, what we are looking at is the mother's face, the noeme of time (Barthes). No one has conveyed this idea more tellingly than Ingmar Bergman. In a memorable scene from the 1966 movie *Persona*, a small boy stretches out his hand in a vain attempt to touch his mother's face, which has taken on the gigantic proportions of a wall, but is ambiguous and elusive (Civitarese, 2012). Before Bergman, Lewin in another valuable insight described the breast as a dream screen. However, one may wonder, is the mother's face only the canvas of the dreams or reveries that we exchange with our patients, or might it also be that of any elementary representation? Is it not always the profound weft of fantasy that underlies any image we create in our minds, if, of course, it is seen as the first organiser of a child's perceptual chaos at birth?

In reality, as we know, sensory perception precedes the image too as the possibility of seeing the Other as separate from oneself—a possibility apparently implied by Meltzer's concept. At an even earlier stage, the mother's face is a bundle of sensations, impressions on the skin, prioprioceptions and rhythms. It is the entire complex of proto-representational and acoustico-musical aspects of the foundations of mental life that "constitute the protonarrative integuments of the self and the world, which are destined to remain the deep structure of, and the implicit background to, every more mature relational capacity" (Barale, 2011, p. 192, translated). For this reason it is significant that in her clinical vignette Dr. Peltz, assisted by her patient's profession as a musician, "retreats" from the painterly to a musical metaphor. The change of vertex—here Bion's term could not be more apt—expresses the intuition of a type of relationality vis-à-vis the object that precedes the "visible". This is the self–other interface at the dawn of subjectivity described by Ogden as "an area of sensation of a soothing sort" (Ogden, 1994b, p. 122), which Merleau-Ponty helps us to see as rooted in inter-corporeality. Compared with the more thoroughly asemantic quality of music, even informal painting implies something less rhythmical and "tactile" than sound, something that is already more structured (if only because of the existence of the frame … of the picture, the museum, or the social context).

The aesthetic experience is an opportunity, which can be repeated throughout life, for the individual to rediscover a fuller sense of conso-nance and contact between mind and body. By the happy interplay of its forms, which make for the constant alternation of moments of integra-tion and non-integration, prior to and perhaps to a greater extent than the satisfaction of id impulses, the aesthetic object sustains the ego. The semiotic order that is so closely bound up with the emotions and the body continues to generate meaning throughout life. As noted authori-tatively by Butler, "In its semiotic mode, language is engaged in a poetic recovery of the maternal body, that diffuse materiality that resists all discrete and univocal signification" (Butler, 1990, p. 112).

In "Primitive emotional development", Winnicott (1945) expressed a similar idea on the general significance of the aesthetic experience. Having emphasised the "normal" presence of moments of non-integration even in mature adults, he wrote, "Through artistic expres-sion we can hope to keep in touch with our primitive selves whence the most intense feelings and even fearfully acute sensations derive, and we are poor indeed if we are only sane" (Winnicott, 1945, p. 150, note 3). In his view, the concept of sublimation is quite incapable of account-ing theoretically for the primitive pleasure in which it is first and fore-most the body that exists and not yet the mind, when, therefore, there is "no repression or repressed unconscious" (Winnicott, 1949, p. 181). It has to do with content and not with form. The theory of sublimation and that of reparation derived from it do not allow sufficiently for the prehistory of aesthetic experience, the aesthetic proto-conflict experienced by the subject (which is not yet, or not yet fully, a subject) at the stage of fusion with the object—or for the intersubjective dimension in which it takes place.

The deepest meaning of aesthetic experience in the contemplation of art, then, might be that of experiencing (or re-experiencing) the happy alternation of non-integration ↔ integration on a pre-symbolic and pre-reflective level. That is the only possible explanation for the absolute importance of form in artistic expression, and for the fact that perhaps the most moving art forms of all are dance and music—but not, for example, painting itself, which appeals to the most intellectual of the senses, sight. The aesthetic object, if successful, is the medium whereby the artist transmits to the spectator his reverie, translated into the primordial language of forms and sensations, and in this way contains his anxieties and helps him to feel more integrated. This may be the root of the sense of wellbeing experienced at the end of an exciting visit to the theatre or an exhibition of fine art.

In another of his incredible insights, Winnicott anticipated our explanation as just postulated of why music thus captures the *rhythm* of being even before the visual element of painting: "Belonging to this feeling of helplessness is the intolerable nature of experiencing something without any knowledge whatever of when it will end ... . It is for this reason fundamentally that form in music is so important. *Through form, the end is in sight from the beginning* [emphasis added]" (Winnicott, 1949, p. 184).

This quotation may help us to understand the sense of Dr. Peltz's work with her patient. Using the harmonic and musical container of the analytic setting, understood in the broadest sense of the term, Ms. M. gradually becomes capable of tolerating the end right from the beginning—that is, separation, transience, and the fragility of life. That is why she, and the analyst with her, can face up to the experience of beauty.

It should be clear from the foregoing that equating analysis with the aesthetic experience is not to invoke a banally ornamental aspect of analysis, the artistic nature of certain dream scenarios and of certain discursive constructions; nor does it involve a description in "elegant" terms of something that has little or nothing to do with artistic experience. On the contrary, the aesthetic experience is, in a strong sense, the deepest element of psychoanalysis, central to the constitution both of the mind and of meaning in the analytic situation. The psychoanalytic experience is fundamentally an aesthetic experience. That is why it is so important to take account of the sphere of aesthetics for the purpose of constructing ever more flexible and precise models in psychoanalysis. It is therefore important to overcome, in both theory and practice, the dichotomy (which began with Freud) between psychoanalysis as a hermeneutics of interpretation and as an aesthetic of reception— between a psychoanalysis of memories and psychic contents and a psychoanalysis of transformations and of the container. Another reason for this conviction is that, as stated by Barale (2011), meaning has a radically aesthetic (and substantially pre-representational) matrix, as do the transformative operations which occur and which we attempt to steer in the analytic field, including the tension toward thinkability, mentalisation, and representability that we seek to develop in that field. (p. 192, translated)

The psychoanalytic theory of Bion (and of Meltzer, Ferro, Ogden, and others) can be described as "aesthetic" both because it restores emotion—*aisthesis!*—to the centre of thought, and because it returns thought to its oneiric foundation, to the operations identified by Freud in the composition of the manifest text of a dream,[2] which are also involved in the dream of artistic creation. Meltzer's concept of the aesthetic conflict, too, can develop its full heuristic potential only if traced back to Bion's primal "aesthetic" idea that inspired it: "In the beginning was the aesthetic object, and the aesthetic object was the breast and the breast was the world" (Meltzer, 1986, p. 203). Freud was still expressing a similar view in 1938: In one of his last notes, dated 12 July, he writes that, in a child, being precedes having and that the primordial mechanism of possession is identification: "I am the breast (ich bin die Brust)"—that is, the object (Freud, 1938, p. 299); it is only later that the consciousness of having, which implies a separation, appears: "'I have it'—that is, 'I am not it' (ich habe sie, d.h. ich bin sie nich)" (ibid, p. 299). This extraordinarily condensed sentence seems once again to emphasise the identity of ego and body. What is more, it also implies that the ego *is* the Other, culture, and social life, and that the first ego is a sensory ego.

In her well-crafted paper, which is completely free of the kind of jargon that often characterises a stillborn contribution, Dr. Peltz offers an example of what is meant by re-dreaming a text, or giving an interpretation that does not interrupt the play of imagination. In rereading Bion and the authors who came after him in a new context with Berger, while at the same time a posteriori projecting their light on to Berger, she does not extract pre-constituted meanings from what she describes, but instead gives birth to new thoughts. The triad of concepts that Bion invites us to espouse as vertices from which to consider interpretation—sense, myth, and passion[3]—inform Dr. Peltz's theoretico-clinical article too. She describes (myth) something she had before her eyes (sense), which she experienced firsthand (passion). This is the same immediacy as that recommended by Bion in the analyst's office together with a long list of paradoxical concepts that could each be seen as perspectives directed toward the achievement of one and the same goal—namely, how to make experience meaningful. These concepts are as follows: forgetting all the knowledge we started out with—this is not a problem because, as Grotstein (2007) wrote, that knowledge will not forget us (!), but will, if we can tolerate remaining in doubt, eventually return in the form of reverie after undergoing unconscious processing in the mind—seeing the patient as our best colleague or perhaps even as a therapist, always encountering the patient as if for the first time, and leaving history and metapsychology in the background as if they did not matter.

All in all, then, it is a question of learning to see. That is why it is worth listening to what Berger has to tell us. We are therefore grateful to Dr. Peltz for bringing Bion and the authors who came after him together with Berger. Having read John and Katya Berger's (2010) *Distendersi a dormire* [*Lying down to sleep*], we shall revisit the Bridal Chamber with all our senses open and alert. It will not be the same as last time. The effect is identical to that of the most felicitous psychoanalytic writings—in which we include the subject of this commentary—on their readers: they convey wonder, pleasure, enthusiasm, and a sense of fullness of life extending far beyond the theoretical and practical field in which they originated and to which they belong. They expand the range of sensations to which we are able to respond throughout our lives.

Another important aspect implicit in Dr. Peltz's text is, in effect, the notion that psychoanalysis should not be used, as it often is, to decipher an artistic text, but that instead art should serve to interpret psychoanalysis. Ideally, in our view, that is the soil in which an aesthetic criticism inspired by the principles of psychoanalysis can thrive anew. This would represent a meeting, a collaboration or an opening, and not the subjection of one to the other. Of course, when we say "art" (including the "art" of psychoanalysis), we are on no account thinking of the naïve but widespread conception that it is a brilliant light that shines down from on high or a pure gift of inspiration, albeit with a weight of its own; we in fact have in mind, aside from creativity, the elements of discipline, work, concentration, and technique. At any rate, it is at once clear that aesthetic criticism and psychoanalytic interpretation as classically understood have both come to grief in the same way.

The reference to art also helps us to explore the area of what the narratologists call "intermediality"—of which Dr. Peltz's text is an example on the level of theory by virtue of her suggested transposition of aesthetic concepts to psychoanalysis—that is, the fact that many art works involve a number of different media, either directly or after mutual intersemiotic translation. For instance, an author may write as if he were playing jazz; a novel may be turned into a film; or music may be used in video art. Likewise in psychoanalysis, as Dr. Peltz notes, we need to be receptive to sensations, reveries, sights, and sounds. But that is not all. An issue that has never been more relevant than it is today is how to confer representability on forms of experience such as traumas that are unrepresentable because recorded in "implicit" or "procedural" memory. This is the context of Dr. Peltz's reference to Levenson (2009), who wrote, with regard to grasping the meaning of the patient's emotional experience: "We embody it".

The idea of truth and a truth drive plays a major part in this way of seeing (and experiencing) psychoanalysis as reflected in art, and, conversely, art as reflected in psychoanalysis: according to Grotstein,[4] these are the principles that inform Bion's entire oeuvre. Hence the value of the model of aesthetic experience. When it is a question of conferring meaning on our lives we do not know what to do with the truths of science because they are purged of emotion. The truth we need in order to give value to and enrich our existence is a truth that moves us. It is an un/conscious, emotional, and shared truth. So one can now also sense what might be meant by a truth drive. It will surely not be the urge to take possession on an abstract level of some system of *true* propositions about reality, but instead the impulse to achieve ever greater levels of emotional attunement to the Other— which, it should be noted, also underlies understanding based on logical and rational thought, albeit only secondarily. This approach overcomes the contradiction between the falsity inherent in perception and thought, on one hand, and the truth (relative falsity) that makes for mental growth, on the other, because it is now reduced to a quantitative rather than a qualitative factor. *Considered in these terms, therefore, the truth drive can be seen as representing the search for this special kind of attunement to the Other*: This is the type of truth that can be said to nourish the mind as food nourishes the body, because every instant experienced in unison introduces order into chaos and constructs the mind.

With regard to truth, however, we are always in the same position as Orpheus. Like him with his lyre, we succeed by means of the fragile but potent theories of psychoanalysis in moving the Hades of memory (Freud: "... *Acheronta movebo*"), in restoring buried memories to life, and causing dead areas of the mind to live anew. To rediscover meaning we too are compelled always to look back—that is basically what is meant by *Nachträglichkeit*—but just at the moment when we see its face it suddenly vanishes, leaving us with an acute sense of loss. Unlike Orpheus, however, we nurture the hope of being able to resume our search at any time. As Dr. Peltz emphasises, and tellingly demonstrates in her clinical vignette, the analyst must have a passion for searching and the courage to feel what he feels when faced with the patient. He can admittedly not overcome his own limitations and go beyond the outcome of his own analysis, but if he has passion and courage—the same qualities as the unfortunate bard of myth—he too can grow psychologically and change together with his patient. Something felt to be authentic and true then occurs, and there forms a pocket of resistance to intolerable pain and the loss of humanity.

We greatly appreciated Rachael Peltz's fine contribution and her successful drawing of a parallel with the activity of a painter who finds the true source of creativity in his relationship with his model. Concepts such as the "pocket of resistance", implying "an encounter, a collaboration, the discovery of a place and the emergence of a face" (Peltz, 2012, p. 282), in our view offer much food for thought on the real work done in the analytic situation. A few points call for particular emphasis. Her remark that "as analysts we strive to establish *places* in which the *faces* of the encounters between ourselves and our patients can emerge" (ibid, p. 282) leads naturally to the idea of characters in the session who can be seen as holograms of the oneiric functioning of the couple. It is in this dreamlike matrix shared by the members of the analytic couple that these characters come to life, after a casting process that permits the emergence of the characters needed at, or by, a particular moment.

The concept of the "psychoanalytic field"[5] can usefully be thought of as representing the space in which the various holograms/characters comprising the resulting cast can move, interacting and undergoing transformation and enrichment in the course of their movements in that space before being assigned to one or other of the members of the analytic couple. This multiplicity of transformative interactions is rendered possible by the idea of non-saturation, the characters (or faces) being deemed to emerge from the waking dream thought which analyst and patient bring to life in the field.

What we find difficult is an excessive shifting of the focus of the discourse on to the aspect of truth. In our view, the need is for an alternation between truth and falsehood. We need the latter too—and for a longer or shorter time. Truth is sometimes burning hot and has to be approached with the potholders or oven gloves of falsehoods or other defences. As Grotstein (2007) pointed out, dreams are a kind of lie in relation to "O". So we are not champions of truth as such, but only of a truth that is tolerable to thought; we can "play" with falsehood and/ or defences for as long as is necessary, trusting that the field itself will, in one of its manifestations—for instance, countertransference dreams, reveries, or acting out—be able to signal when greater degrees of truth can be ventured upon. We sometimes need creative lies. On occasion, our work as analysts teaches us how to play with the alternation of masking and unmasking. The former too is one of the aspects of the "face", as Pirandello repeatedly stressed.

We thought Dr. Peltz's clinical example both excellent in itself and a very good illustration of her theoretical considerations. The analyst with her "soft spoken" patient, seen as a "blank slate", in a zoo populated exclusively by peaceful, herbivorous animals, is able to discern another sound (p. 286). When the patient pronounces the word "gimmick", a whirlwind of different sounds is triggered—the sound, never before heard, of flesh-eating beasts, as demonstrated by a "flash of rage"; "having been slapped in the face"; "the violence in this quiet attack"; and "self hatred" (Peltz, 2012, p. 286). The film now is by Quentin Tarantino and no longer Walt Disney.

What had hitherto been "blandified" can now come to life. Narrative derivatives of a hypothetical sequence of waking dream thought involving "ferocious wild animals" arise from a series of emotional transitions. These include projective identifications, reveries, and enactments: in each case the zoo is enlivened with "faces" that have never before been seen. We have "playing soccer"; "the childhood memory of rage"; "the patient on a cliff"; "the boy in a therapeutic school"; and "the fear of exposure" (ibid, p. 288): the music of the passions now accompanies the sequence of images arising in the session like the sound track of a film.

The emotional field features a constant interweaving of sounds and images, giving rise to a dance of "meanings—faces—passions", each referring to the others in a new hologram-like reality: "smashing the ball"; "yelling and screaming"; "the edge of a cliff" (Peltz, 2012, p. 287). The former Mickey Mouse cartoon is replaced by a new film pervaded with blows, assaults, shouting, and yelling; it is a battle—perhaps the storming of the Bastille or Fort Apache, but at any rate one of the most successful soundtracks ever. The analyst, however, has been the place where new faces have taken advantage of the casting process to tell a new emotional tale—as Ogden might say, a new film that has never been dreamed before.

In the clinical part Dr. Peltz demonstrates the importance of perceiving the patient not from the outside but from within—that is, of having an *embodied* perception of her—as well as the importance in this connection of reserve, hospitality, discretion, waiting, patience, precision, sensitivity, and lucidity. The portrait she paints of herself with Ms. M. "speaks to us", transporting us into a climate of immediacy and special intimacy. She does not trace the outline of the figure from a reassuring distance, but instead allows it to emerge from the composition of colours. Moreover, they are the colours of the emotions of lived experience. Rather than contemplating the scene from without, Dr. Peltz includes herself in the picture and accepts the resulting vertiginous closeness. What is her secret? Pondering how Vincent van Gogh succeeded in becoming the world's most famous painter, Berger claims to have found the answer in his drawings, and eventually reached a conclusion that is equally relevant to ourselves: "He is loved ... because for him the act of drawing or painting was a way of discovering and demonstrating why *he* loved so intensely what he was looking at" (Berger, 2001, p. 87f).

Notes

1. Translator's note: for convenience, the masculine form is used for both sexes throughout this translation.
2. A central aspect of Dr. Peltz's paper is her account of how Bion revolutionised the meaning of the dream work, hence the proximity of art to psychoanalysis. Interestingly, in some respects a similar trend has emerged in contemporary philosophy with Derrida, whose concept of deconstruction is *not* an interpretation that dissects the text, as it is often

misunderstood, but a reading that opens the way to a huge number of possibilities that are only seemingly arbitrary.

3. The following passage from Proust (1931) conveys something of the irreplaceable cognitive function of pain: "Moreover, does it [pain] not on each occasion reveal to us a law which is no less indispensable for the purpose of bringing us back to truth, of forcing us to take things seriously by pulling up the weeds of habit, scepticism, frivolity and indifference."

4. Compare Grotstein: "I put forth the notion that beneath the hidden order that runs through the entirety of Bion's works lies the concept of a *truth drive* and that all the ego defence mechanisms are principally counterposed to the irruption of unconscious truth rather than of libido and aggression" (Grotstein, 2007, p. 52). Grotstein reported that Bion himself mentioned the concept of a *"truth instinct"* to him in 1979.

5. See also Ferro (2006), Civitarese (2008).

CHAPTER FIVE

Spacings

The theme of temporality, of such importance in psychoanalysis, is one of the junctions where the paths of other extraordinarily important concepts intersect: setting, subjectivity, theories of clinical work, the interpretation and understanding of therapeutic factors, the psychoanalytic institution.

In this chapter we address the concept of space–time in relation to Bion's theory of the analytic field. The hypothesis we propose is that the field is a conceptual tool that enables us to modulate in a fine-grained and safe manner the distance between patient and analyst, and to achieve and expand emotional unison—in our view the central therapeutic factor.

We have chosen to use the term "spacing" not only by way of tribute to Derrida (2008) but also to put into immediate context space and time as two terms that imply each other and must necessarily live side by side. Replacing the combination of space and time with the concept of spacing (less abstract than *differance*) allows us to simultaneously allude to the temporality of space and the spatiality of time. Spacing is neither the one nor the other, and is both together.

In its original meaning, the term refers to the act of distributing white spaces between typographic characters. It also suggests the idea of punctuation, that is, the arrangement of graphic signs that generate meaning in the writing of language and ultimately in the unconscious. Furthermore, in architecture, it refers to organising compositional features through the use of open spaces. This alone is a stimulating idea if we think of our use of metaphors such as the Grid, buildings, architecture, mental space, inner holes. Spacing is the very means whereby the subject is constructed. Non-presence is inscribed in presence, the negative in the positive, death in life.

Spacings of subjectivity

Bion has taught us that thinking, giving a personal meaning to reality, which means dreaming reality (doing conscious and unconscious psychological work in order to create new emotional bonds and construct a mental meaning or space), is no trivial act. In fact, it is the measure of how much one can bear (a function of duration) the absence (empty spatiality) of the object (no-thing). If there is sufficient tolerance to frustration, a word simply stops making sense as a name that brings together multiple elements into a stable conjunction; it takes on meaning, and thus faithfully certifies the non-existence of the thing represented.

So it is that the symbol testifies to the absence of the breast and makes it necessary to confront the emotions entailed by the negative nature of any definition. If one cannot tolerate absence, deep down one feels as if one is being killed by a cruel object, and at the same time that one is in turn in the grip of some kind of murderous frenzy, ready to commit "actual murder" on the object (Sandler, 2005).

Thinking implies this sense of vertigo. The price of meaning is a struggle. If one is too afraid of ghosts, one gives up on meaning. One feels the absence that the name covers up, "one sees" what is not there "and the thing that is not there, like the thing that *is* there, is indistinguishable from an hallucination" (Bion, 1970, p. 9) or, according to Bion's own definition of hallucination, from a β-factor. But hallucinating obviously means not being able to use symbols and hence not being able to think.

This point may seem abstract, but in fact it is closely interwoven with the concepts of space–time, object relation and language (the basis for self-awareness) and readily connects with clinical practice.

Spacings in the setting

Some patients, for example, are always afraid of coming late, and for this reason, they put their watch forward by ten or fifteen minutes. This does not stop them from being systematically late. The ploy is usually completely ineffective. The symptom reveals the nature of the fantasy relationship with the object. It is a relationship with an object experienced as if one always arrived late. One senses that a small chasm must have established itself in the self into which the ego is likely to plunge at every step. Putting the watch ahead pre-empts and wards off a painful emptiness, because magically it also brings forward the moment the object reappears. Delay, on the other hand, just as magically makes it disappear. By never meeting it in time, the subject avoids facing up to the bluff and turns into activity the painful impression of being subjected to things.

This is what happens in the situations Bion (1970; Civitarese, 2014) describes as transformation in hallucinosis. The maternal container becomes infinitised and loses its ability to give shape to the infant's violent emotions. This gives rise to not only spatial but also temporal dispersion. If what gives meaning to things is the initially external but then later internalised presence of a container, if this is too extensive, an infinity of time is needed to connect two points (events) that are now at an infinite distance from each other. The container stops being concave and becomes flat. Thus the meaning of things is lost. They are perceived but not really understood. Following Bion we would say that one *has* a conscious but cannot *become* conscious. Things are felt but not suffered.

As one can see, the senses of space and time are not acquired automatically, but are closely related, both taking their imprint from the quality of the primary relationships with the object.

The setting of the analysis itself organises the spacing that is meant to help restore a less anxious sense of space and time, to turn back the hands of the clock if they have been moved forward and vice versa. It is a space-womb (Winnicott, 1956; Bleger, 1967), as a whole, a psychic container, a new semiotic chora (Kristeva, 1974). Its concreteness is regulated by the analytic contract, but it is both a dream space and a theatrical space, where the struggle for meaning with ghosts can go on stage in a state of adequate safety. The possibility this space-field-as-process has of forming (or not) and of functioning so as to facilitate the construction of subjectivity depends on how the analyst concretely regulates (or negotiates) the breaches or adherence to forms of purely notional spacing that are given from the outset.

The possible spacings of setting and theory also depend on those of the psychoanalytic institution, which can vary in its rigidity. This point is only briefly touched upon here.

Spacings in the psychoanalytic institution

This theme of time is one we have addressed in a book edited by Gabriele Junkers, *The Empty Couch*, which looks at the passing of time in the life of an analyst and at the consequences that this inescapable fact has on the personal and professional level. In this case, the hands on the clock are put back. In our article one of the points we underlined was the strong tendency in many psychoanalytic institutes to infantilise young people (candidates). This operation makes it possible to rejuvenate training analysts by some twenty or sometimes even thirty years, giving everyone the illusion of circular time where one keeps going back to school and feels that one has found the elixir of eternal youth.

According to the model described in the previous section, here the container does not become infinite but is all too present and almost threatening. It becomes sclerotic, it loses elasticity, relationships become fixed, time runs (apparently) without change; but in fact it is a denial of linear time.

A structure of this kind also involves fetishising theory, for example, the spacings of the setting.

Spacings in the analytic field

Within the space–time of the psychoanalytic institution and the setting each model tends to define its own rules for representation. Each uses punctuation differently. These rules are based on all the explicit and implicit assumptions of a model, on the grand narratives or metaphors that have inspired it: Oedipus for Freudian psychoanalysis; the phantasmagoric dramatisation of the life of internal objects in Kleinian psychoanalysis; the idea of endless conversation and mutuality in interpersonalism; the mother–child model of the birth of the psyche for the analytic field, and so on. Here we focus on the principal model that we use in clinical practice, aware of course that even if we wanted to we would not be able to stop ourselves (but why should we?) from seeing things from other points of view. However, Bion's model of the analytic field deserves to be illustrated at some length because it has ushered in a radically new way of interpreting the facts of the session.

In the Freudian model the analytic space has its limits in the psyche of the patient, in Bion's concept of the analytic field it is extended to include the couple. It spreads out beyond the visible boundaries of the subject to include the analyst and to form an area of interaction in which each point simultaneously affects all the other points and is affected by them. These influences are of an emotional nature. Bion would call them L, H, K links, i.e., links of love, hate, and knowledge. The tensions that generate these links are the forces of the field. The point of application, the intensity and direction of these forces can be deduced from the "characters" who populate it, and from their actions.

By characters in the analytic field we mean the figures of the analytic dialogue (also understood as an "intercorporeal" dialogue) introduced by the patient and the analyst and which can be regarded as derivatives of waking dream thought. The characters can be anthropomorphic or also abstract, semantic (or representational) in type, in other words corresponding to images, ideas, and concepts, or semiotic in type (for example, sensations, rhythms, tones, gestures). When an image comes to mind or a feeling is experienced, even when these are not expressed in words, they alter the field because they still exert transformational pressure on other elements that are part of it. The effect will be strong or weak depending on the distance between two (or more) elements in play.

The analytic field is a *multi-verse*. Depending on the vertex taken, multiple possible worlds open up. The same character/action may refer to the patient or the analyst, to outside the field or to a quality/element of the field which they have generated together, and in a way that is no longer attributable to the original components. It may also relate to the past, the present and the future, material or mental reality, conscious or unconscious experience.

The subterranean dynamics that bring out the various characters in the field follow the rules of dream work as set out by Freud, which are then identified with the basic psychological principles of mental functioning (the associative work that is expressed in condensation, displacement, and representability) or, in language, with the rhetorical figures of metaphor and metonymy. These rules are the same along the continuum from the early alphabetisation of proto-emotions and proto-sensoriality—the transition from beta to alpha—to dream thought proper, finally arriving at rational thought (in Bion's Grid: the scientific deductive system).

The principle of identity (A = A), when applied to natural and not abstract entities, is based on a metaphorical exchange, such as that between "flag" and "nation". Even rational thinking is infiltrated by dreams. Bion has brought out this continuity by coining the concept of waking dream thought. We dream both at night and during the day. Between primary process and secondary process there is no break in continuity but only varying degrees of simplification/abstraction of experience. In the waking state the psychic function of attention adjusts the breadth of the field of consciousness and the presence of dream elements, and thus reduces (and almost eliminates) or heightens the subjective impression of thinking-as-dreaming.

Unconscious thought, of which the dream is the most direct expression, can be seen as a level of the psyche that is more simplified than raw emotion and less simplified than the concept: a kind of poetry of the mind, the point of equilibrium between body and mind, the psychic place where the "psycho-somatic collusion" between emotions and ideas is maintained, what Winnicott (1970) calls "personalization", and thus where it handles the personal (emotional) significance of lived experience. Since the purpose of analysis is to repair this cohesion when it is broken or to establish it for the first time if this has never happened before, this is the level of intervention (the specific field) of analysis.

The purpose of analysis is to restore the subject's ability to give personal meaning to experience. The word "meaning" inevitably refers to sociality (by definition, non-consensual meaning is what characterises delusion); the word "person", on the other hand, refers to the individual. But in part the distinction is artificial because "person" (that is, according to the etymology, "persona or mask") expresses precisely the idea of sociality involved in shaping the pre-subject, in giving him his face and making him presentable and recognisable to others (but at the same time, paradoxically, also hiding him from others). It makes no sense to talk about a subject outside the symbolic order. The world only makes sense from our subjectivity understood as self-awareness, but in turn we get this from our being part of a wider sociality.

The space of the analytic field is unstable/dynamic. It is ever shrinking or expanding. For example, it shrinks when it is invaded by a violent emotion and imposes an absolute view of things; whereas it expands when the play of the characters makes possible multiple points of view on things. As Bion says, in an ideal sense analysis is the probe that expands indefinitely the very area it is exploring.

The interdependence between the various points (objects) of the field implies a principle of symmetry: unconscious communication between minds is inevitable and constant. However, it is up to the analyst to use rational thinking to bring the spontaneous processes of the field into a necessary working asymmetry, given that the aim is to treat the patient's psychic suffering. In the field, however, there are continuous fluctuations between patient and analyst as to who at any given moment works as a container and who works as a content. Or to put it better: they are active simultaneously, in several dimensions, with multiple and reciprocal relationships between container and content.

The understanding of the dynamics of the field, which is different from their pure perception or recording, enables one to develop tools to influence them. This understanding is always latent, it always comes back *a posteriori*, it can never fully grasp its object, it is recursive. It always looks backwards, and in turning back to this space it becomes temporal, generates meaning and the subject is constructed. The temporality of the analytic field (of subjectivity) is not linear but circular, in the sense that every time a past event reoccurs, it reacquires meaning. In the transverse (syntagmatic) sense the field is the site of events that occur simultaneously at its various points (actually the simultaneity between two events is not absolute but relative to the observer); in the longitudinal (paradigmatic) sense it is the explicit or implicit narrative (chronological order) of these events and how the various "characters" of the field are transformed.

The aim of psychoanalysis and what are considered the seeds of healing are the development of the α function (of the field) and the containing ability (of the field), which is then continually—through micro- and macro-*après-coups*—introjected by the patient. We could say that the analytic session appears like a dream of the minds where different stories coming from different times and places of the field arrive, diffract and overlap. The shared experience results from the circulation of emotional states, feelings, thoughts and characters, with the analyst (who is also a site in the field) there to guarantee and protect the setting and promote a kind of dream-like activity on the part of the analytic couple.

Each session is a pearl, a bead on the rosary-necklace that leads through all the "mysteries" not to the content but to the ability to undertake the journey, back and forth, as in some science fiction films where travel is possible in both space and time. The engine of the analysis and of the narrative-mythopoietic activity is the need of that which is unthinkable and unspeakable to find a space–time and a function that will produce the ability to think and say. Working together on the emotions present in the field, weaving and re-weaving them, leads— through rêverie, through unison—to the development of container/ contained.

The outcome of all the transformative expeditions made session after session is the ability to weave proto-emotions into images, stories of memories previously occluded or even into memories of things that never happened, but which have been constructed in the field and then backdated with continuous movements of *après-coups*. The path taken by the analysis becomes a function of the modes of functioning of each analytic couple at work and the very meaning of a natural process becomes lost. Each pair will have its own way of doing analytical work, and also the events of the analysis, the negative therapeutic reactions, the psychotic or negative transferences (and countertransferences) will belong to that particular couple, or rather to that field.

The session is played out on the level of a reciprocal dream, both when the patient "dreams" (if he is capable of dreaming) the intervention of the analyst or his mental state, and when the analyst "dreams" the answer to give to the patient. The more this reply is "dreamt", the more it will be a constitutive factor, capable of mending any possible defects in the patient's α function. The analyst in the session finds himself in the situation of a driver whose task it is to pay attention to all the instruments on board a very complex car, or plane, although doing so merely serves to continue the journey in sufficient safety. Otherwise there would either be the risks resulting from going off-course (or of serious injury), or else the risks of an analysis that gets wrapped up in itself without getting any further.

Although this is a paradoxical journey, where goal is to learn to travel through perpetually expanding territories, it is still possible to acquire the method. There is a constant basic activity of reverie, which is the way a part of the field continually receives, metabolises and becomes "what" arrives from the (usually several) turbulent areas of the field itself—the patient as verbal, para-verbal, non-verbal stimulation. This basic activity of reverie is the fulcrum of our mental life and its functioning/dysfunctioning determines our sanity, disease and degree of mental suffering.

When the analyst listens, in turn other pictograms are generated by his listening to the patient's narrative derivatives (Ferro, 2002b, 2006), together with shares of alphabetisation of β elements that the patient has not transformed. At this point we have a long-distance dance in which this operation is repeated alternately, or analyst and patient find an attunement such that the α function and the sequence of pictograms and narrative derivatives no longer belong to a specific person and it is the pair that generates meanings and transformations without too many caesuras. A regime of passing from one side to the other in parallel gives way to an endless spiral or worm screw movement. This is the type of functioning that occurs in the analytic field, and that gives life to the analytic field.

From a certain point of view, the analytic field is the "unsaturated waiting room" where emotions, proto-emotions and characters wait before they can be brought back to their saturated fate in the relationship or in the construction. From another point of view, it is made up of all the force lines, all the proto-clusters of proto-emotions, proto-characters and characters that float in the virtual space of the field and gradually take on substance, colour and three-dimensionality. It is as if there were great numbers of elastic bands stretched between patient and analyst, numerous possible storylines to which gradually are attached paper clips—this is the field casting what was indeterminate. At this point, what matters is not the content, but the way in which this operation will lead to the development of tools for thinking. Of course, due to the failure of the α function, not all the clouds of sensoriality or proto-emotions can be transformed into pictograms; some will still be evacuated in symptoms, actings-out, quarrels, phobias, paranoia.

Breaks in the analytic dialogue

Let us now illustrate these theoretical concepts with some clinical examples.

Tizio

Anna enters the room and lies down on the couch. She is two minutes late. She comments that there is never enough time, that she is always anxious about something, and that recently she has often been late. Shortly before that she had turned off the Artemide Tizio lamp that stands on the table between the two chairs positioned in the corner of the room for face-to-face sessions. Suddenly, presumably because of the cooling of the metallic structure of the lamp, we hear a distinct ticking sound, much like that of a clock. It is a rather surprising phenomenon which I have only noticed on rare occasions. It takes us moment to take in the surprise and then we burst out laughing!

Tizio—the name of the lamp is in this case very appropriate (in Italian it is a generic word for a man) to describe the unexpected guest who makes his entrance on the stage of the analysis. Ironically it had taken on what was my (our) job of interpreting—showing without saying, in compliance with the golden rule of any creative writing course—the hypothetical transference meaning of my patient words. This was enough to turn the unconscious experience into something conscious.

I recount this very short vignette, just a few seconds of a session, to introduce the way in which we unconsciously interpret anything that happens in analysis within a broader framework of meaning. In this case, Anna herself turns an event into a dream because she has a sudden revelation: that her complaint about time has something to do with the fixed schedule of the sessions and the frustration that this entails. The ticking of the lamp immediately helps her see things from another point of view. She grasps the unconscious meaning of her outburst, manages for a minute to contain her frustration, and smiles.

Let us now summarise some of the theoretical points this short vignette illustrates: the continuity between unconscious and conscious experience; the hyper-inclusive aspect (the extension) of the field—in a theatre a chair on the stage is a theatrical chair (the principle of the semiotisation of the object); the recursive and backward-facing movement of turning back the clock in the construction of meaning; the bipersonal—but it would be better to say, group—creation of meaning and of events in the field; the concrete metaphor of the intersubjective analytic third (the lamp as a character that came into being in the area of meaning was prepared by conscious and unconscious communicative exchanges between analyst and patient); the function of waking dream thought, in other words, Anna's comment as a derivative of her unconscious activity of transforming proto-emotions and raw sensoriality; the effect of surprise that occurs when it "something true" happens; humour as an indication of emotional unison and an index of the sharing of an aesthetic experience.

The dream of the boyfriend

Sofia, a thirty-five-old psychiatrist, talks about one of her patients who is depressed although she does not understand why. This basic theme is then repeated through the series of characters of other depressed patients she has been dealing with in the day hospital where she works. I do not interpret these characters to her as aspects of herself but through highly unsaturated interventions; I just let the conversation develop.

At the end of session Sofia tells me about a dream her boyfriend had one time he slept at her house (a dream which I consider—whoever actually dreamt it—relevant to our analytic space): she forced him to go on a trip to Paris, but then directed him to a dangerous, awkward path overlooking the sea. Then he found himself inside a cube that ran along a predetermined path that occasionally opened up. He stopped, then set off again for a new stop, and so on. It was a trip that was necessary but afforded no pleasure.

Sofia commented: "Why does my boyfriend think that life together would be precarious, dangerous, and above all a nightmare [in Italian, *incubo*, 'in a cube'] with every stage pre-determined and without anything nice?" In this way she was expressing her doubts about living together, getting married, having children, which she saw as suffocating because the time was not ripe, it was too soon. She did not feel ready because she had not yet experienced sufficient spaces of freedom. These spaces were still obstructed and they frightened her. Giving them up, however, also made her feel quite clearly depressed. In Sofia there was a gap between the time of her actual age and the time of her lived age. At the same time she also felt the gap between herself and the analyst and the intensity of their mutual desires. If "listened to" as coming from her waking dream thought, the space and time of Sofia's story thus became a narrative of the field where she could more easily correct the punctuation. As we know, some people see punctuation as having more of a logical-syntactic function than to serve spoken discourse. It's amazing how a few commas in the right place can make a text more readable.

Stefania

A middle-aged woman tells me at the first consultation that she is haunted by the thought that their children might fall ill. She then tells me that she has been living with this terror for the last nine years; or rather, she has not been living for nine years. Things got worse at the birth of their second child. She is always there ready to pick up on any sign that might herald a fever or whatever.

I tell her that she seems to experience her children like the ball and chain attached to the feet of someone serving a life sentence; sometimes, I suggest, she might even feel the desire to get rid of them, perhaps to run away. She says, "Of course I do! And I understand those mothers who kill their children. Since they were born, no more cinema, no more theatre, no more suitors!" I tell her: "You're living like a doctor in the emergency room".

Sofia tells me that she has the feeling that time has stood still for the last nine years. She is forty-five years old, but she feels as if she were twenty-two or twenty-three. I tell her that it is understandable that the death of the children (whom she loves) would help her get out of her maximum security prison and that she would find a way of living that part of herself that wants to lead "a reckless life, where nothing is ever too late …". She immediately picks up on this theme again by listing all the things she would like and which she thinks she will now have to give up for good! Time stopped at twenty-three. It didn't not go forward. At the (perceived mental) age of twenty-three years old she finds herself with the burden and responsibility of a family that only a woman in full adulthood could bear.

There follows a long story of her mother's illness, which had had the effect of stopping time.

She then speaks of a trip to New York she wanted to make and that she would still be very keen to go on. I tell her that all she needs to do is go to a travel agency and buy a ticket-analysis that will help her adjust to her jet lag and make up for lost time.

Valeria

When Valeria comes into session, I think, "I bet she's pregnant". She then begins to tell me she has something extraordinary to tell me but first she must recount a dream: she was in a room with a worn-out sofa. She was happy because there were a newborn child and the child's elderly grandfather who had been diagnosed as having a disease that would soon lead to his death. Then she tells me her big news: I'm pregnant!

I do not know how I managed to think of it the moment she entered the room.

Valeria recently reached forty years of age, and lately has been enjoying a satisfactory relationship. The time was ripe. Similarly, also the time to finish the analysis is ripe; the plan had already taken shape in one of the previous sessions. There is a child in the flesh and there is a child who is the plan to "terminate the analysis". At this point it is also time for the analyst, who is now a grandfather, to prepare to bow out and accept the linearity of time.

Laura

Laura comes to talk about the end of her analysis in a completely unconscious way when time seems to take the form of a series of steps in which each individual has found his or her own place: Manuela, ten years old, will next year finish primary school; Sandro, thirteen, will finish middle school; and Salvatore will finish high school. She in turn will have to leave the old job that has helped her acquire professional competence as a lawyer and will be opening her own office. The husband will cut the bonds that have kept him tied to his father's company and in turn start up his own consulting firm. The only problem, says Laura with apprehension, is to find an arrangement for her father, who is a widower. Someone has to deal with him and a good nursing home might be the solution. I tell her that everybody seems to have found their place (childish, adolescent and adult aspects) and that the father who has now become a grandfather must withdraw to his own place and leave them free to follow their separate paths.

Lucetta

The situation with Lucetta is one of relative impasse. I point out to her that although we have known each other for a long time I actually know very little about her and that I would not mind if some time or other she would let me take part in her world.

At the next session she tells me two dreams.

In the first she arrives in a place where she sits down on a sofa; in the room there are armchairs, chairs, and a table. She is lying comfortably when she feels something moving in the cushion she is resting on and suddenly she sees droves of black rats that are running out in groups.

In the second dream she is in a similar place; this time, however, there are people sitting around the room, and at some point she realises that the people are mummified, embalmed as in a wax museum.

It is not hard for me to connect these dreams with the request I made the day before, when I suggested that Lucetta should allow me to partake in her world. It seems that this has caused a incredible upheaval. The whole gloomy atmosphere of her childhood, the rats, the black memories have jumped out to threaten and disturb her, without however striking real terror into her heart.

The aesthetic experience of life as spacing

In life we have to deal with a physiological oscillation between circular time, the mental time in which nothing seems to happen, as in an impasse in psychoanalysis, but which is often a time of "pregnancy" ("Under the snow is bread", according to a proverb), and linear time, which is like the time of a one-way train journey from A to B. Both participate in the construction of the mind, because it's like saying identity and difference, the *me* of psychic reality (where the six-year-old boy, the seventeen-year-old adolescent and the twenty-two-year-old student, etc. are always simultaneously present) and the *not-me* of material reality (whose appearance I almost do not even recognise in the photos of years ago, so much have I changed). Things go smoothly if linear and circular time are well integrated.

If time remains circular for too long what happens is like in the story by Dahl (…) in which whoever enters a small hotel near the station of a provincial town is trapped and mummified in an eternal present.

If time only runs forward, we do not have the time to look at and live our emotional landscapes, nor are we capable of having the same experience of poetic nostalgia that Freud (1915) describes in *On Transience*. We become prisoners of events and concreteness. It means that we are avoiding emotional experience.

The *Odyssey* offers a felicitous representation of this oscillation between the linear segments of time (the journey) and the spirals (stages): Nausicaa, Calypso, Circe, and finally Ithaca. It is important to point out that the journey of Ulysses—the embodiment of the wise man who respects the gods—was also possible because someone, Penelope, denied the existence of linear time and night after night undid what she had woven.

In analysis, how can we tie together the circular time of Penelope and the linear time of Ulysses?

Let us take two observations by Bion (1992, p. 149). The first is when he writes that temporality arises from the narrativisation of alpha elements:

> these then undergo a process of narrativization to make them approximate to the emotional experiences of waking life in which the personality is participating in a temporal sequence that accordingly has a narrative quality, so that the emotional experience originating in dream-thought is rendered suitable for storage and waking conscious thought. (Bion, 1992, p. 149)

We have already explained what this means for the theory of the analytic field. Now, however, we would like to emphasise another aspect inherent in the concept of narrative, because in our opinion it plays a central role in psychoanalysis: the tendency towards living an aesthetic experience. This is the reason for choosing a further observation by Bion (1992, pp. 143–144):

> the intellectual leader [as it soon becomes clear, he means the artist, but really it is only meant as a model for how the analyst should be] is someone who is able to digest facts, i.e. sense data, and then to present the digested facts, my α-elements, in a way that makes it possible for the weak assimilators to go on from there. Thus the artist helps the non-artist to digest, say, the Little Street in Delft [Vermeer] by doing α-work on his sense impressions and 'publishing' the result so that others who could not "dream" the Little Street itself can now digest the published α-work of someone who could digest it. (Bion, 1992, pp. 143–144)

What can we take from these two quotes?

First of all, it is clear that Bion equates the analyst's activity to that of the artist and then analytic transformation to aesthetic transformation. Furthermore, it is neither the content nor the style itself (for the analyst, the content and the style of interpretation) that redeem the subject from his alienation, but the style as an expression of authentic involvement of the author/analyst in a certain universal emotional experience and his ability, through his work/interpretation, to become—as it says in the *Iliad*—the "breast that makes us forget our anguish", which transforms evil (the trauma of the real) into meaning and in this way transcends it. In the background there is also the emotional bond that is established with the authors we "love", a fact not to be overlooked in the dynamics of aesthetic experience in art as it is analogous to the emotional investment that enables the mother to "dream" the child and the analyst to dream the patient.

But if the ideal moment—that is, the most happily transformational moments—in analysis are aesthetic in nature, this means that the temporality intrinsic to analysis is that of "dreaming memory" (the stuff of which the analysis is made), not the chronological temporality of the historian. This is taken into account by the caesuras of the setting that mark the passage of linear time. What matters instead is that something new and surprising is born, which is what Bion implies when he says that we need to make the O of the session evolve or ensure that the analyst *become O*; by this he means nothing more than letting oneself be pervaded by the waking dreams that are reverie. From there, when it happens (although it can also take a very long time), sometimes, we can feel that we have been touched by *something true*, because it has emerged from involuntary memory and from the analytic field generated by analyst and patient. The aesthetic experience is one of being in unison, of sharing the same space–time, carrying out (almost) the same spacing in the perceptual chaos of reality. The aesthetic experience inside (and outside) analysis is the ideal balance between circular time (when the same thing is repeated) and linear time (intrinsic to aesthetic experience is the feeling that beauty is ephemeral).

That is why the theory of the technique of the analytic field gives so much importance to reverie, because as an expression of the un/conscious psychological work that the analyst can do if not shielded, that is, if he is sufficiently receptive to the patient's projective identifications, puts him in contact in a poetic way with the alpha-elements and with the emotional truth of the relationship at a given moment.

It is obvious that an appearance of asymmetry must lie in the greater skill of the analyst as a "narrator" and critic ("intellectual leader" or "artist", as Bion puts it) of the stories that are generated in the analytic field.

It should be equally evident, but it is worth repeating, that the full definition of what it means to dream must also involve awakening from the dream; it is also clear that there are always at the same time various levels of waking and dream in the state of waking consciousness and also in the dream itself. This means that the concept of dreaming automatically implies a passage between worlds, thresholds, frames. The sense of wonder we experience whenever we cross the frontier of dreams opens our eyes to the fiction of reality; it founds the internal space and therefore helps our mind grow.

CHAPTER SIX

Analysts in search of an author: Voltaire or Artemisia Gentileschi?

Therapeutic action

Although both set store by the symbolisation process, interpersonal and relational psychoanalysis (IRP) and Bionian field theory (BFT) manifestly have very distinct conceptions of it, because each has a different model of the unconscious, the former as unformulated experience[1] and the latter as a psychoanalytic function of the personality that continuously comes alive and develops in the field while enriching and transforming itself (Civitarese, 2008a, 2008b, 2011a, 2011b). It is important to bear in mind that in the BFT approach there are two possible loci of pathology, on the level not only of the transformation from beta into alpha-elements but also of the formation of dream thoughts and hence of dreaming and thinking. Not all unconscious experience is therefore non-representational/ideational.

The clinical vignettes of the interpersonalists sometimes convey the impression that, first, IRP is based on an interactionism not guided at all times by a model of the unconscious functioning of the individual and group mind as versatile that of BFT, which also takes account of the micrometry of the analytic dialogue; and that, second, IRP sees change as underlain principally by rational understanding and conscious agreement (which admittedly often rest on a reading of unconscious dynamics and on the joint experience of analysis). Paradoxically, in other words, change is ultimately seen as based on insight along similar lines to certain aspects of classical psychoanalysis. This may explain the critique of "irrationality" leveled at some interpretations in BFT and at its tendency to dispense with generalisations.

Rather than seeking to reach a conscious agreement, a BFT analyst sees himself[2] as engaged in an exchange of reveries, and applies the principle of unconscious communication between minds and the paradigm of dreams, which can already be found in Freud, to an extreme degree in which the entire session is seen as a dream. If things go well—that is, if the analyst has a normal endowment of receptivity and a well developed alpha function, is capable of reverie and cathects the patient—he will accept and metabolise the patient's projective identifications. If the situation is less favourable and the analyst is shielded, the projective identifications rebound on to the projecting party and become even more violent. We describe this situation as reversal of the flow of projective identifications or negative reverie (Ferro, 1992, 1999, 2002b). The analyst then needs a "second look" in order to evaluate the signals reaching him from the field and to resume correct functioning. Meanwhile he will derive valuable clues from the accident sustained en route, which will therefore, within limits, be thought of as *inevitable and indeed necessary*. This means that the field must contract the patient's illness, which, however, in terms of the field, immediately ceases to be *the patient's*. Clearly, the field must also contract the analyst's illness, but given appropriate functioning, and so on, this should not happen—or rather, *it happens all the time*, but in a setting that ought, precisely, to enable him on each occasion to regain an ideal position for containing the patient's anxieties, a process that can take place simultaneously on a number of different time scales (of seconds, minutes, months, or years).

It should be noted that when we invoke a reverie or an alpha function in the analyst or evacuative phenomena in the patient, we do so for the sake of expository, and sometimes didactic, simplicity. These are, in fact, shared phenomena and activities that are present in the field. We ought really to refer in each case to the alpha function, waking dream thought or evacuations, and so forth, of the field or present in it.

Material reality versus psychic reality

IRP and BFT share the metaphor of the field, which, however, has very different connotations for each. IRP uses the concept of the field to introduce a principle of consensual truth, the idea of the ineliminable subjectivity of the analyst and of the ongoing and non-conscious mutual influencing of analyst and patient, which, however, is seen as closely bound up with an underlying external reality deemed to be dialectically correlated with its internal counterpart. For BFT, which also espouses these concepts, the field serves to illuminate psychic reality and the unconscious functioning of the couple; while thereby seemingly dispensing with material or external reality, *it in fact seeks to apprehend its subtlest nuances in terms of how they are accommodated in psychic reality.*

Stern (2013) claims to have difficulty in accepting the systematic conversion of anything the patient says into an expression of his internal world. We, on the other hand, wonder how, and on what basis, someone who does not share this model decides to read some elements of the dialogue solely in terms of external reality and others, instead, of psychic reality, transference, dreams, or the field. What is the criterion? Is it one that is truly consistent and can be defended to the hilt, or just the analyst's more or less arbitrary decision?

The problem with material or biographic reality is that it too readily tends to become the locus of unconscious defences of the couple. If a female patient tells us that she was abused by a paternal family friend at the age of six, what can we do in terms of reality? We understand her experience rationally and explain certain aspects of her history to ourselves. At most, if the episode seems to be in tune with something that may have happened, we identify with her consciously. However, according to the BFT approach we must ask ourselves *also*, that is, in addition—without by any means disregarding the result of applying a different psychoanalytic model to the situation, but at the same time *rigorously*—the following questions: What does this account mean hypothetically if read in accordance with the dream paradigm? Who is abusing whom? Is the patient abusing the analyst? Is the analyst abusing the patient? Is a field operating in accordance with a "basic assumption" of this kind? It is in our view useful to keep all these vertices in abeyance, without prematurely hastening to attribute the character "abuse" or "abuser" to one party or the other or to one or other of the many worlds in which we are simultaneously living.

Our "insistence" on psychic reality does not by any means cause us to neglect the past history or the present material reality. On the contrary, while it entails an awareness that every model is provisional, conventional, and susceptible to revision, it also means that when it is used it must be applied with determination and consistency. In other words, there is no communication in an analysis that cannot in virtual terms be the expression of the waking dream thought "of the couple" and hence cannot tell us something about what is happening in the present.

On the other hand, it is much more common for an analyst who "falls back" on reality, including that of psychoanalytic theories (not all of which have the same antibodies in this respect!), to be defending against incandescent contents stemming from the analytic relationship. We wonder whether IRP analysts too sometimes run the same risk. We cannot readily understand how an IRP analyst succeeds in reconciling the aim of attributing significance to the trauma—that is, to the history and hence to the transference in the traditional sense (but, on the other hand, how exactly?)—with, at the same time, dispensing with the archaeological metaphor and then working in the here and now in accordance with a principle of total mutuality. Whereas a dialectic between inside and outside admittedly exists, its assertion is too general to serve as a satisfactory solution in terms of the theory of psychoanalytic technique. Material and psychic reality clearly influence each other. However, addressing the *psychic* traces of external reality and traumas, and modifying them, is a completely different matter. The point—given that we should of course refer to therapeutic actions in the plural—is our conception of what actually brings about the psychic transformation that leads to greater integration: Recovery of the memory in itself? The patient's understanding of his unconscious functioning? Achievement of a rational agreement with the analyst? Elimination of certain prejudices that characterised his attitude? Or the situation of containment that allowed all these things to come about?

BFT is based on Bion's (1992) concept of waking dream thought. If it is agreed that there is no clear-cut line of separation between the primary and secondary processes (Westen, 1999), then it is obvious that we dream both at night and during the day. Transformation into a dream (preceding the analytic dialogue with the phrase "I dreamed that …"; Ferro, 2006, 2007, 2009) is a technical device deployed consciously by the analyst in order to rediscover an internal setting whereby he can see the session as a dream, attune himself to the unconscious communication in the session, and hence focus on psychic reality. As a technique that informs the analyst's listening, it is just one of the possible means of access to the spectrum of dreaming in the session—or, more precisely, to its narrative derivatives. Among other things, over-active monitoring of the analytic conversation would be absurd. It would involve a kind of simultaneous translation from one language to another, whether or not this was made explicit to the patient, and deprive us of the possibility of access to deeper levels of oneiric thought such as, for instance, those expressed in reverie, which put us *directly* in touch with waking dream thought. The analyst in fact constantly alternates between immersion and interactivity. Furthermore, attention to waking dream thought extends over 360 degrees. It concerns not only the patient but also the analyst, what comes into his mind, and what he has just finished saying.

Symmetry versus authority

Does the analytic setting in itself guarantee successful functioning of the analyst as a container for the patient's anxieties? This ought normally to be the case. The setting is in itself already a maternal womb (Bleger, 1967; Winnicott, 1956), while the analyst is an expert in the recognition of psychic suffering and has experience, judgement, knowledge, and a technique. Another capability that should be included here is that of examining a posteriori (*nachträglich*) his own unconscious involvement in the sequence of enactments of which analysis consists (if only because words are manifestly also actions). Of course, the analyst's unconscious involvement cannot be confined to subjective experience without influencing his behaviour too. How indeed might that be possible? After all, *a posteriori* means that the unconscious is not transparent even for the analyst (every single thought is already a self-misunderstanding), that his understanding is always recursive and yet—one hopes—on each occasion sufficient, once he has allowed himself to lose it and then to retrieve an internal setting enabling him to contain the patient's (or rather, the field's) anxiety.

The analyst should possess the capability that Bion calls negative: a hyperbolic use of doubt, the ability to forgo common sense while waiting for theories to return to him as if in a dream and only after filtering through unconscious psychological work. Still on the subject of doubt, we may then wonder whether Bion's principle of listening to the patient "without memory or desire", with a passivity directed toward facilitating the emergence of the work of the unconscious aspect of the mind, is not in fact much more radical than the approach of the IRP analysts, of continuous active and conscious investigation. Might an IRP analyst's constant, intentional self-interrogation not be seen as blocking his (negative) receptive capability, and as adopting a position closer to conscious experience than to the analysis of unconscious phenomena?

Strictly speaking, in a field model it is in fact no longer meaningful to consider analyst and patient as two isolated subjects. A more valid formulation would be that of the capacity of the field for assumption and elaboration as reflected in its various points. The situation is not that the patient is the contained and the analyst the container; these are in fact constantly alternating functions. A number of container–contained relationships are simultaneously active on various levels and in different roles. This being the case, we are surprised that Stern sees our theoretical model and working style as authoritarian. We for our part think of these, and intimately experience them, as the approach that in principle assumes the maximum possible degree of responsibility for the patient and the implications of his unconscious life, thereby taking to extremes Freud's notion of an ego that is no longer master in its own house. On the contrary, it seems to us that attention to external reality, as substantially maintained by IRP in the traditional manner, might often be a way of (comprehensively) avoiding the need to come to grips with the unconscious emotional life of the field in the here and now.

The analyst has a precise role involving specific responsibilities. At the same time as he acts in this role, he uses his subjectivity, which he subordinates to the purposes of the treatment, and makes use of the symmetry of unconscious communication between minds to regain the ideal asymmetry needed to treat the patient. Unconscious communication between minds is not the same as the mutuality, so to speak, of the mutual analysis type, because unlike the former, mutuality is (also) a product of the analyst's conscious ideology—for instance, the idea that reciprocity means taking the initiative and speaking freely about oneself (and if this does not happen, why? What limits does an IRP analyst set to his independent involvement?). This is an aspect of mutuality that surely has nothing to do with the symmetry of unconscious communication.

The impression is sometimes gained that mutuality, in IRP, consists in the constant, systematic, passionate, sincere, sensitive, generous, and egalitarian use of confrontation. An IRP analyst is highly active; he interrogates, struggles, specifies, challenges, and sets himself up as distinct from the patient. One of the most frequently occurring words in the splendid, moving clinical vignettes presented by Stern (1997) is "agreement". However, in the end the agreement in question always appears somewhat unbalanced toward conscious, rational experience. Analysis thus, as Ahbel-Rappe noted, ultimately comes to resemble a wrestling match[3] between the analyst and his own dissociated selves, and between himself and the patient or a Voltairean Candide subject to repeated disastrous enactments. *In spite of the claimed mutuality, however, one of the two protagonists is also the referee, even when he acknowledges that the other was right.* The symmetry of the conversation is interrupted when, by virtue also of the authority derived from his role, he decides to interpret, in so far as he does not use interpretation as the expression of an infallible truth and also sees it as falling within the sphere of continuous enactments—or when he confronts the patient about late payment of his fees.

BFT could thus be said to take inspiration more from the so-called *sacred conversation* between mother and child portrayed in many classical paintings of the Italian Renaissance, and is not only a model of how the mind is constructed. Nor is it an idealisation of analysis. The image by no means excludes the element of violence: in fact, one of us has written a whole book (Civitarese, 2012) on ways in which the mind can self-destruct—even in analysis when the analyst lacks the capacity for reverie. In this case the metaphor is no longer that of the Madonna and Child, but that of decapitation, as depicted in the many paintings of Salome, Delilah, Judith, and others. Hence the playful contrasting in our title of Voltaire as a champion of the Enlightenment and the author of *Candide* with Artemisia Gentileschi, a female Italian painter who was a contemporary of Caravaggio and portrayed subjects of both kinds with exceptional skill.

Interpretation

If one does not accept the theoretical premises of BFT, that is, an exclusive focus on emotion and reverie (as the expression of the satisfactory operation of an invisible, transforming alpha function of the mind), as well as on the importance of thinking-as-dreaming (Ogden, 2009)—an impression of arbitrariness may well be gained if the analyst allows himself to be creative and hazards some audacious metaphors.

While Stern considers metaphor to be useful but precedes it with thought, we for our part believe that nothing we can offer a patient is more valuable than living metaphors, to help him to live. Yet we do not on any account consider that anything goes—that these metaphors are forms of intuition that can dispense with discipline and thought. It is just that we are accustomed to conceive of them differently. Ideally they are thinking metaphors or reveries (Bachelard, 1960), successful dreams, fragments of poetry, psychic productions that restore body to mind and mind to body. They are already the most profound form of thought of which we are capable. As ideas interwoven with emotion, they enable us to see reality from a number of different angles, investing it with a "poetic" ambiguity. They emanate from the unconscious, which is seen here as the psychoanalytic function of the personality that is constantly working to find, or rediscover, a basic psychosomatic integration. This is not because abstractions (etymologically, the maximum possible simplification/impoverishment attainable from sensible experience) are useless, but because it is the combination of emotions with concepts that confers meaning on existence, rather than concepts alone.

The metaphors we use are actually symbolisations and not symbolic equations. Why is this? *It is because what Stern calls "working* within *the dream" and understands within the concreteness of its hallucinatory world is in fact working after having woken up from the dream.* The dream proper is defined by the equation "dreaming + awakening". Only then does the dream reward us with the intuition of living in a number of possible worlds, and of having a completely virtual inner reality even if that reality is, in its way, just as actual as material reality. On the contrary, psy-chotic dreams or symbolic equations are characters of material reality when they are taken only as such and not deconstructed or transformed into a dream. Bion would describe this situation as transformation in hallucinosis, and Sandler (2005) as a "psychosis of everyday life". In Stern's view, dreaming must be preceded by logic. For us it is the other way round. We give precedence to the logic of a dream (a dream from which we have woken up—for what else is a reverie or the choice of a "derivative" of waking dream thought?) over that of abstract reason, because we are convinced that, in the telling formulation of Ogden (2005), the unconscious speaks with a quality of truthfulness that conscious experience lacks.

Notes

1. On this point, see Levine (2010).
2. Translator's note: For convenience, the masculine form is used for both sexes throughout this translation.
3. Cf. Ahbel-Rappe: "Virtually every clinical example in the book includes and features (without being overly confessional) Stern wrestling with his own dissociations for the sake of treatments" (Ahbel-Rappe, 2010, p. 799).

CHAPTER SEVEN

Confrontation in the Bionian model of the analytic field

Gunfight at the O.K. Corral

"This is a sickness: it is an illogical, inferential, inappropriate, unrealistic, and emotional way of thinking and has no basis in fact. Recognize the signs of such thinking and get it under control; do not let influence you": pretending to address an imaginary patient, Langs (1973/4, p. 430) summarises in these words the sense of confrontational interventions. Except in Langs, who devotes an entire chapter to the subject, and aside from its role in Kernberg's structural theory, confrontation is the Cinderella of handbooks of psychoanalytic technique. Etchegoyen (1986) dismisses it a few lines, as does Akhtar (2009, p. 54), who notes that it is neither listed in the index to the *Standard Edition* nor even mentioned in several prominent books on psychotherapy.

This relative absence is surprising because we are all aware of the central importance of confrontation in the classical Freudian model of psychoanalysis. The reason may be that our conception of it may be either wide-ranging—which would explain its ubiquity and protean character—or narrow. The narrow connotation is the better known: basically, the analyst draws the patient's attention to a logical contradiction and asks him[1] to resolve it. A wider conception, on the other hand, would tend to take account of the degree of confrontation implicit in any intervention. In Etchegoyen's view, a simple observation may not be readily distinguishable from a confrontation (although in the former case perception is in the foreground and in the latter judgement; observation invites one to look at something more carefully and more closely, whereas confrontation entails addressing a dilemma or contradiction).

Confrontation in general is directed to matters that are evident to both parties, such as ego dysfunctions, resistances, enactments, or breaches of the setting. If used correctly, it can facilitate integration in the patient, help him to control his impulses, overcome an impasse, tackle the onset of acute symptoms, and preserve the therapeutic alliance. In addition, by way of interpretation it prepares the patient to engage with deeper levels of unconscious life. Some hold that failure to use it would in some cases constitute a deplorable omission, tantamount to implicit endorsement of the patient's destructive behaviour.

Confrontation is bound up with a conception of the transference as a false connection and misunderstanding. Again, if the analyst points out to the patient a contradiction in his attitude, he is by definition appealing more to the patient's capacity for rational thought than to his emotional capabilities. In this way he is setting aside the unconscious communication taking place between the two protagonists in the analysis. This also implies the existence of a sharp line of separation between conscious and unconscious or between primary and secondary process.

An analyst who confronts his patient assumes the position of someone who "knows" and who sets his feet on solid ground, but this might be an illusion, for what is the unconscious meaning of his communication? Might confrontation in the analyst not also lend itself to the expression of aggression, the need to dominate and control, or to reassure himself about his own unconscious impulses by a flight into reality? Could it be that he is thereby disregarding the patient's and/or his own unconscious psychic reality?

Moreover, the use of confrontation has to do with one's conception of the nature of therapeutic factors. It is resorted to mostly by models that stress knowledge and insight, directed primarily to making the unconscious conscious. Other analysts, whose emphasis is more on unconscious communication between minds or on the dream paradigm, make less use of it.

In agreement with Bion we consider the main therapeutic factor to lie not in rendering the unconscious conscious, but in achieving emotional unison with the patient. We try to see what the patient sees. Yet an absolute, point-by-point superimposition of vertices is never possible. The context of each individual's external, and in particular internal, life is too different. Every identification will necessarily also entail a differentiation. If sustainable, this difference, the extent of which varies from case to case, represents a cognitive gain for the other. Enjoying mental health means having a range of viewpoints on things: Bion (1965) writes that this involves the ability to adopt a variety of emotional "positions" toward the object. Hence emotions and their transformations lie at the centre. The subject comes into being from a constant interplay of identity and difference. With regard to difference, however, the matter must be seen from the "environmental" standpoint of sustainability. Anything in the confrontation with the other that is not emotionally sustainable by the patient carries the risk of unmotivated retraumatisation.

Ferro (2010) describes this dynamic with the metaphor of the "fluctuation band". Some patients are thoroughly intolerant of being confronted with views that differ from their own or of being faced with contradictions in their behaviour. It is important to respect these patients' predominant need for identity before moments of differentiation or of overt conflict can also be sustained.

Bion (1970) invites the analyst to forget the contradictions arising out of rational examination and to be in a state of hallucinosis (Civitarese, 2014) in order to be able to see what the patient sees—that is, ultimately, the whole spectrum of the patient's inner life. In other words, the analyst must take seriously all impressions, sensations, and ideas that seemingly conflict with aspects of material reality, because they tell a different story from the apparent one—a story that may perhaps be more "true." In the words of Ogden, the unconscious speaks "with a quality of truthfulness that is different from, and almost exclusively much richer than, what the conscious aspect of ourselves is able to perceive and convey" (Ogden, 2005, p. 73).

If an analyst in supervision mistakenly writes that a patient is fourteen years old instead of his actual age of thirty-four, we take very seriously this indication of an adult who, for all his years, is emotionally on the threshold of adolescence. If the idea for a moment crosses our mind that our patient, against all the evidence to the contrary, is not married, this means that from one point of view—which is not exclusive, but important—he is not.

In all the following vignettes our general aim is to demonstrate how analytic field theory and the type of listening it proposes can be beneficial in several ways. It can help the analyst better grasp the emotional needs of the patient. He will be able to avoid engaging in a confrontation that involves regarding certain facts merely as real and not also as derivatives of waking dream thought. It also shows that it is in fact easier to modulate the pressure of interpretation and confrontation if one listens to the way in which the patient—as a locus in the field— responds to the increases in tension we inject into it by suggesting a different perspective on things. Finally, it helps clarify how on many occasions confrontation can be replaced either by indirect confrontation (through the "characters" of the session—so, apparently talking about something else) or negotiation, that is, when a certain point is no longer regarded as essential and a solution can be found that maintains a proper setting and at the same time recognises the existence in the patient of a threshold of tolerance of difference.

Ada[2]

Ada, twenty-eight years old, had always had a very difficult relationship with her mother. One day I remarked to her that perhaps her mother for her part might have suffered too. She flew into a rage and yelled at me: "You are *my* analyst, not my mother's! You take care of *me*!" In a word, she wanted me to take her account literally (she was right, because on the level of psychic reality it was of course absolutely true).

Mario

Mario is a patient in his mid-thirties. He had displayed extreme violence throughout a very turbulent period of his therapy, and when I attempted to confront him with the evidence of his behaviour, he said: "But, doctor, why are you so much on the defensive?!" It was true. After his comment I relaxed. I stopped summoning him back to reality and became more receptive again. In other words, I was able once more to listen in such a way that the entire session could be seen as a dream.

If a patient goes on sarcastically talking to me about her mother's insensitivity and arrogance toward her, I do not tell her that the transference has given her a mistaken impression of my (presumed) open, benevolent attitude, but consider the possibility that she might in fact have an utterly precise view of me, albeit filtered by the unconscious work expressed in waking dream thought and its derivatives.

Confrontation, then, is basically a useful instrument; however, it is not so much specifically "psychoanalytic" as, in a broad sense, educational. Admittedly, though, an intervention in pedagogic form—that is, an appeal to common sense and observance of rules—on occasion actually serves a deeper-level purpose of containment.

Angelo

That was the situation with Angelo, a thirty years old patient, whom I had to ask to suspend his therapy for a while because his rage was threatening to cause it to explode. In general, however, we are nowadays much more inclined to *negotiate* the rules with the patient rather than to impose them on him and insist that he comply with the terms of the analytic contract.

This new sensitivity could be described by the concept of an oscillation between negotiation and confrontation. We also tend to accept that, while the therapeutic relationship is indeed asymmetric with regard to roles, on the level of unconscious interaction it is virtually symmetric. Whereas this on the one hand destabilises us in terms of authority, on the other it strengthens us because we know that this authority is in part false and that we must take very much more responsibility for our unconscious psychic functioning.

Sara

Sara, forty years old, tells me that she wants to break off her therapy as she cannot allow herself to go on with it; she then says that her husband does not respect her private space, opens her letters, changes the start screens on her mobile phone, and is not interested in her sexually; furthermore, lately they are always quarreling. She adds that her children too are becoming more and more unfeeling and that she feels that the rage building up inside her is increasingly uncontainable.

The traditional approach would be for me to interpret her sexual frustration in transference terms and to point out that breaking off the therapy would not help in any way.

Looking at this vignette from a field perspective, however, I instead wonder where and how such a climate of incomprehension and violence might have arisen *in the analysis*, and whether perhaps some of the responsibility for it might be mine. I would say something to Sara while respecting her own narrative level, and tell her that leaving her home and children on an impulse without asking herself how this sorry state of affairs had come about would be harmful. However, my intimate awareness of speaking from actual experience that involves me in the first person—albeit on the level of unconscious communication—offers better prospects of successfully touching the patient with my words. This is all the more true if the insight into what is happening between us comes to me not from an intentional transformation into a dream (Ferro, 2009), but from a reverie—that is, from a psychic production born of even deeper unconscious psychological work.

There is little room for confrontation in a strict reading of the Bionian model of the analytic field. Confrontation is more likely to occur indirectly by way of the narratives featuring the various characters in the analytic dialogue and discussion of their dilemmas. Rational consideration of the situation does not then cease to be important, provided that it is integrated into the emotional view.

Anna

Anna is twenty-eight years old. She comes once a week for face-to-face psychotherapy and is no longer prepared to pay for missed sessions. One evening she argues with me without a break until I am unbelievably exasperated. The same thing happens two or three more times, and I decide to allow myself to give her a chance. I throw in the towel. Even if she has not *entirely* convinced me, we shall do as she wishes. Given that it is so important to her, OK, we'll leave time for it to be understood and see what happens. Perhaps, I tell myself, for once she needs to deal with someone who is not so abstractly inaccessible to her way of thinking, and who will ultimately enable her to learn from her mistakes. Anna has always experienced her parents as cold and intransigent; by agreeing to set aside the issue of the sessions without insisting on a confrontation, I am accepting her regressive, infantile, or immature sides, which must after all have an opportunity to find expression. In this way I believe I can also help her eventually to assume a more adult level of responsibility.

The concept and practice of confrontation—at least in its "archaic"/ tough "gunfight at the OK corral" version—are not characteristic of

Italian psychoanalysis in particular or of European psychoanalysis in general. We in fact tend to see it in negative terms, as if it meant that the time for negotiation were over and we were fed up with hesitation, so we set off on the warpath heading for a kind of "gunfight at the OK Corral". Rather than in the normal run of discourse, confrontation is observed in connection with problems to do with the setting, such as the number and times of sessions, payment for missed sessions, or vacation dates. Even critical situations like these can often be resolved within the field, without resorting to an open confrontation between analyst and patient.

A typical case where the analyst resorts to confrontation is with patients who engage in dangerous kinds of acting out. Let us say that a patient resists the treatment by acting out conflicts in lateral transferences. It is then worth considering whether the "out" element of acting out could be brought into the sessions to a greater extent. This would involve not only the traditional but also a *molecular* conception of the transference. Is it conceivable that, were we able to focus more sharply on *how* the trauma is produced, or reproduced, in the analytic encounter, patients might not need to act out so clamorously, sometimes even risking their lives in order to make themselves understood? In a word, might we be able to regulate the necessary dose of retraumatisation (which should be tolerable and tolerated only with a view to mental growth)? After all, the relational perspective of the field merely intensifies the centripetal attraction already held in classical theory to be exerted by the transference on acting out, when it is said that certain drive-related impulses reawakened by the analysis are acted out other than in the sessions.

In order to return acting out to the dream of the session, "outside" must come "inside"—not be "forced" to come in, but be accepted within. For in our view excessive attention to the patient's history and objective reality carries the risk of neglecting his suffering. The result is a kind of operational thinking about facts and memories-as-facts, of rationalisations lacking in genuine affective involvement. The predominant feeling in the analyst tends to be sympathy, which is mostly defensive in nature, whereas he is actually abdicating responsibility. He should instead be receptive, listening on the basis of fundamental acceptance of the notions of unconscious communication between minds and the dream paradigm.

Sometimes the real acting out at issue is not a question of the cases about which the analyst confronts the patient, but occurs in the session when he "insistently" has recourse to psychoanalytic theories and "hallucinates" the patient and the analysis. Might this not betray a difficulty on his part in representing, symbolising, dreaming, and remembering? Could this not be the challenge of any analysis—trying to see the patient with new eyes, or rather trying to put oneself in a state of passivity whereby theories can return in the form of reveries—in other words, only after undergoing a process of unconscious work? When the analyst is not capable of always seeing the patient as if for the first time (Bion) and of rediscovering psychoanalysis with him (Ogden), then on occasions the Theory itself becomes a kind of hallucinosis (Civitarese, 2014), in the sense that it offers a hyperluminous understanding whose only purpose is to meet the need to avoid some painful experience, be it only rediscovering himself in the role of the "bad guy" proposed by the patient in the analytic dialogue: for example, asking what responsibility he might have in the "story" told by a patient about having been abused—in other words, avoiding interpreting this communication in part as the result of waking dream thought and of something that is going on in the here and now.

The transparency of meanings contained in our stereotypical interpretations cloaks the invisible repetition in the analysis of the trauma that gave rise to the lacuna of meaning in the patient's psyche. The oedipal element of so many interpretations "given" to the patient is in reality the "incestuous relationship" with theories (!) which we all resort to when in difficulty. This is obviously not simply a matter of models, because any theory can be used not *to see* but to *avoid* seeing. Perhaps, however, some are able to lay in more supplies of antibodies to this danger. In our understanding, field theory focuses greatly on the subjectivity of the analyst and in some respects follows a principle of systematic doubt—this is what we mean by "antibodies"—whereby virtually everything that presents itself as a fact, also as a fact produced by the theory of reference, can if necessary be deconcretised and seen in the light of its possible unconscious meaning.

Respecting the rules

In our experience, even in cases where the setting is threatened, it is usually possible to find a solution whereby the implicit analytic communication can, however gradually, be apprehended.

Renato

The first time I see Renato, who is only six years old, he reminds me of a bison-calf, and this is what he turns out to be, as he contains himself in almost muscular fashion (Bick, 1968) with the hyperactivity he uses to protect himself from catastrophic total dissolution.

There is nothing I am able to say that has any effect on his running, no matter at what level I try to communicate. On the contrary, my speaking seems to goad him, as though my words were bullets. In response he picks up some wooden blocks and throws them at me, almost hitting and hurting me.

I try to tell him I feel like a cowboy surrounded by attacking Indians, but nothing will stop him. The perimeter of his running track extends to the waiting room and he continues to run around with his head lowered. I'm beginning to think that it would take a fence to keep him in and I am actually tempted to make one, at least within the confines of the room. Instead, I am still there in my chair, drawing a fence on one of the sheets of paper I has prepared for him. He stops, more curious than interested.

He picks up a coloured pencil and, making big marks outside the boundary of the fence, says: "And I'm going to break it down, I'm going to break it down". Then he draws a red funnel. I say it looks like a whirlwind, or a tornado, or maybe Red Cloud, who can break through any fence.

Still standing, he says: "Draw more fences!" I obey, wondering if I'm acting out, but at the same time trying desperately to think. He continues to break down the fences with the same coloured turbine. I say it looks as if there is no dam that could hold him back.

I keep making fences and inside one fenced area I draw something like a table. He takes a felt-tipped pen to the wall and on a tile draws "an Indian teepee". I say: "A place for Red Cloud".

On my sheet he draws a teepee, an Indian child and a whirlwind. In the meantime I am thinking about how, while running round, he has not only overturned the toy box but also knocked over chairs, side tables and so forth. It looks like a battlefield. I remember how his mother told me that when Renato has one of his frequent uncontrolled fits in which he tries to break everything in sight the only thing that stops him is cartoons.

He comes closer and, instead of using the wall tiles as a drawing pad, this time he uses the tabletop and draws an Indian boy picking up everything that has fallen out of a basket "With the help of his friend the crab who has arms that pinch without hurting". He continues drawing, "But as the two friends are working somebody shoots at them ... then another cyclone strikes".

The session continues. But now we have these "characters" we have created together in our animated cartoon, characters that will help us give a name to and turn into story what happens in the room and between our two minds. This is the necessary precondition for the recognition, narration and transformation of emotions and feelings, which is what Lussana meant (1993) when speaking of the evolution from Kleinian to Bionian interpretation.

One could debate whether my drawing was an acting out. I would observe, however, that denying oneself a certain freedom in emergency situations would mean sacrificing to formalistic rigour what can in fact be communicated and transformed, albeit with exceptional and apparently improper means. For, basically, my drawings reveal three things: the incapacity to think enough, a need to discharge (like Renato's physical running) and the need for a dam, a boundary, which, once erected, would allow the transformations and shared thought processes to take place.

Needless to say, I considered all the characters of the session to be functions and holograms of the couple and of the emotional exchanges between the two of us. They were a point of departure for the narration of emotions and feelings which turned form an incontinent mode toward a mode in which thought and verbal communication become possible. As proto-characters are born, they bear witness to what I have called "functional aggregates" or "affective holograms". What is at times so difficult to grasp about analytic field theory, in other words the idea that everything potentially belongs to the dream of the session and everything can be deconcretised, appears rather obvious in child analysis, where everything is in fact play. Unquestionably, the analytic field model derives in large part from child psychoanalysis.

Cesare

Another situation that I for a long time found it difficult to deal with was when Cesare, an adult patient in his thirties with severe symbiotic pathology, refused to leave my office at the end of his session. No interpretation or rational argument had any effect.

The next day's session somehow always included traces of communications that made it possible to take up the "problem" again and gradually to digest it to some extent. For instance, the patient would tell me about a heater that was leaking oil and flooded a room, or children who failed to obey the school rules, or his boxer brother who insisted on getting his own way with everyone (myself as a part of him?), and so on. However, the real change came about after fruitless efforts—once I almost summoned a colleague to eject him (literally) from the room—when I decided that when the session was over I would be the one to leave the room. This was admittedly a clever trick, but since the problem was separation, once I had left the room it was solved (maybe not very correctly). After a very long time, during which I never ceased to think about his difficulty, I succeeded in getting him to agree to leave first. The solution I adopted can be seen as "confrontation in action" (Smith, 2013), of a kind and an intensity, however, that the patient was able to accept and make good use of. Moreover, the important thing was that I did not feel confronted with a rigid appeal to the classic rules in dealing with problems of the setting, but felt rather that I was granted a certain amount of creativity.

Laura-the-couch?-No-thanks!

With Laura, twenty-four years old, I was faced with another situation that could have led to us getting bogged down in a sterile argument. Notwithstanding our agreement on all aspects of commencing an analysis, in the first session she refused to lie down on the couch. Having worked with borderline and psychotic patients with whom a face-to-face setting where we could see each other was necessary for a long time until they overcame the persecution anxiety that prevented them from turning their back on me, I have never found this a problem. (For example, I recall a patient with powerful symbiotic nuclei who, having agreed to lie down on the couch, dreamed of being on a slide in a children's playground and discovering during his descent that the landing area at the bottom was made of razor blades that would tear open the skin of his back.)

But the situation with Laura was different. She did not seem to have any psychotic nucleus (it was only later that I learned how terrible it was for her to get in touch with violent emotions and in particular with the shame they aroused), and yet I agreed to face-to-face working for a long time.

After a long period I noticed that I was working badly, and asked her if I could turn my armchair round so that I had my back to her, in order to avoid her scrutiny and the concreteness of the emotions exhibited on her face. This we did.

After a further prolonged phase of therapy, Laura announced that she was going to have to "move". I then remarked that the time was perhaps ripe for us too to move to the armchair and the couch respectively. She eventually accepted this and we agreed that our move would take place on the first Monday of the following month.

The Monday arrived, and Laura, entering the consulting room before me and heading for the "analysis area", in one bound ensconced herself in my armchair! I was dumbfounded. Various courses of action (₩☺₡#? ☒↑✄✂‼☞☜●???✈♥!)³ flashed through my mind. Remarking to her that the couch must apparently be such a terrible experience that she first needed to see if *I* could stand it, I then "calmly" made for the couch and lay down on it. Finally we had a proper analytic situation, even if the roles were seemingly reversed. I was greatly helped in all of this by my experience as a child analyst, which had over time accustomed me to stop holding the setting in veneration, and I enacted what I would later have called a *transformation into play*. To be honest, I was also helped by recalling—perhaps not accurately—that when Marie Bonaparte was suffering later in life from rheumatism she too would lie down on the couch.

For a while we proceeded in this way, until Laura mentioned that her secretary had high-handedly taken possession of an armchair that was by rights hers. It was then easy for me to tell her that someone else was also high-handedly occupying a place to which she was not entitled. With many years of work behind us, in the next session she lay down on the couch for the first time.

In her first session on the couch, Laura recounted a dream: a wicked nurse is about to inject a young woman with a drug that turns everyone red, but a physician stops her and saves the patient. I saw this dream as the first sign of the possibility of opposing a superego structure that used injections of shame to prevent her from coming into contact with herself and her emotions. But this new capacity seemed to have been generated by the fact that Laura was now able to acknowledge my direct and subtly superegoic comment.

Even gentle firmness can make the patient feel understood and contented. The problem is not the confrontation in itself but taking into account—something we do by intuition and experience, as well as through knowledge—the *sustainability* of the quota of difference intrinsic to any confrontation, even one that presents itself without this label and as a simple diversity of points of view. Each different point of view always implies a certain amount of confrontation and this raises the voltage of the analytic field. *The measure is always relative, as is the degree of saturation of the interpretations, and it is the patient himself who constantly gives us directions.* One patient can endure a harsh confrontation, while another, like the patient in the vignette, needs to see his defences respected for a certain amount of time, and reacts catastrophically to homeopathic doses of confrontation. Any intervention, even the most delicate, can in some contexts become something like a gunfight at the OK corral and thus risks being traumatic. Our reservations as to the method of confrontation by itself do not therefore only apply to its "archaic" or old-fashioned expressions or authoritarian models. If the analyst does not take into account the constantly ongoing unconscious communication between minds, the intervention that seems least authoritarian may in fact be precisely that. The question then becomes how much "symbiosis"/unison/understanding (Freud, 1895) is needed to meet the needs of the ego and to facilitate the development of the mind with increasing and bearable amounts of *novelty/difference* (Civitarese, 2004).

This is why using confrontation between characters, that is, the necessary use of indirect confrontation, is a way of measuring out the violence of the interpretation and providing the patient with an excipient that makes the medication palatable. If a patient tells us that his boss is always telling off his secretary, we could point out that she would do well to avoid always arriving late: this could be a way of indirectly raising the issue of the patient arriving late at sessions, but also, depending on the context, a way of referring to the analyst's real or imagined "lateness" in saying something useful to contain her anxieties.

It must be said that the very concept of symbiosis, linked as it is to the idea of two subjects interacting in a certain way, does not respect the original postulate of the analytic field model, which is to consider firstly the transformations of the field that has been jointly created and to set aside the individuality of each party. The symbiosis can never be perfect. Disorder is already a given in nature; order is what is always difficult to achieve. The choice of looking at the field, at something between the two subjects and generated by both is made only because it enables us to better understand what is happening in the encounter between the two subjects and because it seems more transformative, and it is in any case called upon to serve the psychic growth which belongs to the couple (the common mind of the group consisting of patient and analyst) but is also *inevitably* individual: each, as it were, takes home a better method for giving meaning to the experience. Does the instinctive and empathic understanding that the mother has for the child create a dangerous symbiosis or does it provide a background of continuity to the child's existence which puts it in a position to tolerate absence and difference? A symbiosis that annuls the other's subjectivity would only point to an incestuous attachment due to the lack of a symbolic/third function in the mind of the mother who is incapable of adjusting the distance. But in reality for us "containment" or unison, which we prefer to the idea of symbiosis, involves this notion of "good distance" and mutual growth.

There is no definitive remedy for the possibility that field theory can be used unconsciously as a kind of enactment for the purpose of avoiding pain, where there is a danger of falling into a kind of delusion of a transparent interpretation. It is true, however, that a radically critical theory, accustomed to systematic doubt and non-authoritarian in spirit, is better equipped—that is to say, again, it has more antibodies—to counteract this risk or to correct its course.

Etta

In the early days of my work as an analyst, Etta, a young female patient in her early twenties, comes in one day and sits down in my armchair. I feel at a loss; I don't know what to say or do, and am filled with anxiety at the idea of no longer having my place. It then suddenly occurs to me that I announced in the previous session that I was going to be away for a whole week. So I tell her that perhaps she wants me to experience the feeling one has when one's place is no longer available—that by depriving her of the week of analysis I made her feel at a loss, and now she is paying me back in kind. Etta immediately gets up and goes over to the couch.

In many years of analytic work there have been numerous episodes that could have led to quite a drastic confrontation over the setting, but by taking the patient as our "best colleague"—as someone who always has his reasons, at least from a particular point of view—we have been able slowly but surely to arrive at a conception that he too could accept.

Situations not directly connected with the setting may perhaps be easier to manage because it is not the "relationship" in the present, which could readily become the theatre of a "battle", that is in the foreground. After all, given an adequately functioning setting, we are assisted by a strong concept—namely, that of the analytic field.

In the field the internal groupings of analyst and patient are immediately activated and form a group situation. Hence the dramatis personae—whether cast in their roles by the patient or the analyst—are regarded not as real characters or internal objects, but as holograms of the functioning of these groupings. All the characters are seen as modes of functioning assumed by the field at the relevant time. The characters thus act as "navigation" devices that show whether we are heading in the right direction or have taken a wrong turning. In particular, the analyst's (the field's!) continuous transformation of everything that comes to life in the session into a dream leads to new viewpoints that involve constant enlargement of the field. The vertex of the patient cannot be ignored; in fact, from one perspective the vertices continuously presented to us by the characters of the field enable us to find the right road.

This situation is not well tolerated by many analysts, as if they were afraid of forfeiting their role and authority. As Tolstoy writes in relation to the Battle of Borodino—hence our epigraph—although the generals in the field have the illusion of controlling events, these are in fact determined in ways that are much more complex, unforeseen, and independent of their will.

The interpretative line

It is not uncommon for the analyst to allow himself to be captured by an interpretative line that then rigidly dictates his manner of listening (or of not listening).

Filippo

I thought it would be good for Filippo, twenty-eight years old, if we were able to integrate violent, split-off aspects of himself. I had tuned into this wavelength automatically. I discerned "roughnecks" even in wheel "bolts".[4] One day, however, he tells me about the dentist who always X-rays the same tooth and never suspects that his patient's intense pain might originate in other teeth. He then explains that he has had some blood tests that have revealed a large number of abnormal red corpuscles, but that another lab doubts that the procedures used for "this analysis" are correct. At this point I cannot fail to realise that my insistence on a particular interpretative line has led me completely astray.

If we hold fast to some *idée fixe*, we may well fail to listen to the new things the patient brings us each day. Tellingly, Bion (1987) writes that the patient who ends a sentence is no longer the same as the one who began it.

Isotta

Isotta, thirty-two years old, is in her first year of analysis. One Monday she tells me that a patient has escaped from the community where she works; next, that an orphaned cousin they had nearly adopted kept flying into a rage and kicking the door; and then that her mother wept at her nephew's bad behaviour, and when her husband returned she reproached him for not being there to keep the children in order and gave vent to a litany of old recriminations.

The problem here is how to "cook" these various ingredients. Simply decoding them would be easy: because the analyst went away at the weekend, Isotta's rage was so uncontainable that she wanted to kick the closed door and give vent to a litany of complaints at being abandoned.

However, this interpretation would have two limits. It would be the fruit of one mind only and would be automatic and saturated. The analyst would seem like a conjuror who knows and understands everything and pulls the interpretation out of a hat. The alternative, of working with the characters and relationships so as to bring out the emotions between them, might prove too general. A third possibility might then be to "sample" the patient's responses and be guided by them in the session in order to decide what to mention and what not to mention "explicitly".

The same problem had arisen when Isotta had referred to her boyfriend as a "bear" who didn't like accepting invitations to a dinner with friends. In one session I remark that it is hard to deal with the "boyfriend/bear", but that I am also trying to see things from his perspective, and I mention the difficulty he has in being with others. At the end of the session I feel dissatisfied; I seem not to have understood very much.

Isotta begins the next session as follows: "Yesterday the light bulb in my bedroom blew and I was left in the dark". This announcement (presumably pointing out that the session had not turned on any light) allows me—treading with great care and proceeding in a roundabout manner—to show Isotta that being a "bear" might also be a relatively unknown aspect of herself because it was kept in the shade by a more free and easy side of herself, and that her non-stop talking might serve as a barrier to protect the bear. When she tells me about the fine and interesting movie she has seen, I am able to add that on the one hand she likes coming to analysis, but on the other she finds it hard to come and show herself as she really is. She then remembers that as a child she very much enjoyed dancing, but felt ashamed if her family saw her doing so.

Our point is that there is no right or wrong way of interpreting, but that one's interpretations should be constantly modulated in accordance with the valuable clues offered by the patient.

Another function of the analyst appears to be that of dreaming the missing pieces so that the patient's dream can develop. It does not then matter what the dream is, provided that it can develop. Any communication, however seemingly reality-based, can refer to emotional reality and deemed a "narrative derivative of the patient's waking dream thought", as long as we dare to listen from the vertex of transformations into a dream. A completely different kind of listening then becomes possible. This is rendered all the more difficult the more (apparently) reality-based situations, seen as external, close off the analyst's capacity for reception and dreaming, which might thus be lost in the tortuous byways of listening as a social worker, a family-planning adviser, or a supportive psychotherapist—thus abandoning the analytic vertex.

There is also the opposite risk—of an interpretation in the form of a simultaneous translation that strips a story of all intense emotion and decodes it into an intellectualisation lacking in affect. The need is then for interpretation and comprehension in our minds until there is no possibility of extension in the domains of sense, myth, and passion (Bion, 1963). In other words, an interpretation must relate to something of which the patient can see at least certain aspects (to produce the rabbit from the hat, the patient too must be able to see the tips of its ears!); the narration must be hot and come into being on the fly; and the same applies to the characteristic of shared visibility in narrative, visual, and mythical terms.

As a therapeutic factor we propose the quality of the analyst's mental functioning in the session, and in particular his endowment of receptivity, flexibility, and capacity for transformation, tolerance, and patience. When these enter the field, they effect previously unthinkable transformations. In this way, beta elements and emotional or sensory proto-mental contents which were not previously transformed into pictograms (alpha elements) or containable may cease to be "camouflaged", "stored up", split off, projected, or evacuated, but instead become thinkable. The quality of the analyst's mental functioning in the session is a variable of the analytic field and is one of the field's co-determinants, just as, broadly speaking, one's interpretative choices codetermine the opening or closure of possible worlds.

Our knowledge resembles a Swiss cheese that is full of holes rather than an entire Parmesan wheel. It is just that we are ashamed, and afraid to show how many holes we have, so that we spend much of our time creating *trompe l'oeils* to fill them (or to pretend, or to persuade others or ourselves, that we are filling them).

Religions, ideologies, and fanaticism in its various forms are among the principal "fillers" to which we resort. The same applies to the use of theories in a session. In this way we have the illusion of appearing as a densely structured "Parmesan" cheese instead of a minimally trabeculate Emmental. Bion's *Attention and Interpretation* (1970) includes a few lines on the need for lies that enjoin us to adopt a modest posture and accept the extent of tolerance we must deploy both with ourselves and with others; instead of claiming to be "Paladins" of truth, we should be happy to be mere artisans of the degree of mental development that can be tolerated by our patients and ourselves.

Defence against knowledge

The limit achievable in an analysis depends on where the analyst, and hence the analytic couple, dares to go. As to roles, the relationship is asymmetric, with the analyst taking on more responsibility. In order not to go under in waters that are too deep and therefore feared, a common defence is to avoid supplying a culture medium suitable for the development of the characters brought by the patient. The easiest, most underhand, and most craven of these devices is to accommodate the "characters" in the history as persons.

Post no bills

In the first analysis of a patient who had come to me for re-analysis—at the time he had just turned fifty—some of the characters he had brought to his previous analyst over the years (for the sake of convenience, let us disregard the current significance of this narration, that is to say, what they might mean in the here and now of our sessions) remained in effect a dead letter, as if subject to a ban on "posting bills" announcing possible "films"—as if there were a tacit agreement that certain posters would fall foul of the censors. The point I am making is that the analyst who had preceded me had not developed with the patient those narratives from a field perspective: he had not seen them as a dream of the session, as ways of subconsciously representing the functioning of the system comprising patient and analyst. He had only seen them as events external to the analysis.

I still recall some of these "unwatched films":

> One concerned references over a long period to an article by the patient on the suicide syndrome that had been turned down by a journal. (me turning down the prospect of coming into contact with his depressive anxieties?)

Another was the report of a "head-on collision" in a car in which the patient was travelling. Also in this case the subject of the "head-on collision" was never developed further, at least in its "Gunfight at the OK Corral" version. The analyst did not read this communication by the patient as a possible comment on some of his previous confrontational interventions.

The patient also mentioned a tenant in the previous analyst's apartment block—a person he would occasionally run into and who seemed to him to be a "depressive" suffering from severe depression. This subject too was never allowed to come to life in the sessions, that is to say, the analyst did not look at the depressed tenant as a kind of hologram that had become active in the field and that might refer to a depressive quality of his or of the analyst's, and ultimately to emotions still waiting to be contacted and transformed.

Nor was room given to a distant relationship with a notorious Sicilian bandit from the 1950s, a dissolute cousin, a somewhat dishonest uncle (the patient was never given a tax receipt by his first analyst!), or another uncle with autistic traits. None of these stories were seen as possible expressions in the here and now of dynamic aspects of the analytic field or as unconscious reactions by the patient (considered as a "place" in the analytic field and not as a separate subject) to interventions by the analyst (also seen as a place in the field).

In other words, analysts often cut off many of the "possible stories" that could enrich the narrations of the field. Their potential to disrupt more the normopathic aspects thus remains unexpressed.

Psychoanalytic orthodoxy, too, obeys the same law of adapting to the already known and approved. Psychoanalysis itself has forfeited its original "sulfurous" status and become the nth ideology used to standardise and deaden one's conscience.

The Minotaur turned to wood

Stefano, a six-year-old, is in therapy for a selective "mutism" that commences after his parents separated and has gradually worsened. His mother abandoned the family for a new partner. After a short period when Stefano seemed to have adapted to the new situation, he first suffers from enuresis (here we have the theme of incontinence), and after a while completely stops speaking at school (hypercontainment).

At our first meetings, he does not say a word, his eyes are lifeless, and he seems to droop. It occurs to me to suggest to Stefano that he whisper a few words to his father (who comes with Stefano to his sessions and stays as an observer), who thus begins to act as a loudspeaker. Stefano whispers words to his father, who amplifies them and repeats them in audible form.

The first structured game to appear involves a zoo, in which tigers, lions, and gorillas are locked up in extremely sturdy cages. The second game features an exceedingly fierce dog that has to be muzzled. What comes into my mind is the story of Officer Starling and Hannibal Lecter, who is fitted with a kind of muzzle to stop him biting people.

Concealed behind this form of "mutism", or rather of "setting the phonatory gain to minimum", is manifestly the failure of containment, as tellingly depicted in Munch's "The Scream".

It is not only the abandonment by his mother but also her total lack of warmth and closeness that leaves Stefano speechless. When reflecting on Stefano's birth, his mother had commented: "He was always a burden and an obstacle to my career—the career I had devoted my life to, and wanted to go on devoting it to".

A few months into his therapy, Stefano is prepared to let his father leave the room and wait for him in the waiting room. Developing his play, he eventually agrees to write down what the "characters" assigned to him need to communicate in the game in which the analyst gives a voice to other characters.

It is in our view important to apprehend the defensive attitude of "hyper-containment" as an alternative to non-containment, because it will then become possible to work on the deconstruction of the emotional tsunami that terrifies Stefano. The tsunami can be deconstructed into a number of different winds/emotions (the southwesterly *libeccio*, the northerly *tramontana*, the southeasterly *scirocco*, etc., each of which corresponds to an emotion that must be deciphered—for instance, rage, jealousy, or abandonment).

To use another metaphor, it is perhaps useful to develop the container and the figure of a "tamer" of wild beasts so as to ensure that ferocious animals (emotions and proto-emotions) can move about and be contained (not hyper-contained!) by this new function. They will then be amenable to modulation.

From "O" to "K": the dream column

Manuela

Manuela is an accommodating ten-year-old analysand engaged in rivalry with her twelve-year-old sister. After the sister's recovery from a serious illness, the parents buy her the Alsatian puppy she has always dreamed of. Manuela's analyst is annoyed at what he sees as an unwise acquisition and an intrusion into the therapy, as his patient has a "dog phobia". So he decides to talk to the parents, whom he accuses of having heedlessly disturbed Manuela's analysis.

In this way, however, he leaves "a fact" (the purchase of the puppy) in the form of a mere "fact", or, within the therapy, an "O", without transforming it from a "fact-in-itself"—if you will, from β-elements—into K, α, meaning, or narration. After all, in an analysis, any "O" can only be accommodated in column two (yes, the column of lies), in order to be transformed into the subjective truth of the analysis in question. Even then, as Grotstein (2007) constantly reminds us, the result would be a distortion/disguise/transformation of "O."

From this point of view, the puppy could basically be dreamed of as the hooligan feared by Manuela—as something alive and new that arrives in the analysis and in her psychic life—and the parents who bought it as a description of the work of the analyst, who has been able to bring something alive and new into the analysis.

Other vertices are of course also necessary, but would not be so specifically psychoanalytic.

Ultimately, a transformation is brought about by dreaming the "facts" so that they can become narremes in a finished narration. This entails having the courage to see the dream not as a way of getting in touch with emotional or psychic truth, but as a lie capable of bending "O" so as to satisfy our need for meanings and narrations for the organisation of emotions, affects, contingencies, and events.

The theft

After the analyst cancelled a week of analysis for personal reasons, a patient dreams of being robbed by his son, whom he has always trusted and from whom he would never have expected such a thing.

The "fact" in this case is the cancellation of four sessions by the analyst. When inserted into column two, however, it gives rise to the following dream: someone the patient trusted betrayed his trust by stealing something from him. "The fact" of the cancelled sessions becomes: "You, the analyst, have stolen something from me, and I would never have expected such a thing. Can I still trust you?"

Maria and the Snark

In the previous session, Maria, an attractive thirty-year-old woman, asked me to give her a certificate she needed; furthermore, we are about to take a week's break in which she is going to lose four sessions.

P: Today I called Daria to see if she would agree to swap classes with me so I could get away from that strict teacher of mine.
A: A kind of Mrs. Rottenmeier.

P: That's exactly right! Poor Heidi came down from the mountains, was eating her ham perhaps with her hands, and that bitch Rottenmeier was always telling her off.

A: I was wondering which one of us this strictness might really belong to—me or you? Maybe it's you: you don't want to have anything to do with me because if you pay me, that obviously proves that we are complete strangers to each other, so you can't tell me anything personal, anything that has to do with your emotions.

P: Yes, you're a stranger to me. But I had a dream: someone warned me that I was being followed, and I was afraid; then the dream continued with my four dogs running away, taking risks, and crossing the road. They went into a campsite and I followed them; I was afraid that something nasty would happen to them.

A: Does anything occur to you?

P: Only being afraid.

A: Someone following you isn't necessarily a criminal or a stalker; it could be a bodyguard or someone who is interested in us.

P: That way, it would mean it's you!

A: Not only that, but I might also be the dog you're fond of (the sessions you're fond of), and now that we're going camping—on holiday—you are worried in case something happens to me. So you follow the dogs to protect them ... following can also be out of fondness ...

P: (A long silence.)

A: Do you know the story of the Snark?

P: No, tell me.

A: It's a tale set in the days of sailboats. A young captain is terrified of an enormous fish that constantly follows his ship. Whenever he sees it, he ducks out of the way so as not to be seen, hoping he has got rid of this terrible fish, but each time he sets sail he catches sight of a huge fin in the wake of the ship. To cut a long story short, he finally discovers that the fish is following him to give him a letter from his father containing a treasure map.

P: Theoretically, there's some truth in that. Will you give me the certificate for the hospital?

A

(handing it to her):   Perhaps it's true on the practical level too, because I'm giving you the chit ... like in the story.

The characters cast in their roles by the patient or analyst are seen to undergo constant transformation so as to allow the expression of what progressively becomes thinkable in the here and now of the session. It is not a matter of historical facts or the bringing of things from the past into the present; the emphasis is instead on the attempt to develop the patient's—or rather, the field's—capacity to think (to dream), by way also of ongoing transformation of the patient's communications into a dream.

Luigi and reading

Luigi is a seven-year-old boy diagnosed with "severe dyslexia"; he is restless, often unrestrainable at school, and hyperactive.

The interview with his parents immediately takes an unexpected turn. The mother says that as a child she too was dyslexic, and goes on animatedly about her "terrible experience with the vice-principal" of the school where she was a teacher: he persecuted and attacked her, making her life impossible, never showing the slightest degree of understanding, and eventually causing her to take early retirement. The father pooh-poohs everything, saying that he is worried only about important things, such as the loans they have taken on, which he is afraid of being unable to repay.

It seems clear to me that the minds of both parents have been and remain virtually closed to Luigi and his anxieties. They are like rooms lacking in space, peace, and quiet—two rooms exposed to swirling whirlwinds that turn everything upside down.

It is as if sheets of paper placed on the table are being scattered through the room so that they cannot be read. The only emotions that are read and recognised are persecution in the mother and catastrophic anxiety in the father. In effect, Luigi's parents have at their disposal only a kind of two-letter alphabet that stands in the way of any emotional reading of their own reality.

It is understandable that Luigi can only evacuate, resorting to hyperactivity, restlessness, and mental states that he is unable to read. A person who cannot read his own mental states is in a kind of fog that renders every sign, letter, and alphabet indistinguishable. The first alphabet to be learned is the emotional alphabet, to be followed afterwards by the cognitive alphabet, at least in so far as the latter is based on the former.

Luigi's sessions take a characteristic course. He arrives in an utterly disorientated state, moving about continuously, calms down and "organises" himself in the middle of the session—when the analyst begins to read for him the emotional states of the characters in his play and constructs a kind of emotional syntax that enables him gradually to address the more complex connections between emotions—only to become disorganised again as the end approaches.

In a typical session, Luigi begins by smearing an incredible number of sheets of paper with a mixture of every available colour. Next, figures begin to appear, in step with the analyst's interventions that contain his anxiety. Then a "face" takes shape, described by the analyst as "always in a rage, but also terrified and desperate"; after which Luigi draws a boat, a little man, and the sea. The analyst suggests reading the drawings as a sequence: "Maybe the face is the face of a man in the sea; perhaps he has fallen in and is terrified in case he drowns".

While seemingly on the level of the manifest text, the analyst creates links, connections, readings. He forgoes a premature reading of the transference aspect—"When we are not together I/you feel that you are going under in a sea of anxieties and are desperate"—as that would be like trying to teach logarithms to first grade schoolchildren.

Luigi goes on drawing and tells of a boat trip with his parents, of the danger of big waves, and says he thought that if the boat were to capsize, they would need life rafts and lifeboats.

Luigi's response is logical and emotionally consistent.

The session proceeds with a narrative co-construction that always involves boats, ferries, hazardous crossings, waves, and the risk of shipwreck—a precise description of the emotions that are coming to life in the therapy room.

Toward the end of the session, Luigi draws waterspouts, speeds up his play, and talks about pirates "who are not ... in *legge*"[5]—and from then on it is impossible to read the emotions present in the narrations and his play, which has now become mere evacuative turbulence.

Sessions like these recur, gradually revealing more and more clearly the bond of survival that has arisen between Luigi and his analyst, until it eventually seems appropriate to increase the number of "lifeboats" to at least three a week.

High noon or the ambush cook?

In the field, the "tsunami" (or "battle of the century") fragments into a large number of places, times, and forms of turbulence, so that these can be managed more easily—as if a natural transition from confrontation to negotiation were actually taking place, that is, between moments when there is no room for negotiation and one part of the working pact is regarded as essential (and some things are essential, but in fact ever fewer) and moments when an agreement can be found, with each moving away from their starting positions. Ultimately one has to relinquish one's authoritarian attitudes as far as possible—and even with regard to what is meant by the "truth" of an analytic fact. Moreover, the concept of restricted and classic confrontation seems to us to put too much emphasis on rational understanding at the expense of emotional factors in the relationship.

Whereas confrontation may be a legitimate part of other models, in our view the boundary between the acceptable and something that calls for a battle is movable:

a. The physical presence of the patient in sessions was not negotiable, now other worlds may be opened up with Skype.
b. In the case of the mutiny on the *Bounty*, perhaps the field had become so persecutory that, Captain Bligh having failed to apprehend the unmistakable signals reaching him from it, the inevitable outcome was an explosion in the form of a rebellion by the crew. His deafness to the situation was an additional detonator.
c. Although we have moved on from the patient who "attacks, misunderstands, and distorts" to the patient who is our "best colleague," we must be capable of understanding what this best colleague is telling us even if he sometimes does so in forms that are not immediately comprehensible. However, if we look at these too through the eyes of the patient, we shall find our way out of the difficulty. While the patient is often the Minotaur with whom we may feel tempted to join battle, he is always, too, the Ariadne who quite inscrutably offers us the thread whereby we can escape from the most complicated of labyrinths.

In other words, from a field perspective we are interested not in confrontation or discussion of presumed truths, whether historical, reconstructive, emotional, psychological, or otherwise, but in expanding the degree of emotional unison (the patient's ability to accept more possible points of view) and in developing his alpha function (Ferro, 2010; Civitarese, 2008, 2011a)—that is, the instruments for containing and metabolising previously indigestible emotional facts.

Notes

1. Translator's note: For convenience, the masculine form is used for both sexes throughout this translation.
2. The analyst is GC in the first five vignettes and AF in all the others.
3. Of course, these little icons between brackets are meant to represent in a playful and ironic way, as in cartoon speech bubbles, the intense turmoil the analyst experiences at this point in the session.
4. Translator's note: A play on words in Italian: *bulli* means roughnecks and *bulloni* bolts.
5. Translator's note: *Legge* is the Italian word for law—that is, the pirates are outlaws—but it is also the third-person singular, present tense, of the verb *leggere* (to read).

CHAPTER EIGHT

A Beam of Intense Darkness: a discussion of the book by James Grotstein*

T he title of this book (*A Beam of Intense Darkness*) by James Grotstein (2007) and its dedication (*To Wilfred Bion. My gratitude to you for allowing* Me *to become reunited with me—and for encouraging me to play with your ideas as well as my own*) deserve some preliminary comments.

A "beam of darkness" constitutes an antidote to the tendency, often found in the human species, to carry out "transformations in hallucinosis" (Bion, 1965), to impose meanings on what has no meaning because of our incapacity to wait for shreds of meaning to emerge. Like snails which produce slime, we are a species that continuously "s limes" meanings because we cannot bear the darkness of our not knowing. In the book's title we find a sort of celebration of that "negative capability", the capacity, that is, to remain in the paranoid–schizoid position without feeling persecuted—the mental state which, more than any other, should belong to the psychoanalyst (and, indeed, to any man or woman).

---

* A. Ferro is the author of this chapter.

We are the victims of that excess of light continuously produced by our pseudo-knowledge which pollutes our minds and prevents us from truly expanding our authentic knowledge. Let us switch off the lights and wait for something to emerge, even if it is only its shady shreds … If successful, such an operation will simply allow us to reconnect us to ourselves, to weave threads of meaning with the parts of ourselves which were kept disconnected or which were denied, and it will open our minds as wide as our current degree of evolution will allow: it will let us play with our ideas with the same intensity, seriousness, and also enjoyment that we find in children playing with their toys, that is, with the dwellers of their internal world and with the phantasy ones of their relational world. More generally, our species causes the greatest disasters when it ignores the playful dimension of things and tragically takes them too seriously.

I could go on with more observations inspired by the book's suggestive title and its dedication, but that would make it impossible for me to review this book because it would inevitably lead me to the writing of another one about it. If I were given the task of drawing a map for such a rich and beautiful landscape, I would find it almost impossible to reduce it to a geographical scale of less than 1:1.

This book is, to some extent, a dream about Bion's whole work and, as such, it allows us to indulge in an infinite number of associations— not a dream to be decoded, but one that is continuously opened up to new thoughts and helps us develop the capacity to think. After I had finished reading it, the first feeling I experienced was one of gratitude for this "gift" which its author has given us, and at the same time one of fear as I wondered whether I would be able to describe at least some of the flavours and moods it evokes.

From the first lines, one will immediately notice Grotstein's implicit generosity towards American psychoanalysis (which, I believe, has not yet received in Europe the credit it deserves), his *self-disclosure* as he recounts an episode of his own analysis with Bion, and then an *enactment* by Bion himself who, during a session with Grotstein, was reading a letter (the one which gives the book its title) from the correspondence between Freud and Lou Andreas Salome.

The focus of Grotstein's volume is immediately turned on to Bion's mystical aspects—aspects that have nothing to do with the religious sense of that term, referring instead to the analyst's capacity not just to operate from "O" towards "K", but also to be "at one with 'O'" (Grotstein,

2007, p. 2), and to experience reverie, intuition, and compassion with one's patients. Bion is aware that the field of psychoanalysis is that of a non-linear science, exposed—as is inevitable in the relationship with another person—to violent upsets and fundamental transformations. The mystic is someone who can tolerate uncertainties regarding the nature of the cosmos and, I would add, of the micro-cosmos where the only sense is that of experiencing, feeling and dreaming one's own emotions, and helping the patient to develop similar mental faculties.

From the very beginning the author also provides us with much information, as yet unknown to me, on which, however, I shall not dwell here. He emphasises how Bion had moved from being a little-read author to one whose presence can be found everywhere in psychoanalytic circles. We learn about how "his ideas have spread beyond the ghetto of his Kleinian roots to every major school within the psychoanalytic framework" (ibid, p. 4). We also learn that Bion is the author who has more than anyone else attributed importance to the concept of flux or evolution ("Yesterday's patient is not today's patient" (ibid, p. 5)) and how that same concept also applies to psychoanalytic ideas.

In the *caveat* at the beginning of the book I discovered many shared viewpoints. The book does not take into consideration *The Tavistock Seminars* (Bion, 2005a) and *The Italian Seminars* (Bion, 2005b) since this would have involved quoting them word by word. (I know this well, having encountered the difficulties of reviewing them (Ferro, 2007) with a limited amount of space available!)

"Don't try to understand *me!* Pay special attention to *your emotional responses* to me!" (Grotstein, 2007, pp. 7–8). Grotstein stresses the importance of offering a "holographic" reading of Bion, in order to allow us not to miss any of his multiple viewpoints. The same, of course, would apply to our reading of Grotstein's own book, which can be read throughout at different levels, including the level of his personal experience with Bion: what better definition could we give of the "Language of Achievement" than the one Grotstein gives us on page nine? (I also take part in this game by not giving you the answer!) Such a dialogue was carried out also with Francesca Bion and many other privileged interlocutors—among them, Bleandonu, Grinberg, Sor and de Bianchedi, Paulo Sandler, Joan and Neville Symington, Eigen, Lopez-Corvo and Ogden—whose works have contributed to our knowledge of Bion and to the development of his thought. Several interesting pages explain why Bion is considered by some, or by many, as an obscure author. The most convincing explanation, I think, is the one offered by Grotstein himself, about Bion as a writer in direct contact with what his mind is dreaming ("wakeful sleep" (ibid, p. 15)).

The author then changes register to deal with certain aspects of Bion's own life, such as his refusal to "supervise" in Los Angeles and only accepting to offer "a second opinion" (ibid, p. 12), following his war experience of the military headquarters giving ill-informed orders because of their distance from the scene of action—hence the idea that only the analyst can have an intimate understanding of his patient. In a privileged position among his interlocutors we find Ogden; Grotstein reports Ogden's view that Bion wrote in such a way that his text could then be recreated afresh by each new and different reader: "he must become the author of his own book (his own set of thoughts) more or less based on Bion's" (Grotstein, 2007, p. 14).

One of Bion's characteristics is that he managed not to answer questions, but rather helped everyone to find their own answers, however one-sided these may have been—hence the comparison with Socrates and his method. Often emphasised is the fact that Bion was a highly cultured man. Grotstein offers us a number of enlightening comparisons or metaphors, portraying Bion, for instance, as "Prometheus bound" and the difficulties he experienced with some of his London colleagues, or as "Prometheus unbound" and the spreading of his ideas, taking on a place of great importance in Latin America, and especially in Brazil, and today in many other countries too, Italy included. I shall go on indulging in the game by remembering how surprised I was, and then comfortable immediately after, the first time that I saw a huge portrait of Bion in the headquarters of the old institute of the Sao Paulo's Psychoanalytical Society where I had gone to run some seminars.

Grotstein then reflects on the huge quantity of intellectual tools and techniques that Bion has given to the whole psychoanalytic community:

> Language of Achievement, containment, reverie, "binocular vision", "reversible perspectives", "multiple vertices", "abstraction", "common sense", "correlation", "public-action", "spontaneous conjecture" ("wild thoughts") and "rational conjecture" … "abandon memory and desire" […] and models like "α-function", "α- and β-elements", and the "gastrointestinal tract" and the "synapse". (Grotstein, 2007, p. 23)

The image that comes to my mind is that of a kitchen being progressively better equipped with new utensils: new saucepans, new pots, new dippers, and new cooking tools. (I have always associated the alpha function to that tool always present in an Italian kitchen, the tomato-sieve, and the beta elements to the tomatoes which, transformed into alpha elements by going through the sieve, give us that sauce which lets us paint pictograms.) These utensils have not only allowed us to cook better our emotional ingredients, those sensorialities and proto-emotions that all patients brings to their sessions, but have also made it an analytic goal to develop those very tools. A beautiful metaphor is that of Bion–Nelson, that Nelson who, when at the Battle of Copenhagen his admiral asked him to withdraw because the enemy outnumbered the British fleet, put his telescope to his blind eye and, claiming he saw no signal, gave life to the battle which would eventually be famously won by the British Navy.

We can then focus on other key concepts such as:

> (1) the selected fact, (2) the constant conjunction, (3) the reversible perspective, (4) multiple vertices, (5) an absence of memory and desire, (6) the reversibility of progression and regression between PS and D, (7) the importance of binocular vision, (8) reverie, (9) negative capability, and (10) the importance of context, imaginative conjecture, abstraction, and myth. (Grotstein, 2007, p. 24)

Grotstein then brilliantly presents and discusses Bion's two different souls: the more rational soul and the more intuitive one, which the rational one tries to harness. This is also explained in terms of the Indian and the British souls. Thus we find ourselves here in the company of a "dreamer Bion" and a "thinker Bion", a Bion who, without pontificating, started each of his presentations (without reading any notes) by uttering: "I can hardly wait to hear what I have to say" (ibid, p. 23). Grotstein also offers us the gift of a dream he had about Bion, so that Bion is presented to us in a bite-sized and digestible form—a rich and very tasty food indeed! Grotstein has come so close to Bion's "O" that it is no longer easy to tell him apart from Bion, to differentiate the theoretical level of his discourse from the experiential and personal one. But that is why this book has such a magic quality that allows us to enjoy reading it all in one go, as well as to study it as an emotionally charged summary of Bion's work as a whole. A book to relish, and a book to mull over.

I found Grotstein's playing around with certain interpretations which he remembers having received in the course of his analysis with Bion to be both enjoyable and helpful. The game involves labelling them as either "Kleinian" or "Bionian" or "Kleinian and Bionian" or even as "a very Bionian interpretation". He gives us a taste of his sessions with Bion and with considerable honesty he tells us that "often when Bion spoke I did not understand much of what he was saying—and he said a lot—but I did seem to resonate with it preconsciously. It always had an effect" (ibid, p. 33). He offers us a glimpse into an extremely rigorous analyst and I was particularly impressed by the description he gives us of him, following an interpretation:

> I do recall, however, how impressed I was that virtually every one
> of the words in my associations was taken up, used, and rephrased
> so that I was receiving from him a somewhat altered and deepened
> version of what I had uttered. (Grotstein, 2007, p. 29)

I shall report here just one of Bion's interpretations, offered in response to Grotstein's description of his depression as "beyond words". Bion replied that "he believed that it was not only 'beyond words', it was 'before words'" (ibid). Today I would describe it as an unsaturated interpretation (Ferro, 2002a), which at the same time indicates how that mental state could be perceived before being expressed; how the relation between projective identifications and reverie was constantly at work "underneath"; and how the reverie allowed something to be grasped which had not yet been verbalised. Grotstein also engages in a discussion on how "Kleinian" Bion really was, but I would rather not comment on this point here as I have my own personal views about it (Ferro, 1996), even if I entirely agree with Grotstein's statement that it would be impossible to have access to the depths of Bion's thought without going first through Klein's. What I am also impressed by is the quality of "reality" which Bion seems to attribute to some of his patient–Grotstein's communications. For instance, the brilliant one about his sister (ibid, p. 31), even though I wonder why this "character" was not deconstructed into the emotional parts which she undoubtedly conveyed to him. I could perhaps reply that this reflection of mine already belongs to an "after Bion", even if it could only exist "thanks to Bion".

As I said before, this is a book that can be used at different levels. It is invaluable for students of psychoanalysis because it will help them enter in a lively way into the Bionian world. It is an invaluable book for those who have to teach Bion, as it offers some extraordinarily synthetic explanations of Bion's main concepts. Furthermore, it is also an invaluable book for scholars who already have an in-depth familiarity with Bion's thought because it allows them to reflect on how Grotstein has re-elaborated Bion's concepts and reached his own "O", so that one could develop Bion's own way of thinking in increasingly complex ways.

Bion's relationship to Freud's and Melanie Klein's theories is very clear (see Grotstein, 2007, p. 36). Bion is adamant about the crucial importance of the space of emotions and of a boundless imagination. What is so central for him is the relationship with the other, or rather the other is indispensable to us in our efforts to get into contact with our internal world. Freud insisted on the importance of infantile neurosis and sexuality. Klein considered recovery as reparation and a journey towards the depressive position: "in other words, the infantile portion of the personality must renounce its hatred, envy, greed, and omnipotence" (ibid, p. 38). For Bion, patients, thanks to their negative capability, must accept to "be at one with their emotions—so as to keep their rendezvous with their infinite creative self" (ibid).

Using unforgettable words, Grotstein synthesises for us the various pilgrimages through his four analyses: in the Freudian one it was the question "to recover buried memories and to keep my rendezvous with my acknowledgment of my repressed libidinal drive" (ibid, p. 39). In the one inspired by Fairbairn, "my pilgrimage was mainly with buried memories in terms of objects" (ibid). In the Kleinian one, he had to face his destructiveness and his death drive. Finally, with Bion he recognized "how cut-off I was from it—and how my anxieties and symptoms were but intimations of my inner 'immortality' and infinite resources" (ibid).

The author then explores in detail the other main differences between Bion and Freud: how could I not mention here their different ways of understanding dreams? For Bion the dream is an ongoing mental activity at the basis of our unconscious thinking. Grotstein calls "mentalisation" the first part of the move from sensoriality to image, and calls "thinking" the next stage during which the alpha elements are placed in a sequence and give shape to narratives. Dreaming also makes it possible for an impersonal "O" to become a personal one which everyone can tolerate.

As to its relation with Klein's thought, we are all familiar with Bion's extension of the concept of projective identification, which he understands as a normal modality of communication for our human species, as well as with his idea of a continuous oscillation between PS and D, no longer seen as consecutive stages, not to mention the central place he gives to the emotions and reverie of the analyst. This last concept, in particular, no longer belongs just to the Bionian model, for it has now been universally accepted by psychoanalysis. Reverie is a transformative response to the stimuli from the patient and must be differentiated from the countertransference which stems from the analyst's infantile neurosis. In the end, Bion's patient:

> must be analytically contained and thereby be able to suffer, not blindly endure, the pain of emotional experiences. Each time an individual feels (suffers) his emotional pain, he becomes reunited with his godhood self, his infinite self ... and thereby evolves. (Grotstein, 2007, p. 42)

Chapter Five is extremely rich, complex, and original, and because it presents us with a number of unexpected perspectives it could give rise to many fruitful discussions. If he were to summarise the essence of Bion's contributions, Grotstein would say that Bion has led Freud's and Klein's positivistic psychoanalysis "into the new, uncharted realms of uncertainty: from the strictures and prison of verbal language to a realm beyond and before language" (ibid, p. 44). To begin with, we are presented with the linear scheme that goes from beta towards alpha, and we are introduced to the important concept of "exorcistic dreaming" to describe the work of the alpha function in its task of detoxification— a function that will be later introjected by the child (patient). Grotstein then postulates that the child is born with a "rudimentary (inherited) a-function with which it is prepared to generate pre-lexical communications and to receive prosodic lexical communications from mother" (ibid, p. 45). The child is therefore seen as being endowed from the beginning with the emotional equivalent of the "transformational generative syntax" as a "semiotic entity" (ibid). This entity can communicate and utilise projective identifications whenever verbal communication fails. Grotstein then adds that the child projects not only "the fear of dying" but also "its fear of 'unassisted living'" (ibid, p. 46). This opens up for us a whole range of thoughts concerning the signals which patients send us in the course of their analysis to prepare us for their messages. It is here that we could place a trigger point of many negative transferences, psychotic transferences, or negative therapeutic reactions.

We also find here the intriguing idea (which I entirely share with the author) of the existence of balpha elements: these would be those alpha elements preceding the beta elements insofar as they were generated in the child's mind by Ideal Form, if still only in a rudimentary way. What is postulated here is a whole continuum between alpha and beta elements, in different situations and at different stages: something that also happens for those thoughts without thinker which are waiting for a dreamer-thinker. The use of models (Grotstein adds to those proposed by Bion some of his own: the immune system, the Krebs cycle, the dialysis) allows us to operate within a separate, yet parallel, system. Through it we can describe analytic scenarios and events in a provisional and flexible way, better than could be done by already established theories, because these, after all, prevent us from working "without memory and desire" and make us run all the time the risk of polluting our eyes with an excess of light, like in the big cities where it is almost impossible to see a starry sky.

This chapter's final pages, where the author engages us in a discussion about the question "What is a β-element really?", are both profound and difficult. Perhaps "the β-element is the emotional sense impression of O: the ghost of O?" (ibid, p. 59). He suggests "differing degrees of maturation" for the alpha elements while the beta screen is considered to be "a degraded α-screen that menacingly hovers around the projecting subject awaiting the recognition that had been denied it" (ibid, p. 60). Alpha elements which are not accepted and are degraded to beta lead us towards an extremely complex world where Grotstein continually surprises us by making us consider things from new and unexpected perspectives. Sentences such as:

> The real and most important difference between a b-element and an a-element, consequently, is that the former connotes the impersonalness of Fate (O), whereas the latter, the α-element, indicates that the subject has attributed personalness to the experience and personally claims it as his own. (Grotstein, 2007, p. 61)

I believe, consequently, that β-elements may be reconceptualised as follows: When O intersects our emotional frontier and makes an impression there of its presence, the initial response is the formation or appearance of an a-element (personal). It may either continue in its transformational course into dream elements, contact-barrier, and memory, or come to be rejected by the mind and degraded after the fact into "β-elements" and thereby remain "impersonal", "unclaimed" in the "dead post office" of the mind. May not Bion have also thought of this idea when he selected "b", which follows "a" in the Greek alphabet? Moreover, α-elements are, in my opinion, continuations of their Anlage as "thoughts without a thinker" that have been thought all along by "godhead" ("godhood")! (Grotstein, 2007, pp. 61–62)

Grotstein seems to adopt towards the beta and alpha elements the same procedure that Bion had used in relation to PS-D; no longer, that is, a linear movement from beta → alpha, but an uninterrupted oscillation beta ↔ alpha, without a specific finishing line. This complicates, but also makes more lively, unpredictable, and in this sense also open-ended, the activities of thinking, dreaming, and feeling.

Grotstein describes an infinite Unconscious that continuously expands through the tracing not of indelible motorways but of what would rather resemble the forces of a magnetic field in a state of uninterrupted transformation. Grotstein, as is common with him, disturbs our universe, even if it would occasionally prefer to be left alone, by asking us whether transformations really take place (let's say in whatever beta ↔ alpha direction), or whether it is in fact we who alter our way of perceiving beta and alpha.

As to what concerns Grotstein's "disturbance", I must admit that before reading this book my theoretical universe was sufficiently stable, while now it has been so severely shaken that I no longer know what its effects may be. One of the issues which I had given up trying to deal with, was that of thoughts without a thinker—those thoughts which are waiting for a mind that could think them. A new thought for me has been to imagine these thoughts as balpha elements, by which I mean that they have reached a level of development beyond which they cannot go without a mind capable of dreaming them or thinking them. This could be the result of an alpha function of the kind that only operates up to a point, waiting for further "cooking" of these thoughts. I believe we are those "neurons of God" which build the world of Ideas. Grotstein's position, clearly similar to Bion's, is that there exists something above us and which comes before us, a sort of Platonic world of Ideas: "I believe godhood (aka 'godhead') to be the 'ghost writer' of the 'thoughts without a thinker'" (ibid, p. 78). It seems easier to me to think about which thoughts have been thought and later split off and evacuated, and which then request to touch base again in order to be developed.

Grotstein has a comfortable familiarity, foreign to myself, with the complex philosophical ideas of Plato, Hume, Kant, and is anyway capable of "upsetting" parts that we would have found it easier to ignore, or at least to force us to reflect upon them. Two lines of thought are in a state of conflict here (or should we try to integrate them?). The first tells us that "the mind had to be created in order to accommodate the emergence of 'thoughts without a thinker'—in order to 'mind' (bind) them into constant conjunctions: that is, thoughts with names" (ibid, p. 69). The second one is easier for me to follow:

> It is a model for a transaction that transforms β-elements, the sensory stimuli of emotional experience (O's imprint on the emotions), into α-elements that are suitable for mentalization—that is, for notation (memory), repression, for reinforcement of the contact-barrier, and for a continuing supply of dream elements for dreaming. (Grotstein, 2007, p. 80)

After all, the first line of thought is more mystical, it is related to incarnation, with inspiration and intuition, while the second one is closer to evolved and more complex physical or biological systems. The following sentence from Chapter Six would on its own deserve to be the subject of a whole conference and debate: "The individual who lacks an apparatus to think (dream) the thoughts may either project them elsewhere as untransformed β-elements (degraded α-elements, in my opinion) or regard them as religious or messianic epiphanies" (ibid, p. 67). I entirely agree, however, with statements such as the following: "The α-elements are mentalizable by and for the mind, unlike β-elements, which are somatic and inchoate emotional sense impressions. Alpha-elements constitute the elementary alphabet of thoughts" (ibid, p. 68). However, sentences such as:

> The ultimate source of the stimulus lies in Bion's (1965, 1970) concept of O the Absolute Truth, Ultimate Reality, infinity, godhead.

> Put another way, a-function, the hypothetical model, and/or dreaming, the living process in actuality (to which I refer as the "dream ensemble"), screens and transforms raw intersecting impression from O (as β-elements) and, as stated above, transduces and "translates" them into information (thoughts) and appropriate responses. (Grotstein, 2007, pp. 68–69)

are again for me the obscure Bion (with whom Grotstein feels most comfortable), who claims "that thoughts are primary and seek a mind to think them" (ibid, p. 69).

I entirely agree with Grotstein that Bion has been responsible for a radical transformation of psychoanalytic technique. From the beginning Grotstein focuses his attention on five points, but I could just summarise everything with the following simple words: *the analyst dreams the session*. This takes place in a rich variety of ways: the analyst deconstructs the patient's communication, transforms the beta elements into alpha ones, uses these latter ones to reinforce the contact barrier, to create memories, and most of all he develops tools for thinking (and for dreaming) for the patient. This chapter is important, but I shall not dwell on its subject, as it has already been at the centre of my interests for the last few years (Ferro, 2006). I shall only focus here on a few key passages:

> Descend into a state of reverie [...] receptive to your (the analyst's) unconscious emotional resonance with the patient's emotions and be able optimally to recruit them. (Grotstein, 2007, p. 83).
>
> The analyst must "dream" the analytic session—that is, he must "dream" the patient's as yet undreamed or incompletely dreamed emotions (O at large). (Grotstein, 2007, p. 83)

Grotstein claims that Bion uses a Kleinian technique, even if of course he does so in an exquisitely personal (Bionian) manner. Here I disagree with Grotstein because I think that a technique that entirely relies on all the tools that Bion has made available to us must inevitably bring about a radical change to all previous models. Insaturity, oscillation PS ↔ D, selected fact oscillation ↔, negative capabilities, projective identifications to communicate and reverie can hardly coexist with those models where urgency, a perspective on anxiety, destructiveness and the death drive are fore-grounded. It is also true, though, that Grotstein considers the death drive as having a defensive function and does not attribute a major role to it. He agrees with Bion that it is emotions that are at the core of analysis. To experience one's own emotions (they are "O"s ambassadors) is the ultimate goal of analysis.

Grotstein strongly believes that the newborn baby already possesses a rudimentary alpha function available to him (he would create alpha elements from the start, and not just evacuate the beta ones). Furthermore, and I find this to be of particular interest, Grotstein believes that projective identifications kick in when there is a failure (however temporary) of communication, a situation analogous to that of the evacuation of the beta screen when the analyst is felt to be unreachable.

This obviously introduces us to the great importance of micro-communications in the session, and leads us to "the patient as the analyst's best colleague" the only one capable to communicate to us these micro- (or sometimes macro-) fractures. Grotstein points out how all earlier theories are overcome when the fulcrum of the analysis is moved: "It is only when there is a disruption or breakdown in their communication that the infant is reduced to having to use projective transidentifica-tion (heightened emotional display) with the not-so-containing (at the moment) container-mother" (ibid, p. 92).

The author also considers the alpha element as a sort of precursor of the beta element. In this respect, I wonder whether Bion was not more Kleinian in the way he practised analysis than his model would allow us to be today, by which I mean whether his model and the tools he has given us could go beyond his own technique. On the other hand, Grotstein states:

> Bion [...] instituted the notion of "evolving O", which I have interpreted as "ever evolving truth", that is, a "truth drive", which exerts pre-eminence as the content of the repressed [...]. By "truth", both Bion and I mean "emotional truth". Thus, the analyst is always searching for the analysand's hidden emotional truth in every analytic session, with the death drive in a secondary position—as defensive armament that is mobilized or recruited by anxiety to attack one's awareness of and links with his dependent relationships on objects that are the occasion for the pain of emotional truth in the first place. According to this reasoning consequently the death instinct is always secondary, never primary, and is defensive against the awareness of mental pain at the cost of the

consciousness of relationships. It attacks links with objects that
inaugurate the pain. (Grotstein, 2007, pp. 96–97)

The new task is to become evolved enough to be able to allow
for the acceptance of Truth as truth, by which I mean the transformation of impersonal Truth into personal truth. (Grotstein, 2007,
p. 97)

In the central part of his book the author goes deeply into the main features of Bion's thought and its philosophical implications, not always
easily distinguishable from Grotstein's own. If, on the one hand, there is
a great capacity for abstractions, particularly in relation to all the implications of "O", this is done without ever losing sight of the psychoanalytic perspective. We are thus offered reflections on such key concepts
as that of "obstructive object" (ibid, p. 103), of negative reverie, and
of the consequence on the mind of a child who has to interact with an
emotionally unavailable mother: "psychotics could not think or feel:
because they could not allow themselves to suffer emotional pain"
(ibid, p. 103).

His reflections on mysticism, the godhood incarnation, deserve personal and careful reading. The concept of "O", difficult as it is to define
(witness Grotstein himself, who feels the need to give us a whole series
of definitions of it in order to provide us with a complex overall impression), must be considered to be of central importance in Bion's way of
thinking:

O can be defined as that Ultimate Reality always in flux, that is
free of representations, images, or symbols [...] O as the Absolute
Truth (about) Ultimate Reality, but he also associates it with infinity,
β-elements, the Ideal Forms, noumena or the things-in-themselves,
and godhead (godhood). (Grotstein, 2007, p. 106)

The work of analysis consists in the re-appropriation of lost and split-
off parts and even in letting them evolve "as a finite fi infinite self by
receiving the legacy from his infinite, immortal, godly self. I call this
state the attainment of the 'transcendent position'" (ibid, p. 107).

According to Grotstein, what Bion blames Klein for as his analyst is
that she did not take into account his need to get back in touch with
the Bion who had died in the war on 8 August. What makes it possible
for development in analysis to occur is the "Language of Achievement",

which is the language of emotions before these can be represented by concepts or ideas, even if the "binocular vision" implies the need to use also the "Language of Substitution". "O" is the goal of the analysis as a whole; getting close to "O" is the goal of each single session. An "O", of course, which from being impersonal would then become subjective and specific. "The instinctual drives—particularly the death instinct in Kleinian theory—would be relegated to the status of mediators of O" (ibid, pp. 114–115). And, he adds, "Knowledge (transformations in K) constitutes, consequently, an intermediary position, an obligatory detour, in the process of the person evolving as an individual in consonance and in parallel with evolving O" (ibid, p. 116). The concept of "O" transforms existing psychoanalytic theories into defences from absolute truth and ultimate reality. In particular certain Kleinian views are considered as a "digitalisation" of "O"'s chaotic, infinite and non-linear complexity.

Grotstein describes a "truth instinct" or drive which leads us towards "O". However, he also raises a question concerning the danger of curiosity insofar as it could force through the contact barrier.

> It is as if the unconscious works like a Hollywood producer who might characteristically say to an actor auditioning for a part: "Don't call us. We'll call you!" This is how the Eternal Forms, O, godhead becomes realized in human experience as a conception. (Grotstein, 2007, p. 142)

This concept is not dissimilar from my own idea of "casting", by which I mean that ongoing activity of the oneiric thinking during the waking state in order to find characters and situations in which they can be emotionally embodied—a track, this one, which runs parallel to the one where:

> every perception, conception, or act in external reality must be "dreamed" in order to become a part of the unconscious as well as become conscious as a result of initial unconscious processing. Put another way, every perception, conception, or act in external or internal reality must be accompanied by the creation of a corresponding unconscious phantasy. (Grotstein, 2007, p. 145)

Another theme is that of the gradient "falsehoods" → lies → Lies. It is clear that only "the lie requires a thinker to think. The truth, or true thoughts, does not require a thinker—he is not logically necessary" (ibid, p. 149). Truth can be burning hot and, like a saucepan with hot panhandles, it often needs a couple of more or less thick oven gloves (lies of different degrees) in order to be "touched".

Chapter Sixteen, on container/contained, is a complex one. Grotstein finds in it the roots of that concept, already present in "Development of schizophrenic thought" (Bion, 1956), and points out how our first ideas relate to a negative container which fails in its function. Only later can the concept of a positive container be formulated. The $-♀$ derives from an "obstructive object" which is the result of a mother's process of inverting the flux of projections in order to cope with her inability to tolerate her child's projections of unbearable emotions. Furthermore, the child "hates" his mother as a result of having been rejected by her. This is a child who can only communicate through projective identifications. The $-♀$ becomes a superego which deprives all evolutionary steps of any meaning. Such a superego is not just an "'hypocritical moral system', but also a pathologically 'protective' agent for the now demoralised infant who is denied a reasonable container-mother into whom to project" (ibid, p. 154). Such a superego offers a sadistic security. The container is not simply a "processor" of the child's proto-emotions, but it also generates independent thinking in response to his beta elements. Grotstein then describes the container's complex functions. When functioning in a receptive mode, the analyst (or the mother) becomes a channel between the patient (or the child) and her own unconscious.

Grotstein's interesting hypothesis concerning Bion's symbols $♂$ and $♀$ is that he chose them because of their associations with the penis, and with the mouth and vagina, as prototypes of creativity in the Primary Scene. Obviously the functions of $♂$ and $♀$ alternate on the analytic stage and in the relational interactions between child and mother, giving rise to an ongoing "co-construction". The introduction of $♂$ and $♀$ (and of course $♀$ will then be internalised by the patient) leads us to an intersubjectivistic perspective on the analytic relationship, where what counts and is of value are the characteristics, qualities, functioning and dysfunctioning of $♀$—and this not just in terms of the patient's phantasies, but also in terms of how $♀$ realistically does or does not function.

If I can be forgiven for a brief digression here, I will say that my view that the development of $♀$ into a field theory (such as it is derived from Madeleine and Willy Baranger's early writings (M. Baranger &

W. Baranger, 1961–1962)) originates from the introjection of the emotive threads which develop between analyst and patient within the field itself. They create a containing network which makes it possible for increasingly intense emotions (♂) to "dance around" almost as if they were acrobats feeling they could jump from trapeze to trapeze without fear, knowing that they were surrounded by a 360° three-dimensional safety net.

Closely connected with this chapter is the very meaty chapter which follows it, dealing with the complex theme of projective identifications. Grotstein starts by clarifying how Klein's projective identifications are profoundly different entities from Bion's. Klein's are a one-person phenomenon and an intra-psychic phantasy, while for Bion they also include as a necessary component the fact that "the projective identifications into the object became continuously modified by the responses of the object as container" (Grotstein, 2007, p. 169).

For Grotstein, Bion considers two aspects of projective identifications: (a) a normal communication (alpha function of the child—alpha function of the mother); and (b) an abnormal communication when the child employs such a mechanism, after a failure of normal communication. The projective identification in Bion's sense is called by Grotstein "projective transidentification" to emphasise that it involves two persons and the space between them. The theory of projective transidentification includes yet two other processes: "(1) a sensorimotor one—that of gesture, prompting, priming on the part of the projecting subject—and (2) spontaneous empathic simulation within the optimally receptive object" (ibid, p. 170). Projective transidentification operates by establishing an inductive resonance: "Consequently, projective transidentification would function by establishing an inductive resonance between the internal-object images formed by the projecting subject, on the one hand, and those counterpart images formed by the external object of the subject, on the other" (ibid, p. 180). Grotstein emphasises time and again that communication normally takes place within the alpha function and that only when this fails do we have a transidentification.

The difference between projection and projective identification is of course extensively discussed here, also taking into account the contributions and clarifications offered by Kernberg, Ogden, and Grinberg. Grotstein's personal contribution to this subject is to consider that the child (or the patient), when under the pressure of cumulative emotions, will induce:

> a symmetrical state in the vulnerable-because-willing mother (or analyst) so that the mother/analyst unconsciously surveys (self-activates) her own inventory of past actual or possible experiences within her conscious and unconscious self, selectively recruits the most pertinent of them for conscious consideration, and then generates thoughts and/or actions (interpretations) to address the distress in the infant or analysand. What the mother or analyst contains, consequently, is not really the infant's or analysand's projections but, rather, the emotional results of their corresponding unconscious recruitment of the mother's own experiences, which constitute her own subsequent reconstruction of the infant's experience to which they resonantly correspond. They remain self-contained in the presence of the emotional induction by the infant/analysand. (Grotstein, 2007, pp. 184–185)

For Grotstein projective identifications are the engine of every transference, whether it concerns past or present states of mind.

In the projective transidentification:

> the analyst, upon experiencing the evocative or provocative induction (sensory, ultra-sensory, or even extra-sensory) stimulus from the analysand, summons within himself those corresponding symmetrical phantasies that match the analysand's experience. This is how a mother functions in maternal reverie when she is attending to her infant. Thus, when the analyst seems to act as a container for the analysand's reported experiences, I postulate that the analysand unconsciously projectively identifies his emotional state with his image of the analyst in the hope of ridding himself of the pain and of inducing this state in the analyst by manipulating his image of the latter. The analyst, who is willing to be a helpful co-participant in this joint venture, becomes open and receptive to the analysand's input via a state of empathic resonance. This resonance eventuates in the analyst's counter-creation of his own image of the analysand's projections (β-elements). (Grotstein, 2007, p. 186)

I believe the concept of projective transidentification allows us to clarify and enrich our understanding, but I also think that there is still a lot of work to be done on the theme of projective identifications. I think that many more things than we currently know and recognise actually occur between one mind and another. As far as the analytic session is concerned, I believe that emotional upsets really can pass from one mind to the other, especially if we consider that patient and analyst form a field of emotional forces which belong to both of them. In this sense the analytic field, which is made up of beta elements, alpha elements, balpha elements, oneiric thinking, narratives and characters, looks like what Ogden describes as the "analytic third", and can be considered as being less saturated and more expanded in space and time.

It is not a coincidence that Madeleine Baranger (2005) derived the concept of field from Bion's work with groups, where "each person can be thought of as a group of subpersonalities, and the group can be thought of as an individual as well as a group" (Baranger, 2005, pp. 190–191). The meeting itself of analyst and patient generates the sparking off of proto-emotions, expectations, needs, and desires which the setting itself can circumscribe and allow analyst and patient to experience them within a transpersonal space generated and inhabited by both. The transformations in the field will then be introjected by analyst and patient. I am firmly convinced that the time is ripe for us to approach that area which comes to life when we combine Bion with all those little-known concepts about the field and with those other equally little-known concepts derived from narratology and semeiotics.

Grotstein then takes us by the hand to reconsider Bion's writings on psychosis by showing us the seeds of future formulations they each contain, starting from his "The Imaginary Twin" ("Bion unmasks the many personas that comprise the imaginary-twin ensemble, including the 'unborn twin'" (Grotstein, 2007, p. 198)). I think this paper already indirectly opens the way to such concepts as that of "the patient as the analyst's best colleague" which we will find described in a more advanced form in his *The Italian Seminars* (Bion, 2005b) and which anticipates the concept of "character" going beyond that of "personification". In a "field dream" perspective, we would not consider characters as people; it is rather as if in the analytic field we had a dream shared by analyst and patient which turns characters into the holograms of their mental functioning (Bezoari & Ferro, 1991). With his "Commentary" Bion shows us his reconsideration in *apres-coup* of all his writings on psychosis. Grotstein helps us see both the indications and the formulations not only of Bion's new way of thinking, but also of this totally new framework that was being opened up for the whole of psychoanalysis once the focus had been moved from the instincts to "O", and from the domain of positivism to that of evolution, uncertainty, intuition and of what for the time being can only remain unrepresentable. This gives us access to an entirely new world, of which Grotstein writes: "Bion is about to 'cross the Rubicon' and bring us into a new psychoanalytic worldview, the outlines of which we are only now beginning to grasp" (Grotstein, 2007, p. 200).

It is in *A Theory of Thinking* (Bion, 1962a) that we find Bion's main new ideas. Among them, I would like to highlight those concerning the formation of an ideogram (image) when the absence of the breast is felt to be tolerable. It is from such an ideogram that the capacity to dream and then to think will eventually develop.

The chapter entitled "Transformations" is among the most complex and deserves careful reading. It begins with the famous example of the poppies and it deals with the theme of invariance. But what does the Transformation operate on? The answer is obvious: on "O". But what do we mean by it? Here Grotstein helps us to understand that the answer must be a double one. On the one hand, "O" is a collective term for *noumena*: "O seems to be a collective term for noumena, Ideal Forms, Absolute Truth, and Ultimate Reality, at least from the inner world: that is, from the unrepressed unconscious" (ibid, p. 214). On the other hand, the other aspects of O "are the sensory stimuli of our emotional responses to our interaction with external (as well as internal) objects" (ibid). This leads us to reflect on the fact that those who have mostly attributed the source of "O" to the first hypothesis tend to consider Bion as a mystic, while those who have chosen the second hypothesis would not have done so. It seems to me that Grotstein helps us to see these two ways of considering "O" as being in a necessary state of oscillation, just like Bion when he suggests that: "somebody should, instead of writing a book called *The Interpretation of Dreams*, write a book called *The Interpretation of Facts*, translating them into dream language [...] in order to get a two-way traffic" (ibid). This would lead us to the need to differentiate between two categories of beta elements which I am tempted to call beta 1 and beta 2. By beta 1 I mean the "un-repressed unconscious" and by beta 2 "the sense impressions of emotional significance" (ibid, p. 217). In the course of the cycle the beta 2 would be transformed in alpha elements, while the beta 1 would be transformed from preconceptions in realisations.

The "'food for thought' is *deconstructed* into its elements and then *reconstructed* into more suitable elements so as to be absorbed" (ibid). What is the "invariant" in "the food for thought" are emotions and, in the end, the "truth about emotional relationships" (ibid, p. 218). This is the relationship whose variants are the "narrative derivatives" (Ferro, 2006) and what matters is the emotional state underlying them. Such an emotional state is all the more meaningful for taking place within a relationship. Grotstein writes: "'just as reason is emotion's slave' (Bion, 1965, p. 171), so emotions are slaves to (containers of) truth. Thus, truth is the invariant, and emotion is its vehicle or container" (Grotstein, 2007, p. 218). It is worth noticing that it is not the truth itself that undergoes transformation, but it is the truth-observing mind which is put through several transformations "by applying a system of filters to darken the blinding glare of untransformable O" (ibid). It is after all, as if the human mind were at the same time something that continuously elaborates stimuli and a defence from "O". "All we can do is fictionalize—mythify—our perception, our experience of Truth (O)" (ibid, p. 219).

I found the passages in the book about "rigid motion" transformations, projective transformations and transformations in hallucinosis to be extremely interesting. The first ones, which involve a displacement from the past to the present without undergoing any change in the process, have an "as if" quality. The second ones belong to a more concrete area and are typical of those patients who, being incapable of tolerating frustration, expel it by using their muscles as if they were a mind.

Another important idea is that of "publication", the process through which the analyst helps the patient transform an unconscious experience into a conscious one, a "public one to himself" (ibid, p. 223). Here we would have to consider the meaning of publishing clinical material.

In every mind there are ongoing transformations in hallucinosis, but these are concealed by other modalities of mental functioning which cover a number of different phenomena. It would be interesting to compare how these have been understood by Meltzer (1978) and by myself (Ferro, 1996) and to consider the links they have with other models of the mind (I believe there are many), even if described in very different languages—and I am referring here in particular to Andre Green's *A Work of the Negative* (Green, 1992).

A child who can tolerate (or who is helped to tolerate) frustration can then build a hallucinatory image, which then becomes the starting point for the development of thought, of thinking and of the mind. It is also worth mentioning the "autistic transformations" and it would be helpful to compare these with Ogden's contiguous–autistic position. In contrast to the transformations into hallucinosis are the ones I call "transformations in dreams" which are continuously performed by those analysts who are capable of reverie.

Before moving on, I want to emphasise that Grotstein has reminded us that Bion used the term "mystical" in a highly idiosyncratic way: as the ability to be in "touch with O—to 'become O'" (Grotstein, 2007, p. 230). This, as I have already pointed out, has no religious implications.

We are well familiar with the significant difference between Bion's and Freud's ways of conceiving dreams. For the latter the dream work consists of a kind of agency delegated to cryptograph the dream content; for Bion, on the other hand, the dream serves the function of providing the "building blocks" for thinking, feeling, being oneself. Bion's way of thinking about dreams radically changes our way of considering psychoanalysis; if the symptom and psychic suffering stem from an insufficient capacity to dream, it is then clear that the focus of psychoanalysis moves from the dream contents to the apparatuses which produce dreams. At this point Grotstein's reasoning becomes extremely complex, because it attempts to give a holographic view of the problem of dreaming in Bion. Grotstein postulates here a "dream ensemble" made up of various operative functions. We can consider them in their synergetic functioning (alpha function, dreaming, contact barrier, oscillation container–contained—and this in their connections with the pleasure principle/reality principle, finite/infinite) or else we can look in depth at each of these operative sub-units. I think that Grotstein succeeds in performing both operations here, by showing us a complex system at work, in some respects similar to the work of the Grid.

The elements beta 1 and beta 2 (using my own lexicon) are intercepted by the alpha function which begins to give them a first rough priming, to be followed later by the activity of dreaming which takes place in the conscious part of our minds. At first we have a process of mentalisation, and later another process which leads to the development of thoughts and to the capacity to think them. We thus have an extremely complex and organic model of the mind at work. Its highest operative level is due to a Truth Principle that reorganises work towards the deepest possible level at which "O" can be known.

The dream work, for Bion, is of course uninterrupted: we have the dream during waking life and then the night dream. It is clear how the latter could be understood in a different way if we held that a sort of an alpha mega-function could be at work here on all the alpha elements stocked up during the day, rather than if we believed that what is at work at this level is a different organising function which does not dream alpha elements again, but instead edits and links together sequences of alpha elements. Obviously, what we are describing here are just models, and I think everyone should be aware of the limitations and of the advantages of the model he or she may choose to adopt. However, Grotstein does not stop here but goes so far as to consider that our species has a need to tell stories and to listen to them. Narratives at increasingly more complex levels become ways of making "O" as personal as possible. It is the story, the tale, the myth, the dream which let us get as close as possible to the various aspects of our own "O". I also value Grotstein's idea that we would request people who are important in our lives to become our co-dreamers.

Let us now consider more closely some of Grotstein's observations which, in their figurative way, succeed in helping us understand a number of complex concepts:

> The emotional vocabulary furnished by a-function is used in dreaming to construct imaginative, preponderantly visual narratives as truthful "archival fictions", which contain emotions that have emerged from transformed and transduced β-elements. These β-elements result from sense impressions on the subject's emotional frontier cast by intersections (interactions, confrontations) with the evolution of the "Absolute Truth" about an infinite, cosmic, impersonal "Ultimate Reality", "O", into a mercifully tolerable, finite, and personally acceptable truth about one's own personal, subjective relationship to one's objects in inner and outer reality. In other words, impersonal O becomes transformed into personal O in a "transformational cycle" with detours in K, and failing that, –K (falsehood). (Grotstein, 2007, p. 261)

Or again:

> The α-elements are thereupon selectively distributed to notation (memory), repression, further thought processes, and support for the contact-barrier between consciousness and the unconscious and for deployment as constructive units for dreaming. The deployed

α-elements, as they proliferate and link together to form more complex structures, are like letters of the alphabet ("a–b") that combine to produce versatile images, symbols, words, sentences, and, ultimately, thoughts or dream narratives. (Grotsteing, 2007, p. 263)

Dreaming functions as a filter that sorts, categorizes, and prioritizes emotional facts that are stimulated by this incoming data. (Grotstein, 2007, p. 264)

Grotstein presents us with a set of models which help us see both the details of the activities of each sub-unit of dreaming, and the operation as a whole. Thus we have the model of the Mçbius Strip, of the Reversible perspective, of the Binary opposition, and of the Binocular perspective.

One would have to quote here in their entirety the at once poetic and accurate definitions of "dreaming" that Grotstein provides us with, but here we would be faced again with the problem of the geographer who is so fascinated by the beauty of the landscape and by the importance of each detail as to be tempted to draw a map in the scale of 1:1. The only antidote to this is my suggestion that you read the book yourself, as in this review I obviously cannot repeat it all word for word.

A quotation I cannot resist reporting here is the following: "the psychotic suffers not from too much primary process but from a defectively functioning primary process—that is, defective dreaming" (ibid, p. 268). And again:

I hypothesize that a-function implies the existence of at least two mirror-image binary-oppositional structures, each consisting of dialectically opposing primary and secondary processes—and that they both subserve dreaming. (1) One binary-oppositional (binocular) structure—a-function 1—exists in the unconscious and is responsible for the transformation (mentalization—dreaming) of β-elements into α-elements, which are then relegated for use as dream thoughts, repression, memory, and reinforcement of the contact-barrier. Although this structure consists of the dialectical operations of both the primary and secondary processes, it is under the hegemony of the pleasure principle. (2) Another binary-oppositional structure–α-function 2—situated in consciousness and/or in the preconscious and under the hegemony of the reality principle, transforms (dreams) β-elements emanating from stimuli in the external world so as to render them unconscious. In other words, there is spectrum of a-functioning that extends from the most elemental to the most advanced. (Grotstein, 2007, p. 271)

"The act of dreaming strongly suggests that the human being must be born with a propensity for story-telling, story-seeking, and story-responding, one that issues from the aesthetic vertex" (ibid, p. 275). For the analyst, dreaming is an "observational technique" (ibid, p. 279), which allows him to get in touch with his own and the other's emotions (which, let us remind ourselves, are the invariants of transformations). "Through dreaming, the analyst 'becomes' his own, native version of the analysand" (ibid). Dreams furthermore

are ingeniously conceived "archival fictions" or "novels" that maintain the integrity of Truth as an invariant in the context of a protective fictive backdrop arranged by encryption or encoding, so that the integrity of System Ucs. and System Pcs. can be maintained and continually restored. (Grotstein, 2007, p. 280)

Furthermore, dreaming "monitors and repairs the Unconscious Systems (Ucs. and Pcs.) by reconfiguring unconscious phantasies that can collectively, as a phantasmal or mythic network, subtend and support System Cs. and the far reaches of our being" (ibid).

Finally, some consideration should also be given to the second column of the Grid in its function as "a container—dreamer—thinker function" (ibid, p. 284), because each individual can only bear a subjective amount of truth; and anyway this, in order to be tolerable, needs to be distorted to various degrees. In the end, there is in each of us a different degree of tolerance for suffering and for acceptance of the truth.

I found the last pages of the book to be intensely beautiful. They show their author's courage in recognising the revolutionary change brought about by the work of Bion who, unlike Freud who had tried to gain scientific consensus, postulated (and, I believe, with good reasons) the need for psychoanalysis to be based on a different science.

Bion, the intrepid tank commander, took a different direction and attacked science's flank. "Scienc", he claimed, was appropriate only for inanimate objects. The "science" that is apposite for psychoanalysis is a "mystical science", a science of emotions that are infinite and consequently complex and non-linear in nature. (Grotstein, 2007, p. 328)

I'd like to quote here a sentence from Grotstein's book which sums up Bion's viewpoint: "We become what we agree to suffer" (ibid).

In conclusion, I would now like to say that this is a book that I had been waiting to have for a long time—a book that was in my "memoirs of the future". This book is a hologram of Bion's thought that can be deconstructed in its constituent parts and then reconstructed again and again. It is Grotstein's dream about Bion, but a dream that enriches his thought, transforms it and makes it more readily available. It is a book that I will certainly use with my students in seminars on Bion's thought, and I will encourage others to do the same. It is a book, in my opinion, that all analysts, including those of a different orientation, should take most seriously. It is a book that dares to disturb that universe of knowledge that any reader had before reading it. It is a book which is "thought for thinking", but also reverie, as well as representing the closest we can get, for the time being at least, to the global "O" of Bion's thought. Evolution, however, does not stop here.

CHAPTER NINE

Between "other" and "other": Merleau-Ponty as a precursor of the analytic field*

Intermediacy

According to Pontalis, Freud is "a thinker of conflict rather than of the intermediate" (Pontalis, 2007, p. 316). Two kinds of thought coexist in him: binary thought, made up of dichotomies such as conscious/unconscious, primary process/secondary process, pleasure principle/reality principle, or narcissistic libido/object libido; and ternary thought, as with the threefold division of the first topography into *Ucs.-Pcs.-Cs.* or the *ego-id-superego* structure of the second topography. However, even if what predominates in Freud is dualism and the idea of psychic life as essentially based on the conflict of agencies, forces, quantities, and wishes, he was keenly aware of the need to conceive of the intermediate, or, to use a more abstract term, intermediacy. This is suggested by his evocative neologism[1] of the *Zwischenreich*, the "in-between realm" or "half-way region." The term already appears in a letter dated 16 April 1896 to Fliess, his Berlin friend and correspondent (Freud, 1985,

---

*G. Civitarese is the author of this chapter.

p. 181), in which, though, it is not quite clear what Freud is referring to. Jeffrey Masson, the editor of this edition of the correspondence, notes that, according to Schur, he is alluding to the unconscious and the body-mind relationship, and that Fliess was subsequently to make use of it in connection with the subject of bisexuality.

In "Remembering, Repeating and Working-through" (1914), Freud uses this word again, in order explicitly to denote the transference, the realm that lies between illness and reality. The transference neurosis is merely an "artificial" disorder, he explains. It is contrasted with what is natural; it is an artifice, a surrogate, an expedient, an illusion. The *Zwischenreich* is thus the locus of infinite transformations, a "playground," which, while provisional and virtual, is, Freud explains, precisely for this reason "accessible to our intervention" (Freud, 1914, p. 154). The term occurs on two other occasions in his oeuvre, to denote fantasy and art (Freud, 1913, 1917). His interest in the intermediate space is also reflected, finally, in the essays on telepathy and the processes of thought transmission or thought transference (*Gedankenübertragung*) involved in this phenomenon (Freud, 1921).

I mention these concepts in order to emphasise that the history of psychoanalysis, from Freud on, is the history of exploration of the intermediate space. Considering only the principal authors after Freud, for whom, as we have seen, the *Zwischenreich* is first and foremost the in-between realm of the transference and then of fantasy and art, for Klein it is the area of play; for Winnicott, the potential/transitional space (the idea of "betweenness"); for Lacan, the stage of the mirror and of primitive alienation that lays the foundations of the subject as seen reflected in the other's gaze; for Bion, "O," or the "something *between*" patient and analyst that is the object of analysis; for Green, the "third" in analysis; and for Ogden, the "intersubjective third" of analysis.

This paradigm in its most radical guise is represented by the concept of the analytic field (Ferro & Basile, 2009; Civitarese, 2008a, 2011a), which is underlain by the conceptions of intermediacy of Merleau-Ponty and Bion. For scholars of the French philosopher's thought, the good news is that Merleau-Ponty is totally up to date, as his teachings can be applied to the most advanced notions in contemporary psychoanalysis, such as the neo-Bionian school and inter-subjectivism; the bad news is that, with rare exceptions, analysts are unaware of this.

The field ego

Merleau-Ponty is very seldom cited in the psychoanalytic literature.[2] Yet, together with Derrida, he is perhaps the only one of the great philosophers to entertain an extremely close relationship with psychoanalysis in a circularity of projective and introjective exchanges. Like Derrida, he took much from psychoanalysis, but also gave a great deal back to it, both directly, by in part inspiring the concept of the field according to the Barangers' first formulation (Baranger & Baranger, 1961–1962), and indirectly. For their conception of the analytic field, the Barangers explicitly drew on Kurt Lewin, Heinrich Racker, and Enrique Pichon Rivière (León de Bernardi, 2008). Other influences were recognised only later: Churcher (2008) reports that Lewin already influenced Bion and his first analyst, Rickman, and that in 1945 the latter presented a paper on field theory to the British Society; he also points out that in the second, revised version of the Barangers' 1961–1962 paper, as republished in 1969, the name "Lewin" is replaced by "Merleau-Ponty".

Present-day psychoanalysis is called upon to take account of intermediacy and intersubjectivism, of the (bodily) forms of implicit memory and of the inaccessible or fetal, and hence unrepressed, unconscious (Bion, 1997; Civitarese, 2013a). Not everything can be traced back to perception (as we naïvely imagine) and to consciousness, because there is a *fleshly* "perception" that is not representational—a level of sense that can be described as semiotic but not yet semantic. For this reason, Merleau-Ponty can once again be seen as a vitally important interlocutor of psychoanalysis. Among other things, he must also be credited with having, so to speak *in advance*, presented a radical critique of the cognitivist paradigm, focusing on the role of emotion and affectivity in perception. Learning to speak is in his view not a purely intellectual matter, but is bound up with identification with the environment, with the obscure assimilation of customs, and with the system of relationships established with others. It is equivalent to the structuring of an affective grammar.

In the introduction to his Sorbonne lectures on child development, Merleau-Ponty examines the subject of jealousy. Commenting on a case observed by Rostand,[3] and applying the two-stage temporality of *Nachträglichkeit*, he describes how, when a little brother arrives two months later, a small girl assigns new meaning to the powerful emotion experienced when she saw a bitch suckling her puppies and immediately acquires new linguistic competence, in the form of the use of the imperfect, the appearance of four verbs in the future tense, and repeated recourse to the words "me" and "I". An emotional crisis gives rise to a transformation resulting in mental growth. Jealousy causes the girl to become more of a subject/agency. This passage inevitably reminds one of Melanie Klein's famous lines on the letters of the alphabet, which were quoted by Derrida (1967) in *Of Grammatology*:

> For Fritz, when he was *writing*, the lines meant roads and the letters ride on motor-bicycles—on the pen—upon them. For instance, "i" and "e" ride together on a motor-bicycle that is usually driven by the "i" and they love one another with a tenderness quite unknown in the real world. Because they always ride with one another they became so alike that there is hardly any difference between them, for the beginning and the end—he was talking of the small Latin alphabet—of "i" and "e" are the same, only in the middle the "i" has a little stroke and the "e" has a little hole. (Klein, 1923, p. 73)

One reason for analysts' relative disregard of Merleau-Ponty may be the critical dismissal by Lacan (some of whose seminars he had attended) of his concept of the unconscious, in which, according to Fielding (1999), Lacan concludes that:

> … although there are a "few whiffs of the unconscious to be detected in his notes [which] might have led him to pass" into psychoanalysis, Merleau-Ponty's phenomenology is ultimately dependent upon a Cartesian ego and an abstract eye, and is, accordingly, incompatible with psychoanalysis. (Fielding, 1999, p. 185)

When I first read the pages on infant development in Merleau-Ponty's course and saw how he quotes the psychoanalytic literature, at one point I, too, wondered: whatever has become of the unconscious? In particular, why does Merleau-Ponty never mention something that, partly and indirectly thanks to him, has become an increasingly vital notion for us today—namely, as Freud (1912) puts it, communication from unconscious to unconscious? Now on the one hand he seemingly accepts Freud's idea of the unconscious, as he would otherwise be unable to conceptualise—as he does—the distinction between emotional ambivalence, which is unconscious, and ambiguity, which is conscious;

or between racism as a reaction formation, an expression of character rigidity and rejection of ambiguity, and projection. On the other hand, however, Merleau-Ponty is interested primarily in the cognitive unconscious in the broad sense (that is, the procedural, non-repressed unconscious); he is interested in the background of intercorporeal, preverbal, or presymbolic "pre-communication" that precedes and then always accompanies linguistic or symbolic communication. This is indeed not the classical Freudian unconscious of the first topography, which is a representational, repressed, and dynamic unconscious.

For Merleau-Ponty, the ego is a field of intercorporeal relations. A child communicates with the world through the medium of the parents. His perception of it from birth cannot dispense with sociality. If the psyche is seen as isolated, this process is inexplicable. Communication with the body precedes communication in words. Intercorporeal communication precedes linguistic/symbolic communication. *The other is my own skin*, Merleau-Ponty notes. The individual is immediately part of a "system" or "field of relations". The body is impregnated with what it touches, sees, feels, and tastes. Consciousness of one's own body is never, even when an ego is established, that of an "isolated mass", but a postural schema that is not fixed once and for all, but results from the position occupied at every instant relative to the environment. In addition, it is always a *"certain style* of action" (Merleau-Ponty, 1951, p. 147). No one has given a better description of this interpenetration of bodies than Merleau-Ponty: "Husserl said that the perception of others is like a 'phenomenon of coupling'. The term is anything but a metaphor", he comments significantly (ibid, p. 148). Nowadays it is often said, in the context of the field, that the sexuality reported by patients is a narrative genre and that what is described is the coupling of minds in the session (Ferro, 1999). As in Merleau-Ponty (Vanzago, 2012), sexuality (the drive) is referred to affectivity.

To emphasise this essential dimension of personal identity, Merleau-Ponty substantially relates the distal senses (sight, hearing, and smell) to proprioception and touch. He gives precedence to the latter over the former. *He sees all perception as tactile perception.* In this way he succeeds in conveying the insight that the subject is part of a totality, of a system in which everything is in motion and in which every component interacts intimately with every other component. In this connection, the metaphors of ordinary language are revealing. We say, for instance, that one's eyes *rest* on an object, or that words can *caress, touch*, or *wound*.

Touch is the sense of continuity, of contact, of syncretic sociality, of the metonymic contiguity from which metaphor stems. The visible is traced back to the invisible, and the body (a concept that separates) to the flesh (in effect, a concept of continuity of sentient/sensible substance). Again, one need only hear one's own recorded voice to have an experience of depersonalisation. It is coloured by a "tactile" sound that does not reach us via the outwardly directed sense of hearing and that does not appear in the recording, but traverses us, passing through our flesh and bones, contributing to the definition of our sense of self.

Compared with the other senses, sight and hearing are, of course, bound up more with consciousness, because it is language that makes consciousness possible by linking up with the image of the thing. More-over, even if it does not contain word presentations but only thing pres-entations, in Freud the unconscious itself is intimately connected with language. It is the negative of the conscious mind. Words have their source in the conscious mind. In Merleau-Ponty, on the other hand, we may discern an insight into the so-called "procedural", non-repressed unconscious. The intellect is referred to its material, bodily substrate, but here too, as with the repressed unconscious, it is never outside the perimeter of "existence"—that is, of the symbolic. The concept of existence in the philosophical sense—Heidegger's *ex-sistere*—would be meaningless if applied to animals, because it entails knowledge of self. *In this way, however, the concept of the unconscious is extended to the under-standing of corporeity*. The body preserves the traces of older traumas that have not succeeded in being represented, but if the subject is con-sidered not in isolation but as a node in a network, the shadow of the repressed weighs on these, too, by maternal contagion. As Lacan notes, we are caught in the toils of the symbolic even before birth.

In Merleau-Ponty, the organisation of subjectivity commences in the prelinguistic phase (the phase of *"pre-communication"*—1951, p. 148) of child development, in which "there is not one individual over against another but rather an anonymous collectivity, an undifferentiated group life" (ibid, p. 149). This includes all the dynamic forms of spatialisa-tion of bodily activities, such as respiration, posture, the sensitivity of the oral cavity, etc.—what analysts call the relation to the breast. The other is initially felt to be only an experience of wellbeing or ill-being in the body. In particular, this state, or process, of "syncretic sociabil-ity" (ibid, p. 149) is never abolished. In a passage in "The Child's Rela-tions with Others", Merleau-Ponty gives the example of a little boy who disobeys his parents, picks up a glass, and then puts it down. Immediately afterwards, he hears the sound of another glass breaking. The boy immediately becomes agitated, as if he were to blame. No process of more abstract thought has had time to unfold. Instead, it is as if his hand retained a sensory memory of the glass. In this way a kind of magic link (a transference) becomes established between the order of representation and that of the procedural, between the prohibited gesture and the fragmented shards of the object. So it is that the repressed casts its shadow even on to things to which the body assigns meaning on a purely pre-reflective level. As Merleau-Ponty (1951) remarks,

> there is a sort of spatial synchronism—i.e., a presence of the same psychic being in several spatial points, a presence of me in the other and the other in me. In a general way there is an inability to conceive space and time as environments that contain a series of perspectives which are absolutely distinct from each other. (Merleau-Ponty, 1951, p. 177)

In psychoanalysis we say that the interiority of the analyst, like that of the patient, is a place in the analytic field. This is a key principle, upon which an absolutely innovative theory of analytic technique rests: instead of the unilateral decoding of the patient's unconscious with a view to annexing increasingly large portions of it to consciousness, reveries are exchanged, thus contributing to dyadic expansion of the un/conscious as a psychoanalytic function of the personality.

Merleau-Ponty's emphasis on the body owes a great deal not only to phenomenology, but also to psychoanalysis. While his starting point is Husserl, this is only in order to bring him closer to the unconscious of psychoanalysis (Stawarska, 2008). The unconscious passes through the body. Although Freud's theory is admittedly centred on the concept of representation, he was the first to invoke a non-repressed unconscious—the ego as a projection of the surface of the body. The very concept of the drive, on the boundary between the bodily and the mental, bears witness to his constant attention to the body. Freud repeatedly stresses that the ego is a bodily ego. As late as in 1938, in one of his last notes, dated 12 July, he writes that being in a child precedes having and that the primordial mechanism of possession is identification: "I am the breast" (*ich bin die Brust*)—that is, the object (Freud, 1938, p. 299)—while the consciousness of having, which implies a separation, appears only later: "'I have it'—that is, 'I am not it'" (*ich habe sie, d.h. ich bin sie nicht*) (ibid, p. 299). This extraordinarily condensed sentence seems once more to stress the identity of ego and body. Furthermore, it also implies that the ego is the other, culture, sociality, and that the first ego is a sensory ego. The first *Zwischenreich* (the first *between*) is "an area of sensations of a soothing sort" (Ogden, 1994b, p. 174), the thin film that forms at the interface between subject and object. Merleau-Ponty had in fact anticipated this: "in so far as others are felt only as a kind of state of well-being in the baby's organism because he is held more firmly or more tenderly in their arms, we cannot say that they are actually perceived" (Merleau-Ponty, 1951, p. 153) The object is not yet perceived as separate, but its stamp is noticed. In an ingenious summing-up, the expression "I am the breast" marries intersubjectivism and corporeity. Again, the theoretical fantasy that pervades Freud's entire oeuvre is that of the "poetry of the mind":[4] the images that populate the psyche are abstractions of external perceptual afferences that gradually *condense* as they ascend to the brain (Freud, 1891). Hence the concept of condensation (*Verdichtung*) in the dream work—and hence also, later, Melanie Klein's vividly dramatic representation of the earliest unconscious fantasies, which is entirely based on the body and the fragmented body, and which is so well represented on the figurative level in the deconstruction of women's bodies in cubist painting.

However, with the concept of projective identification in particular, Klein develops an extraordinarily advanced intersubjective theory of the psyche that in some respects complements that of Merleau-Ponty. According to Angelino, Melanie Klein:

> on the other hand fascinated Merleau-Ponty, because her writings are rich in highly concrete, and indeed brutal and almost shocking, descriptions of our relations with others and with things, which confirm his ideas about the role of corporeity and the drives (libido and aggression) in our relations with the world. (Angelino, 2005, p. 374, translated)

By her detailed, obsessive study of the mechanisms of the first introjections/projections and identifications within a partially undifferentiated situation, and while accepting the existence of a primitive ego right from birth, Klein develops a valuable model for representing the relationship that links the subject to its environment and to the other, not only at the stage described by Freud's concept of primary narcissism, but also when the subject is no longer at such an elementary phase in the constitution of the ego. As noted by Kristeva:

> the fragile ego is not truly separated in the sense of a "subject" separated from an "object", but it incessantly consumes the breast from within and ejects the breast into the outside world by constructing-vacating itself while constructing-vacating the Other. (Kristeva, 2000, p. 62f.)

As it were in tune with Klein, Merleau-Ponty organises his philosophical researches by choosing the two key metaphors of the field and, later, the chiasm (in *The Visible and the Invisible*, 1964). Identity is conceivable only in difference, in the intersection of one's body with the world of things and of others. One can be oneself only by projecting oneself outside one's self into the other, and vice versa. The subject (S) is constructed only by alienating itself in the object (O), which is thereby transformed (O'); and then, by re-introjecting from the object what it had deposited in it, the subject is in turn modified (S'). (The structure of the chiasm—the notation derived from it seems to allude ironically to a kind of distress call to the other—would be SOO'S'.)

Oddly enough, the unbalance toward the unconscious and psychic reality in effect causes Klein to neglect the "fleshly" dimension—that of the feeling and the felt—of the body (even though the body is absolutely the protagonist of the subject's unconscious fantasies); conversely, by virtue of his concentration on the body as experienced, Merleau-Ponty's propositions in fact closely resemble contemporary theories of the non-repressed or "sensory" unconscious and of procedural, non-declarative memories.

The fact is that, while paving the way for the undermining of positivist epistemology and a one-person approach to psychology (hence Derrida's charge of logocentrism—substantially, the conviction of arriving at an ultimate truth about things), neither Freud nor Klein has abandoned that conception. Their intersubjectivism is incomplete; nor could it be otherwise. Such was the epistemological framework of their time. The direct contribution of Merleau-Ponty to psychoanalysis is only very tangential—and, aside from the Lacanian excommunication, continues, precisely, through the Barangers; however, he must take the credit for having been the first to demolish the idea of the isolated subject.

Since Merleau-Ponty, thinking of the subject has meant thinking of the intermediate space, which I suggest calling intermediacy. His conception offers psychoanalysis a more abstract and wider-ranging theoretical framework, while also bearing out the insights stemming from clinical practice.

While never quoting him and notwithstanding the explicit reference to the Hegelian conception of the subject, which can be subsumed in the master-servant dialectic, Reis (1999) claims in a brilliant contribution that the profoundly intersubjective inspiration of Ogden's thought fits better into the framework of Merleau-Ponty's philosophy. This is an important point in favour of the French philosopher because Ogden is one of the pacesetters of contemporary psychoanalysis. For in Reis's view, the basis of Hegel's version of intersubjectivism as a dialectic of recognition is already that of two isolated minds (an interpretation that Benjamin (1999) considers to be somewhat "crude"). I wonder whether the shift from the body to the concept of the "flesh" might not have the same significance for Merleau-Ponty—that is, of attempting to overcome what had remained in *Phenomenology of Perception* (Merleau-Ponty, 1945) of a philosophy of the isolated subject. The concept of the countertransference, for example, is not genuinely intersubjective because the analyst's subjectivity is seen only as the place in which the patient "creates" that phenomenon. The analyst as a person remains outside it. "For Hegel subjectivity remains equated with the conscious subject in competition with the other […]. But it fails to speak to a level of 'innate intersubjectivity'" (Reis, 1999, p. 378). It takes no account of the pre-object phase of life. For Merleau-Ponty, on the other hand, the subject does not arrive, but is born of intersubjectivity.

The analytic field

The field model is but one of the utterly innumerable models that could be constructed to represent the relationship between human beings in terms of intermediacy. Other perspectives are always possible. One should not make the mistake of assigning an ontological value to a particular model, as Merleau-Ponty himself sometimes tends to do.[5] After all, the notion of the subject too is a construct. It works well in many different contexts, but, while necessary, is nevertheless always a fiction. One need only consider how it has changed since Freud. The point, instead, is to ask ourselves what model is most suitable for describing a particular phenomenon because it tells us more about it or makes it more readily understandable, brings out new aspects, and, in a word, serves our purpose better. This was the case with the introduction of the concept of the field in physics or that of the Gestalt in psychology.

The field can also be thought of as a new metaphor that, as Kuhn (1962) clearly explains, impels scientific research to ask new questions, to look in new directions, and to reexamine old acquisitions in a new light. Field theory is a new and deeper-going theory of unconscious communication between individuals, because it involves a *more radical* notion than other models of the unconscious and of oneiric functioning in the session; it modifies our idea of therapeutic factors and of interpretation; and it offers a more accurate description of the functioning of the analytic relationship.

By analogy with the electromagnetic and gravitational fields of physics, analytic field theory postulates that there arises, between patient and analyst, a field of invisible forces that powerfully influence their interactions. These forces are not knowable directly, but can only be deduced from their derivatives. Investigation of the intermediate space of the field facilitates understanding of how communication between one unconscious and another takes place (Freud, 1912).

Once established, a field takes on a life of its own. It dispenses with the subjects that generated it, in the sense that it is more than the sum of the initial components. Of the objects that inhabit it, it is no longer possible to say to which of the two subjects they belong.[6] This would be feasible on the basis of the manifest text—who said what or did what— but not of the latent text. In the unconscious text, the asymmetry of the unencoded text is lost. The deep structure of the analytic dialogue is very different from its surface structure.

However, what is the field made of? A psychic field stems from the intersection of mutual introjective and projective identifications. The subjects absorb and emit "psychic" rays. This of course involves psychological processes in the minds of analyst and patient, connected with each other like two dynamic systems interacting in real time. While the field could be said not to exist outside the minds, that is actually not so. It also includes everything that furnishes the place where the physical persons are situated, as a possible source of stimuli, as well as the more or less subtle actions performed by each in order to force the other to accept projective identifications. After all, both members of the couple unconsciously seek to impress a particular shape on reality by their transferences, or, as Bion would say, by their transformations in hallucinosis. Externalisation of one's fantasies (unconscious schemata or scripts, narratives that combine a number of elementary representations) is a way of conferring familiarity, and hence knowability and bearability, on reality within a dialectic of identity and difference, of assimilation and accommodation.

Compared with Merleau-Ponty's hypothesis of the field ego and Bion's of the proto-mental area, the concept of projective identification proves to be extremely valuable in terms of explanation, because it so to speak renders "tangible" the channels of communication whereby this shared unconscious psychological area can become established. It imparts "visibility" to the *way* in which the psychic recombines with the sensory-tactile and to the concrete, indispensable points of contact that mediate the processes of interindividual psychic influencing. Reflections of this concept can be found in the terms used by Merleau-Ponty (1951), some of which are borrowed from Wallon: "sympathy", the "postural schema", "transfer of conduct", "contagion", "capacity for 'collection' and 'inward formulation' of gestures", "mimesis", "transitivism", and "syncretic sociability".

To distinguish between simple psychic projection, which is applied to one's unconscious image of the other and is therefore an exclusively intrapsychic process, on the one hand, and projective identification, a process that is also interpsychic, on the other, Grotstein (2005) invented the concept of "projective transidentification". It may be speculated that, after all, projective identification and projective transidentification are one and the same phenomenon, varying only in intensity—ranging from a zero level of modification in the subject's mind to, ultimately, unconscious behaviours aimed at influencing the other and forcing the other to act as a container.

The field is pervaded with forces of attraction and repulsion resulting from the collision of these particle beams of projective identifications traveling in opposite directions. Every place in the field exerts a gravitational force on any object within it. The interactions may be weak or very weak, and hence difficult to detect, or they may be strong. Things too are invested with projections, transferences, and magic thought. One will of course react differently to inanimate objects than to a person, because in the former case one's specific reactivity to a fellow human being is lacking—a reactivity that we now know to be based also on specific neurophysiological functions.

Personality is the outcome of the work performed by certain functions, such as, for instance, the alpha function of the mind, a central component of which is dream thought. In other words, we possess innate structures that can, however, develop only in favourable environmental conditions, which represent apparatuses for symbolisation. A first law of the field is that unconscious communication can be neither prevented not controlled. A second law is that this dream thought is active both at night and during the day. A third law of the field is that, the higher the "temperature" of the relationship—that is, the greater the level of emotional involvement (passion)—the more intense the forces of the field will be. Frequent sessions and the prolonged duration of treatment have the aim of raising this temperature to an optimum point. For Freud, this point marks the triggering of the transference neurosis.

Oscillation between symmetry and asymmetry in the analytic field

The patient-analyst relationship is not asymmetric in an absolute sense, because it is not possible to identify the unconscious contributions of each party. It is certainly asymmetric on the manifest level, but not necessarily on that of unconscious communication. The fear is sometimes expressed that the analytic field model entails the disappearance of the concept of the subject. This fear is unfounded. Both the viewpoint of the subject and that of intersubjective dynamic interaction are merely models or conventions, and not the thing itself. They are constantly evolving perspectives that we extract from reality in order to acquaint ourselves with something to which we lack direct access. Here again, continuity or discontinuity is evident: intersubjectivism is not antithetical to the concept of the subject, but complements it. In fact, however, even if only in part, the subject is ousted once again, and more radically, from the house of the ego; not only is it driven back toward the unconscious, but the individual unconscious itself is referred to sociality.

The therapeutic relationship is asymmetric because the patient has all the space he desires for expression in words; the analyst is a professional and, furthermore, has already undergone treatment in the form of his own analysis; pathological projective identifications normally travel from patient to analyst. Yet temporary interruptions or inversions of asymmetry do occur, as there would otherwise be no such thing as negative reverie or a negative therapeutic reaction. The analyst must identify these, because if they become chronic their effects will be harmful rather than therapeutic.

The distinction between symmetry and asymmetry, however artificial, enables us to describe two modes of functioning of one and the same process. The secondary process tends constantly to reestablish asymmetry, but using unconscious thought and symmetric communication. This can nevertheless not be taken for granted. It involves work. What is, or should be, taken for granted are only the external aspects of the relationship—namely, responsibility, purposes, means, levels of personal suffering, and so on.

Conceptualisation of the intermediate space in this way has consequences. In principle, interpretation is no longer directed to the patient, to modifying something in him, but instead to improving the narrative capacity of the field, understood as an un/conscious narration à deux. Whereas it is seemingly addressed to the patient, from this vertex it addresses him only as a place in the field, as a point in dynamic interaction with all other points. The point is to improve the general level of the text composed and performed à deux by analyst and patient. Hence each intervention aims to increase the couple's ability to dream the problem that cannot be dreamed, and to construct narrative maps of places that do not exist—or rather, that exist only in imagination. As a rule, an unsaturated interpretation, or interpretation in the transference, expands the capacity of the field to dream much more than a "closed" interpretation. Where this approach succeeds, the "oxygenation" of the room improves, the patient finds it easier to breathe, and the analyst too emerges changed from the encounter.

The analyst chooses appropriate interventions on the basis of this aim, whether they are intended to reveal the patient's unconscious dynamics to him or are mere discursive openings or punctuation marks in the dialogue. As a guide, he follows the figures of the discourse, the characters of the session seen as affective holograms or functional aggregates of the analytic field. These represent the thermometer that measures the emotional temperature of the field, the fluctuating index of emotional unison, and the associated tolerance range (Ferro, 2010). They furnish information on the state and quality of the field's oneiric functioning—that is, on the capacity of the system to perform a certain un/conscious psychological work of transformation of emotions. The analysis is no longer the struggle between good and evil, as in Freud between reason and the diabolical drives seething in the unconscious, but between meaning and the absence of meaning, between the ability or the inability to use the po(i)etic-constructive-aesthetic virtualities of the unconscious.

How could this be expressed in the language of Merleau-Ponty? The analyst must preserve the sense of opacity of the body. He cannot use a purely technical operational thought that does not draw, like art, on the "fabric of brute being" (Merleau-Ponty, 1964, p. 123), on the mysterious source of sensations, but is himself a "working, actual body" (ibid, p. 124). His body is "both seeing and visible [...]. It sees itself seeing; it touches itself touching; it is visible and sensitive for itself" (ibid, p. 123); "things are an annex or prolongation of itself; they are incrusted in its flesh, they are part of its full definition; the world is made of the very stuff of the body" (ibid, p. 125). So it is not easy for him to know who is seeing and who is being seen, where one ends and the other begins—as Bion says with regard to analysand and analyst. Vision is not the absolute transparency of a picture of the world that presents itself to the eyes as an act of pure thought: "Immersed in the visible by his body, itself visible, the see-er does not appropriate what he sees; he merely approaches it by looking, he opens onto the world" (ibid, p. 124).

Another particular strength of Merleau-Ponty's philosophy is represented by his considerations on art. For some time my interests have centred on the idea of aesthetic experience as a model of what actually happens in psychoanalysis (Civitarese, 2011a, 2012, 2013b). Being, like Freud, perhaps insensitive to music, Merleau-Ponty is more concerned with painting. "Music," he writes, "is too far on the hither side of the world and the designatable to depict anything but certain schemata of Being—its ebb and flow, its growth, its upheavals, its vortices" (Merleau-Ponty, 1964, p. 123). In fact, precisely because it is on the hither side of the world, music—perhaps even more than painting—affords an insight into the birth of identity; precisely because of its "tactile" quality, which creates less distance than painting, it is the most moving of all art forms. Music, more than painting, is an immediate immersion in things. In *Ethics of Sexual Difference* (1993), Luce Irigaray criticises Merleau-Ponty for undervaluing the tactile, and attributes this attitude to a parallel devaluation of the feminine (Murphy, 2008). This author also argues that, in intrauterine life, the sense of touch (and of hearing) precedes that of sight, so that the priority assigned to it by Merleau-Ponty is not justified. It is precisely with reference to intrauterine life that Bion invokes the "inaccessible unconscious". The fact is that the philosophy of perception continues to presuppose a subject-object duality, albeit with a view to overcoming it. It is this duality that Merleau-Ponty sought to surmount with the new concept—for which traditional philosophy still lacked a name—of the "flesh".

The very idea is dizzying. There must be a limit to subject-object "confusion", as any vision would otherwise disappear and meaning would be absolutely lost. The result would be an absurd "no-person psychology". Yet the analytic field model is perhaps the only *practical*—in so far as clinical work is done—realisation of this conception. The events of the field, characters of the discourse, figures aroused deep inside the patient or analyst, are dynamic events of the emotional field of analysis. They are "vertices" (a term coined by Bion precisely in order not to give precedence to one sensory channel over the others) from which to see and to be seen. They are "interpretations" that are at one and the same time conceptual and sensory, conscious and unconscious of self, of the other, of self-with-the-other, and conversely of self as seen by the other and by the intersubjective field. Can Merleau-Ponty's idea of the "fundamental *narcissism* of all vision" be associated with this model? Does the fact that a character can be assigned to all and to none not correspond to the concept of the "anonymity" of the flesh? When we say that the point is to expand the narrative-po(i)etic-aesthetic capacity of the analytic field, are we not invoking a principle of "visibility in itself?"

Merleau-Ponty's late concept of "flesh" calls to mind representations of the world of atoms. Consider Hofstadter's approach to it in *I Am a Strange Loop* (2007). We could in my view furnish a much more radical and de-subjectivised version of it. But we could identify it with Bion's "O" or Lacan's Real; Merleau-Ponty must then specify that the flesh is divided into "flesh of the world" and "flesh of the body." Perception is the "dehiscence" of the flesh between the visible and the see-er. He is basically reintroducing the subject, but by a route that actually enriches rather than invalidating the results of his *Phenomenology*. In other words, if the subject is thrown out of the door—and in this connection psychoanalysts from Freud on need not take lessons from anyone (except perhaps from Dostoyevsky or Nietzsche)—lo and behold, here it is coming straight back in through the window.

The symmetry of unconscious communication could be redefined as "the experience of the reversibility of dimensions" (Merleau-Ponty, 1961, p. 369). Quoting Cézanne, Merleau-Ponty repeats that colour is "the place where our brain and the universe meet", but for analysts, colour is emotion. The "painterly" depth of the vertex of the analytic field finds in emotion its naturally "self-representing" quality where the eyes of patient and analyst constantly intersect, and they see themselves seeing; it arises from this internal animation. The outlines of things are transfigured. As in Monet's *Nymphéas*, the figurative becomes ever more evanescent and we are transported into our interiority and at the same time into the heart of things. Merleau-Ponty writes that "it is simply a matter of freeing the line, of revivifying its constituting power" (ibid, p. 372), and this could be the motto of analytic work. More accurately, we could call it "transformation in dreaming": the lines

> … were supposed to circumscribe the apple or the meadow, but the apple and the meadow "form themselves" from themselves, and come into the visible as if they had come from a pre-spatial world behind the scenes. (Merleau-Ponty, 1961, p. 372)

In the words of another painter, Mark Rothko,[7] the painter's instruments are faith, clarity, and intimacy:

> The most important tool the artist fashions through constant practice is faith in his ability to produce miracles when they are needed. Pictures must be miraculous: […] The picture must be for him, as for anyone experiencing it after, a revelation, an unexpected and unprecedented resolution of an eternally familiar need. (Rothko, 2002)

Again:

> The progression of a painter's work, as it travels in time from point to point, will be toward clarity: toward the elimination of all obstacles between the painter and the idea, and between the idea and the observer. As examples of such obstacles, I give (among others) memory, history or geometry, which are swamps of generalization from which one might pull out parodies of ideas (which are ghosts) but never an idea in itself. To achieve this clarity is, inevitably, to be understood. (Rothko, 2002)

And lastly: "I paint very large pictures because I want to create a state of intimacy. A large picture is an immediate transaction. It takes you into it" (ibid).

This can surely not fail to remind us, respectively, of Bion's concepts of faith, absence of memory and desire, and the special intimacy of two dangerous and ferocious animals, as he saw analyst and patient. Yet even if we are with Rothko, who prevents us from continuing to appreciate Rembrandt? Or we might agree with Merleau-Ponty that, while we may be with Cézanne, that does not mean that we must dispense with the masters of perspective. In Cézanne, Juan Gris, Braque, and Picasso, we find objects—"lemons, mandolins, bunches of grapes, pouches of tobacco [...] which, so to speak, stand 'bleeding' before us" (Merleau-Ponty, 1948, p. 93). They project out beyond the surface of the picture toward us or to draw us into it, to include us. Painting as an aesthetic experience is an experience of authenticity. However, just as, in the paintings of Cézanne, the viewer is included in a "space which the heart feels" (ibid, p. 54), so it is in analysis with the concept of emotional truth and the truth drive. The body is, "as it were, embedded" in things, and thereby gains access to their truth (ibid, p. 56):

> As the thing, as the other, the true dawns through an emotional and almost carnal experience, where the "ideas"—the other's and our own—are rather traits of his physiognomy and of our own, are less understood than welcomed or spurned in love or hatred. (Merleau-Ponty, 1964, p. 12)

Notes

1. To express a new concept for which he lacks appropriate words, Freud coins new and often brilliant terms. Another example is *Vorstellungsrepräsentanz*, which ingeniously conveys the idea of the gradual transition from the sensible presentation of perception to its reproduction in memory (*Vorstellung*) and to the actual symbol (*Repräsentanz*)—in effect, the transfer from body to mind, another in-between area.
2. On Merleau-Ponty and psychoanalysis, see Fielding, 1999; Angelino, 2005; Stawarska, 2008; and Orange, 2010 (the only psychoanalyst).
3. "Grammaire et affectivité", *Revue française de psychanalyse*, 14: 299–310.
4. See Freud (1891, p. 53): "We can only presume that the fibre tracts, which reach the cerebral cortex after their passage through other grey masses, have maintained some relationship to the periphery of the body, but no longer reflect a topographically exact image of it. They contain the body periphery in the same way as [...] a poem contains the alphabet, i.e., in a complete different arrangement serving other purposes, in manifold associations of the individual elements, whereby some may be represented several times, others not at all".

5. Some authors read his philosophy as a metaphysics of the body (Reynolds, 2004).

6. See Ogden: "The task is not to tease apart the elements constituting the relationship in an effort to determine which qualities belong to whom; rather, from the point of view of the interdependence of subject and object, the analytic task involves an attempt to describe the specific nature of the experience of the unconscious interplay of individual subjectivity and intersubjectivity" (Ogden, 2004, p. 168).

7. Translator's note: The following quotations are taken from various Internet sources. They all appear, translated into Italian, in Rothko (2002).

CHAPTER TEN

Carla's panic attacks: insight and transformation*

This paper is an initial reflection on the subject of panic attacks, based on the presentation of clinical material from the ongoing analysis of a female patient with severe pathology, of which such attacks were from the beginning the most conspicuous symptom. This clinical description is useful in my view because the "panic attack" is often attributed in the psychiatric literature to organic factors, so that analysis is held to be contraindicated. My chapter concludes with an attempt to define the general theoretical model underlying this symptom.

I wish to share with you the adventure in which I have found myself engaged with Carla and shall therefore come straight to the point. On my first meeting with this patient, the basic diagnosis I made to myself was agoraphobia and claustrophobia. In general I prefer as far as possible to avoid in-depth diagnosis, for fear of imposing an excessively rigid pattern on the material observed and its elaboration. I therefore relied on my countertransference feeling that it was right to take Carla

---

*A. Ferro is the author of this chapter.

into analysis; I felt that there was room in my group of patients at that time for one who was more seriously ill, and was also prepared to accept the difficulties and frustrations that might be involved in pursuing the associated line of research.

I knew from experience, too, that patients with severe agoraphobia have significant and even substantial psychotic nuclei, as Segal (1954) pointed out, and so, although I had never previously analysed agoraphobic patients who also presented the range of symptoms known as the "panic attack", I acceded to Carla's demands for an analysis.

I have noted elsewhere (Ferro, 1994) that, having done a great deal of work with seriously ill subjects, I tend to choose my patients not so much on the basis of the classical concept of "analysability", whether in the more open form of suitability for analysis (Limentani, 1972) or in that of "accessibility" (Joseph, 1985), as on that of the ability of the analyst and the analytic couple to withstand the "trial" entailed by the possible difficulties of an analysis.

This approach of mine is very close to the view of Puget & Wender (1987) that in limit situations we are still in the realm of analysis provided that a psychoanalytic function is activated that can give rise to the comprehension and semanticisation of the unconscious that has hitherto remained uncomprehended and unconceived in thought, thus resulting in relief from mental pain.

Carla's analysis falls conveniently into discrete periods.

Problems of the setting

After the initial idyllic sessions, Carla had a massive regression that called the setting seriously into question: she experienced everything that felt like a "rule" as imposition and exploitation. She would constantly try to subvert anything in the analysis that smacked of regularity; it became impossible to end the sessions on time, and she was unable to lie down on the couch (I gave up insisting on this from the outset) or to tolerate the frustration of not getting answers to her urgent questions.

Her "primary school classmate" now took the stage; she had the same name as the patient herself, "Carla", was "terrible, intolerant of any discipline", already on drugs at middle school, behaved promiscuously and would not stand for any rule, however minimal. Of course, the appearance of this "character" (a split-off part of herself) allowed me to start elaborating and interpreting what was happening in the sessions.

Carla would repeatedly put me off my stroke with behaviour I had never come across before: once she sat down on the table (instead of in the chair, on the floor or on the couch as she usually did), and left it only when I thought of Italo Calvino's novel *Baron in the Trees*, in which a teenager feels so alienated by the behaviour of his parents and of the human race in general that he withdraws in indignation to a life in the trees. When I gave an interpretation to that effect, Carla immediately came down from her table/tree.

Although I am accustomed to working with seriously ill patients and children, I was put out perhaps most of all by one particular instance of acting out that violated one of my own taboos: on entering the room, Carla immediately headed for and sat down in my armchair. I was dumbfounded, turned to stone, and thought: "But she can't possibly be occupying my space and leaving me without a place of my own". This countertransference experience enabled me to make the interpretation which gave me back my place: I realised that her "occupation" was a response to my cancellation of one of the previous week's sessions. This had upset her, arousing anxiety about not having her own space, in such a way as to inspire the same anxiety in myself, albeit unconsciously. When I interpreted to that effect, Carla "returned to her place".

In fact Carla typically responded very positively to appropriate interpretations, but showed indifference or opposition whenever something did not convince her or was not adequately "tailored" to her individual situation.

When Carla brought a funny story into the analysis one day, it proved helpful for a while in working through the difficulties of maintaining a setting. The story of the "despairing horse" also introduced to the analysis some seriously dysthymic aspects of Carla's personality, at the same time indicating that she experienced the setting as an exploiting *claustrum* or—the only possible alternative—as something over which she could triumph by violating it. There would therefore be a constant oscillation between impotence and exploitation, in which she was in effect staging a phallic-narcissistic conflict situation like the one she had been involved in from a very early age with her older brothers. The funny story, which was highly significant in itself, was about a man who owned horses, one of which spent the whole day in its stable, from morning until night, crying its eyes out in despair, so that he was at his wits' end. He therefore organised a competition, with a prize for anyone who could cure the horse. No one succeeded, until an unknown person asked to have a go, on condition that he was allowed to be alone with the horse. Suddenly the animal was heard to snigger. The happy owner gave the man the prize, but after a while the horse's constant hilarity became just as intolerable to him as its previous state— indeed, even more so. Summoning the unknown man again, he asked him to restore the former situation. Back he went to the horse, which, shortly afterwards, resumed its desperate crying. At this point the ani- mal's owner was prepared to pay anything to find out how this could have happened, and the answer came by telegram: "The first time I told him: 'Mine is longer than yours' (implying the penis), and the horse started sniggering; the second time I showed it to him and he lapsed into despair again".

The long road to the couch was to present major difficulties. After lying on the couch for the first time, Carla dreamed that she was on a chute like the ones in seaside amusement parks, but made of dozens and dozens of razor blades, so that she suffered terrible cuts sliding down it. These persecution feelings were gradually metabolised and the fact of lying more stably on the couch led to an account of her first trip abroad, her first impressions on hearing a new language, the onset of menstruation, which had occurred during that trip, and the wedding she had attended on that occasion. All these emotions were connected with those activated in the present situation by the assumption of a new, more mature position in the analytical consulting room. The posi- tion on the couch gradually stabilised and problems associated with the symbiotic nuclei took the stage.

Symbiotic nuclei

These had already been mobilised by the "recumbent" position, which she experienced as a serious loss compared with being able to "eat me up with her eyes", as she had done when it had been possible for her to look at me and "devour me" throughout the session. The greater distance gave rise to mourning. However, she persisted in her tendency not to differentiate between herself and me, and to confuse our posi- tions: she would have liked me to lie down beside her on the couch. This was the time of the appearance of "Marco", a three-year-old boy to whom she had been "engaged" when she was very small—indeed, she had once even been through a marriage ceremony with him. In the absence of containment by the mother and father, she had spent whole days with him, and they had lived together in complete symbiosis for a number of years. Then Marco had been snatched away from her when his father had moved for work reasons, and the two had been separated by an enormous distance. For a long time, fusional closeness and despairing distance were the two modalities that prevailed in the consulting room.

Towards a theory of mind: the mother's womb

In one session during this period, she asked about a perfume called 'Fahrenheit' that she could smell in the room. This enabled me to introduce the theme of "degrees", marking differences in temperature and hierarchies within a field that she preferred to see as uniform, undifferentiated, homoeothermic and homoeostatic; I interpreted to that effect.

In the next session she told of a passionate young boyfriend, Giovanni, whom she described as "one of those boys any girl would be happy to have beside her, even if only once a week". The climate of the session seemed to me to be excited and vaguely false; I was left with an unsatisfied taste, as if something had remained hidden and unsaid, even though I had tried to connect the presence of "Giovanni" with what I had told her on the previous day. That night I dreamed of a small shark, which turned into a torpedo.

On the following day, Carla arrived for her session in a state of extreme crisis: she had dreamed of a little girl whose mother did not have a womb ... a little girl without an umbilical cord ... in fact, there was no mother, but instead a man ($\male$) ... The little girl was starving to death ... She added that she had thought of suicide ...

I then felt that my interventions about "Fahrenheit"—*degrees, gradients, differences* and *hierarchies*—although centred and active, and although they had satisfied the more adult parts of the patient (as witness the appearance of "Giovanni"), had amounted to an "overdose" for the more infantile part, the little girl who still had foetal needs, which had been deprived of its life sustenance: a full acceptance of emotional availability ($\female$), total mental receptivity on my part, rather than precise interpretations that left the little girl/shark starving and aroused the explosive threat of suicide.

I use the symbols ♂ and ♀ as a deliberate allusion to Bion's (1962b) conceptualisation of the "contained" and the "container" and their mutual vicissitudes, because the problem in the session seemed to me to be connected with the archaic themes of the reception and return of primary mental states and proto-emotions, which needed to be accepted and transformed; it was too early to give back the full interpretive meanings. Only later would it be possible to deal with other levels, which involved sexual identity.

The first interpretation of "Fahrenheit" might, with a different patient, have been a good reverie-based one, but was premature in this case given Carla's limited receiving capacity. I had made her aware of an excessive difference between us—between myself as active thinker and herself as recipient of an unexpected truth that she lacked a space to accommodate. This caesura had therefore activated potentially explosive jealousy, rage, and dissatisfaction within her.

My countertransference dream put me in touch with the emotions that had been kindled in her, which she had put back into the field. This helped me to discover the meaning of the previous day's communications and to tune into Carla's emotional capacities and needs. I realised that she was still far from being able to tolerate interpretations of content and that she needed my mind/womb to contain the meanings that could not yet be expressed.

A place for the spilt-off parts

Meanwhile Carla's split-off forms of functioning, which she used her brothers Piero and Stefano to name, were becoming increasingly evident. I felt that the time was ripe to tackle these splits, but Carla's mind was plainly not yet equipped to contain these aspects, which I had perhaps not yet metabolised sufficiently.

Indeed, she arrived in a state of extreme anxiety—even hearing "voices in her mind"—for the session that followed my interpretation that the brothers' functioning stood for forms of functioning of her own. I realised that this interpretation had been premature and attempted to restore the split, by speaking once again about Piero and Stefano as "her brothers" with whom she was in a constant state of conflict ("Piero" had to do with violent greed and "Stefano" with aggravated narcissism). The acoustic "hallucinations" then disappeared.

For a long time we allowed these characters to retain their names. She subsequently dreamed of the greedy part (or form of functioning) as a big octopus, whose tentacles enfolded me, but which clung to her during separations in the analysis; I was equipped to withstand them, whereas they suffocated her ... She then dreamed of a talking buffalo, which came into the session on condition that it was allowed to leave and not forced to stay. Meanwhile, "the brother who would not tolerate any learning" was having English lessons and gradually acquiring a knowledge of the language. Then came another dream: there was a tower in orbit a long way above the earth, and a landing apron had been built for it; a man was climbing the steps of the tower and, at each step, the tower came closer to earth by the equivalent of one step, until it was suddenly resting on the ground. As the man continued to take small steps, the tower began to burrow into the earth. This dream was followed by the patient's acknowledgement of her own greed and narcissism, which she had hitherto named as characteristics of the "brothers". There could in my view hardly be a better representation of the small steps necessary for the integration of splits without the generation of excessive persecution feelings.

The patient as the analyst's best colleague

More than four years had passed since the beginning of Carla's analysis, and it seemed to me that things were moving, but then something happened that took me a long time to make sense of. Just before the summer holidays, Carla told me that she had been in touch with the psychiatry department of a university clinic in a nearby town, a unit well known for its organicist approach. I connected this decision with the approach of the holidays and with her need for containment and a point of reference (although in the past, whenever holiday time came, I had given her the name of a colleague who would be available in emergency). I imagined that the problem would disappear once the sessions resumed.

But come September, Carla told me she had decided to go into hospital for a period of in-depth diagnosis. I was flabbergasted. Carla was admitted to hospital, but was allowed out for her regular sessions.

At this juncture something began that I was unable to explain for a long time and that I experienced as an attack on the analysis. The hospital's diagnosis had been "panic attacks", for which "analysis was contraindicated"; she was treated with drugs, with serious consequences and side effects.

The analysis was—or at least, so it seemed to me—increasingly called into question and the threat that it might be broken off hung over it. A repetitive element entered the sessions, and my interpretations were based on the idea of negative therapeutic reactions, attacks on the analysis, terror at change, envy, and impasse—at any rate indicating some kind of fracture in communication (Barale & Ferro, 1992; Ferro, 1993).

The climate constantly worsened. The risk of interruption of the analysis seemed to me to loom ever closer. Carla's fellow patients in hospital appeared in the sessions—in particular, and increasingly, Daniele, a boy who was seriously ill, paralysed by obsessions and phobias.

I continued to listen to her account "on the external level", as if Carla were telling me something external to the analysis. After a long period of anguish, I suddenly came upon a new point of view; the way I had interpreted with Carla since September appeared to me to have been quite absurd. I said to her that perhaps she had put on everything that had happened, or rather that she had made happen, since September with the deliberate aim of telling me its analysis—the same analysis, but from a different point of view—and that sometimes, when she was full of panic, analysis was contraindicated because it was too painful; it was up to me to receive it better and contain it, and to realise that my words were like drugs that had serious side effects, and above all that the *hospitalisation* was to be understood as a way of bringing into this room, in their own right, the most suffering aspects of herself, precisely so as to make it possible to tell of them and to make them visible.

In this was I again became able to see Carla's communications as communications in our relationship. The climate of the session changed from one moment to the next. Carla eagerly set about describing her fellow patients at the clinic and she re-entered into possession of her analysis. Soon afterwards she was discharged from hospital. For my part, I recognised her need to bring into the analysis "psychiatric hospital aspects", about which she had no other means of telling me, and to which I had been unable to give sufficient space; her acting out had been necessary in order to find this "place". Carla then told me that she had met a "strong and reliable young man", to whom she was getting engaged.

She confirmed that her admission to hospital had also been a way of protecting herself from excessive pain, as well as, in particular, of opening up new spaces for thinkability.

The following material is taken from a session during this period.

P: May I have something to drink?

A: Perhaps you are missing yesterday's "water"? (a reference in our usual language to the lack of a session on the previous day).

P: Of course. But why are you making such a face?

A: What sort of a face?

P: Detached, as if you were going to Palermo, or like a mother telling a child she is no longer its mother but a paid employee.

A: (I reflected in amazement that the cancellation of a session, which I was yet to announce to her, and about which she could not have known, was due to a seminar that I was to attend precisely in Sicily.) You mean you are afraid I am "detached", "far away", not really here for you?

P: Exactly. That's it, but I have a question for you. And don't give me that analyst's crap for an answer. Who else can I ask but you? I want to know if I am male or female. Roberto, whom I don't understand because he is very fond of me, told me at the restaurant that I remind him of one of those girls in old westerns, full of pep, red-haired, freckled and with a pigtail … who needs to be picked up and given a spanking … and that it is exactly the kind of woman he likes. OK, but am I male or female?

A: (I felt it would be premature to interpret sexually because the level involved was much more primitive: "male" meant "needing to evacuate projective identifications" ($\male$) and "female" stood for "capable of accepting interpretations" ($\female$).) OK, I can tell you, putting it in your terms, that it is certainly not easy to tame you … we have already talked about the efforts of "Petruchio" (a reference to the male hero of *The Taming of the Shrew*).

P: But I am making an effort … because I love Roberto, to dress in a skirt … to put on a fur coat … to do my hair nicely … I am making a terrible effort …

A: (Here again, I felt it inappropriate to mention problems of sexual identity, castration anxiety or penis envy; I felt that we were speaking principally from a mental position tolerant of dependence and receptivity.) And perhaps too, it is "because you love me and with an effort" that you agree to abide by the rules ... to lie down on the couch ... and to respect the end of the sessions ... I must tell you something—that ...

P: Wait ... wait (with an air of anxiety—of panic). Not now ... not now.

A: I am remembering those terrified children when they had to have an injection ...

P: Wait ... wait ... I am having a panic fit ... because I thought you were going to tell me that there would be no session on Friday ...

A: As soon as something to do with detachment and loss arises, you have a fit of panic ... that really does not equip you properly to face up to these things. The problem is that I cannot be here next Friday at 7.30 p.m.

P: Can we have the session at another time?

A: Certainly: at 10.30 that morning.

P: I am full of drugs today. I have been to see Dr. Pivati ... he told me he wanted to make me relax with autogenic training ... I said to him that, if he touched me, I would kill him ... and then I took to my heels ... I wanted to talk about the analysis, but I cannot stand it ...

A: I am now Dr. Pivati, who is touching you, and talking about the analysis ... who is making you have a fit of panic ... and you want to kill me.

P: Roberto and I had a trial of strength with our arms ... he won ... he is stronger.

A: You felt exploited by our communication, which you are forced to accept.

P: I have two—no, three—dreams. In the first I was running away in terror; in the second my mother wanted to marry Roberto; and in the third Roberto was with another girl—it was like playing Monopoly (a board game in which each player must have cards for different plots of land or roads in the right order so as to build houses or hotels); he was not giving me the things I needed to build houses.

A: It seems that you are running away from me when I inflict violence on you by taking away the session that is dearest to you, the Friday evening session, like the mother taking away the person who is dearest to you, and when I go away I cheat on you and don't give you the four cards/sessions in the right place, which you need to build houses.

P: (on her way out) Thank you for the Friday morning session.

Commentary

I had indeed come along to the session "cluttered up" with worries about how to break the news of the missed session to her; that is perhaps why I was defending myself and had adopted a more detached attitude or expression. Carla, who has a particular capacity to "read inside me", had immediately noticed my less receptive mental state and pointed it out to me.

I usually choose the end of a session to tell patients about holidays, cancelled sessions or other matters; however, in Carla's case, because I knew that any change in the setting gave rise to intense anxieties connected with the "agglutinated nucleus" (Bleger, 1967) that was stratified within the setting, I preferred to make such communications within the session. This allowed time for immediate metabolisation of these anxieties and did not leave her to deal with them alone, which might have resulted in acting out. I do not usually "replace" sessions I have to cancel, but I chose to do so with Carla, because I knew that she could not endure a week with only three sessions.

At this point I attributed the panic attacks mainly to the breaking of the symbiotic link; I had not yet understood the importance of the element of unexpected activation of uncontainable emotions by which she felt flooded and swept away with no possibility of escape.

However, the choice of "replacing" the missed session had consequences of its own. Standing outside the door at the beginning of the replacement session, Carla motioned me to go into the consulting room first, contrary to our normal practice; I made a mental note of this, while moving further aside to allow her to precede me as usual.

She then began the session by telling me about a friend of hers who suffered from panic attacks; she wondered—mentioning the names— which analyst she should send her to, Dr. X, Dr. Y or Dr. Z. She then described a rectal exploration she had had to undergo prior to a painful operation.

Some dreams then followed: she was dancing so well that someone fell madly in love with her and wanted to be with her always; then there was an analyst who did not have a degree, but he was good, so she left her own analyst for him, and the analyst who did not yet have a degree in turn left his fiancée for her, because she danced so well and caused men to lose their heads.

I was now able to interpret to Carla that she did not know whether to see the cancellation of the session as painful surgery to which she had to submit (the operation and the rectal exploration) or to imagine that, because I had given her the replacement session, I had lost my head for her, that I had fallen madly in love (the implication of having lost my head), and wanted nothing other than to be with her. The trouble was that then I would have to "go into the room first", which meant that our roles would be exchanged: I would be the patient and she the one who was to cure me, the madman.

But in this case, to whom—to which analyst—should she send her friend—a part of herself—who was suffering from panic attacks? That, of course, had been her history: having to look after parents while no one took care of her—a root cause of the panic attacks.

Insight and transformation: what comes out of the cracks—monsters or nascent thoughts?

At the same time as her new boyfriend "Roberto", whom she trusted and was very fond of, a teenage boy she had met in the hospital now took the stage, as mentioned earlier, and became more significant; she drew close to him and looked after him increasingly.

The panic attacks now tended to come on suddenly and to disrupt Carla's normal activities; meanwhile she had resumed her studies, graduated, got officially engaged to Roberto and was planning to get married. She also began doing odd jobs. But all of a sudden a "panic attack" would come on, characterised by terror, sweating, vertigo, fear of fainting, tachycardia, and extrasystoles.

Increasingly taking the form of "panic attacks of the heart", they started occurring in the sessions, putting her more in touch with unexpectedly activated emotions. Any change in the room, however slight, was now liable to trigger one: a new carpet at the entrance, an armchair or seat slightly out of place. I thought of the agglutinated nucleus and the way in which it is deposited in the setting, and in which, as Bleger (1967) says, it is activated by the slightest of violations of the setting.

Carla then found a "key" in the family's old property; it was made of iron (*ferro* in Italian, which is also my surname), was said by antique dealers to be several centuries old, and would presumably unlock some door in an unexplored cellar somewhere underneath the house.

She and her fiancé eagerly set about exploring the property.

I was also struck by the fact that, whenever Carla entered the consulting room for her sessions, she noted every detail, every smell, and seemed to be looking for something, for some trace.

I abstained from immediate interpretation, because I felt that something important was taking shape. The focus of attention shifted to Daniele and his admission to hospital for a brain operation. Carla described Daniele's pathology to me: he lived in a constant state of panic and terror, had to control everything, and exhibited avoidance behaviour because the tiniest of stimuli, changes, unexpected things or emotions, triggered indescribable terror within him.

I now felt the time had come to put things together: now that she trusted me—as she trusted her fiancé—she really could use the "iron (ferro) key" (my interpretations) to explore her cellars and make contact there with her most catastrophic anxieties: "Daniele" was nothing other than the *way* she could tell both me and herself about her panic and terror.

Her response to my interpretation was intense in the extreme: she had an experience of bodily transformation, for a few moments living and feeling herself to be Daniele, with Daniele's face; she met with and recognised every one of Daniele's states as her own.

A fertile period of work ensued, during which Carla's terrors and fears gradually moved out of her external life and increasingly found a place in the analysis.

One dream played a vital part in the further metabolisation of these aspects: as she calmly entered a room, all of a sudden out of cracks in the wall came monsters, which, however, were made of foam rubber, but dangerous all the same … they came out shooting … if you were hit, you would be infected by a virus and have to be isolated … She said that she had then woken up in terror, but had fallen asleep again immediately because she had wanted to deal with the situation. The dream had continued as soon as she had gone back to sleep: she had confronted the monsters, she could not remember how, but in the company of her fiancé, and the monsters had dissolved. After a short silence, I was about to say something, when I saw that Carla's expression had changed and her face was distorted: I asked what was happening. "Nothing … nothing … Or rather … it occurred to me that I was rather pleased to have told you the dream and to be here, so pleased that I would have liked to come into your arms ... but that is not possible in analysis ... so I felt disappointed, hurt and humiliated; I felt like crying".

I interpreted that we had been given the opportunity to live out the dream directly: first there had been feelings of calm and pleasure, but then the "monster" had been activated; the "*crack*" of my brief silence had been enough to make her fear that her burst of communication had not been received and that I was keeping her at a distance: the monster was the fear of rejection by me ... it was a "foam-rubber" monster from her childhood ... but, if we could together confront this terror of being rejected and not wanted, we would be able to defeat it and make it disappear.

Carla now calmed down and the session continued with the possibility of making her see other "monsters" that had been activated. We also understood how for a long time, so as not to be "infected" by the monsters, she had indulged in behaviour aimed at avoiding or magically cancelling out negative thoughts about me or the analysis that came into her mind; these thoughts had first made their appearance in the analysis in the form of the avoidance behaviour of the "character Daniele", and had subsequently emerged directly in the consulting room as places inside it that Carla had to avoid at all costs, so that she made strange detours to reach the couch. It was now possible to confront these monsters and discover their infantile roots. A long period of work on the "monsters"—on all the emotions *activated by any fracture in communication*—then ensued.

If anything sounded to her like a criticism, or if she thought she might have criticised me, then she was afraid that we might hate each other and tear each other to pieces. So everything had to be gone back over again. That applied to any emotions that were activated—not only jealousy and hate, but also love and passion. At first these were all extremely dangerous monsters, which she was afraid were *limitless*, except that she was able to discover from time to time that they could be confronted and metabolised.

Symbiosis—or rather the old wish for symbiosis—was seen as a protection against these terrors; it was necessary (as portrayed in a dream) to construct *a stomach to digest fiery food*, to allow affects and feelings instead of turbulent emotional vortices to emerge from the cracks.

In her dreams, the "cracks" gradually became a place for the budding of flowers and plants, emerging among what had appeared to be sterile cobblestones.

From the here and now to history and the outside world

Now that Carla had a *stomach-mind that could contain and metabolise emotions*—as we shall see, this is what Bion in *Learning from Experience* calls the "apparatus of 'thinking'"—it henceforth became possible in her analysis to shuttle back and forth between the here and now of the sessions and the rediscovery of a childhood history that had profoundly marked her; this could not have been done without the diminution of the violent emotional turbulence inside her.

It was the history of a passionate little girl who had never met with an appropriate response or had a container to facilitate the process of transformation. From a very early age, she had taken refuge in religion and had intended, as soon as she was old enough, to become a nun "in an enclosed order". For this purpose she had for a long time associated with religious communities, where, however, she had always found herself the target of violent attacks: she had been beaten, ill-treated and more than once almost sexually assaulted.

We reconstructed a childhood history in which she had increasingly had to split off her own emotions and passions, to the point of building a "cloister" to protect herself; but sometimes these split-off emotions nevertheless came home to roost, acted out by various characters (cooks, sextons or gardeners), whom she had unconsciously provoked or seduced.

As an alternative to the "convent", in her teens there had been long periods of sexual promiscuity, nights on the tiles, and nights spent with tramps, prostitutes, and drug addicts under the city's bridges. None of this had induced the parents to intervene in any way. The mother, tired, despondent and herself at grips with a mother suffering from serious manic-depressive psychosis, had been struggling to avoid falling into a severe depression of her own.

Carla had then toned down these aspects of herself, even regaining control over them by long periods of expiation and religious practices, until the split-off aspects burst forth again uncontrollably.

She remembered a recurring childhood dream: she was on a small island that suddenly caught fire and there was nowhere she could escape to. The panic attacks thus resulted from the irruption of passions and proto-emotions into a mind that was literally on fire, without any possibility of escape, there being no parents to help contain these burning emotional states.

However, it had not been possible to work through the oedipal aspects of Carla's history either; her father had so feared contact of any kind that he had forbidden her, even when she was a little girl, to hold his hand, in case anyone in the street thought she was his young lover. Meanwhile, the mother had imposed the strictest of silence on her children in regard to their problems or difficulties, because she was afraid that her husband might die and that she would be left behind without any means of support.

There was, of course, a constant counterpoint between the here and now and historical reconstruction. The here and now became the place in which it was possible to work through what was being repeated, with a view to accommodating it appropriately in the history; the historical baggage was gradually enriched, while at the same time Carla's present life became increasingly free of the shadows of the past.

I shall now give a brief account of the development of Carla's external life up to this point in the analysis. About a year into the analysis, Carla began to do odd jobs, even working as a cleaning lady despite her father's professional background; she then took a position as a "night porter" in a rather shady hotel; and finally she resumed her philosophy studies, which she had broken off a long time before, obtaining a brilliant degree with a thesis on the "psychology of children of junior school age".

After a number of love affairs, some of them tempestuous in the extreme (always connected with phases in the evolution of the transference), two years later Carla married Roberto, a young public official, and moved to a town not far from Pavia. She now normally comes to her sessions by car, train, or coach, no longer a prey to the terror of panic attacks. Last year she gave birth to a little girl, whom she cares for with great devotion.

The panic attacks have gradually diminished in intensity and frequency in her external life, finding a place in the analytic consulting room instead. The more it has become possible to pinpoint their meaning and onset in the sessions, the more they have continued to decline. During the last summer holiday break, Carla did not have a single panic attack.

They recently recurred in the analysis when I told her that I was going to have to cancel her sessions for the next two weeks, but disappeared again as soon as the normal rhythm was resumed.

Considerations of space preclude an account of the meaning of all the aspects of Carla's external life for the analysis, but there was certainly not a single communication that did not have a meaning assigned to it in the consulting room, before being reattached to other, sometimes external, entities.

I should also like to mention briefly Carla's psychiatric history. Before the analysis she had been treated with drugs and had had behaviour therapy, but without any lasting benefit. For the first two years or so of the analysis, she had also—with my consent—been in the care of a psychiatrist colleague, who had prescribed drugs for her. I had always preserved my position as an analyst, trying to understand "what" was the nature of the drug that Carla told me about "in the sessions"; mostly it was "an antidepressant", made up of minor infringements and transgressions of the setting (not lying down on the couch, or delaying the end of the session by a few minutes). As the analysis progressed, both the drugs and the transgressions of the setting gradually disappeared from the scene.

Discussion

The implicit theoretical model on which this paper is based is that of Bion, combined with the concept of the field due to Baranger & Baranger (1961–1962) and Baranger, Baranger & Mom (1983).

In *Learning from Experience*, Bion (1962b) has already provided us with a provisional, unsaturated model of the mind, a central function of which is the elaboration of "sensory impressions" and "emotions" (i.e., perceptual stimuli of any kind and origin—so-called β-elements) into α-elements, which are like pictograms, which are therefore visual, and which synthesise in images every instant of relations with self and others. (There are also non-visual—that is, acoustic or kinaesthetic— α-elements, but for simplicity Bion says that these can be disregarded, adding that what applies to visual-type α-elements also applies to all the other types.)

This transformation of β-elements into α-elements is wrought by an unknown factor, with only some of whose constituents we are familiar; it is, of course, what Bion calls the a function. The α-elements are placed in order and form the "dream thoughts" and the "unconscious waking thought" that accompanies all our mental operations, even during the daytime, without our being aware of it. Once formed, the α-elements may belong to the conscious or the unconscious system; at any rate, they constitute the building blocks of thoughts.

Once the "thoughts" have been formed—by the process described above, namely: (sensoriality/emotions/β-elements)—α-elements—unconscious waking thoughts—Bion (1962b) postulates the necessity of a system, and more precisely of an "*apparatus of 'thinking'*". In the absence of this "apparatus", or if it is deficient or its capacity is exceeded, thoughts are treated like b-elements and therefore evacuated.

Bion (1962b, 1970) thus distinguishes two "loci" of pathology. In the first and more severe locus, the a function is deficient (so that the subject is unable to transform sensoriality and emotional turbulence into α-elements and consequently evacuates β-elements, giving rise to hallucinatory or psychosomatic pathologies or characteropathies), whereas the second, in which the a function is intact, is observed when the "apparatus of 'thinking'" has insufficient capacity to handle and cope with thoughts that have already been formed.

In terms of these concepts, it seems to me that, at the beginning of the analysis, Carla needed her panic attacks in order to evacuate the part of her emotions that she was unable to metabolise (into α-elements), or, put differently, to envisage mentally or symbolise. She therefore had a deficiency of the a function, or at least of the "apparatus of 'thinking'" (Bion, 1962b, 1963), which gave rise to the evacuation of emotions that were not yet thinkable.

The only alternative to the evacuation of β-elements (sometimes acted out in Carla's characteropathic behaviour) was their encapsulation through the singular feature of an inelastic, rigid container that Meltzer (1992) called the "claustrum".

When Carla found in the sessions that her proto-mental states (Bion, 1965) were being received in a way that allowed transformation, it became possible for these states to be gradually transformed in the direction of thinkability (a b), but also, and in particular, for an effective a function and an efficient "apparatus of 'thinking'" to be progressively introjected (♂♀; PS D).

This involved both a gradual transformation of emotional turbulence in the direction of thought and the replacement of the claustrum by a ductile container capable of performing transformations, thereby permitting the operations defined by Bion as the development of ♀, of ♂, and of ♂ (Bion, 1962b).

Great importance therefore attaches to the quality of the analyst's reverie in the session, and to his tolerance for receiving the patient's emotions, which are often conveyed by projective identification, as well as his capacity to modulate interpretations in accordance with their tolerability to the patient; an overdose of interpretation generates persecution, because it overtaxes the "apparatus of 'thinking'".

The concept of the field due to Baranger & Baranger (1961–1962) and to Baranger, Baranger and Mom (1983) helped me to see the theme emerging at any given time as stemming from the current interaction with the patient (Ferro, 1991; Bezoari & Ferro, 1991). For this concept focuses on the mental functioning of both patient and analyst, and implies that transformations are possible only if that of both members of the analytic couple is modified. However, I have discussed this subject many times.

To conclude, there are different ways of understanding the "characters" who appear in each session, according to the reference model used. They may be seen either as having mainly historical and external relevance or predominantly as internal objects of the patient, which may also be projected in the transference, or else as an expression of the internal group formed by the patient, the analyst and their constant interaction. The latter conception greatly reduces the importance of the historical aspect and the idea that these characters belong solely to the patient's internal world, so that they become mainly an expressive, narrative modality of the emotional movements taking place in the consulting room.

In my understanding, the character can become a function, a derivative, an expression or a form of naming of the modality of mental functioning of the analytic couple, which is modified, changed, transformed, and leaves or takes the stage in accordance with the variations of the relational and interactive situation within the consulting room (Ferro, 1991, 1993).

My theorisation of this view is based on Bion's conceptualisation of the α-elements as visual; the characters, stories and anecdotes presented by patients could also be considered as narrative derivatives of α-elements (Ferro, 1994).

This last way of conceiving the characters, of course, alternates with other conceptions of them (as historical figures or internal objects).

However, the "character" also becomes the entity that permits the weaving of a narrative fabric that will lead to insight on the part of the analyst or the patient (Bezoari & Ferro, 1991, 1992).

"Daniele" enters the field in order to make it possible to tell of the deep mental states of the patient, but also of those of the analytic couple while it is still avoiding the monsters, when the "stomach" ("apparatus of 'thinking'") has not yet developed sufficiently, so that it even has to leave the stage when the lumps of unthinkability of which it is composed begin to be digested.

In our view, the linguistic emotional text woven with the patient— what Faimberg (1989) calls "listening to listening"—can also show when the process has "gone astray" and the "transformational richness" has been lost; this may occur when, at some place or time in the relationship (a dream by the patient, a countertransference dream, material brought by the patient, images of the analyst's own, acting in, acting out etc.), there emerge drifting lumps of β-elements that are not received and transformed, or anxieties and proto-emotional states, which, however, must *necessarily* be received and transformed in order to give rise to a b a trend.

I believe that the foregoing justifies the constant attention to the tiniest details of the session and the here and now of the relationship; it shows that the right approach is not to use saturated, exhaustive interpretations, but to share with the patient a working method that can be introjected and does not involve the decoding of pre-existent equivalents, but instead the construction of meanings that can be shared.

REFERENCES

Ahbel-Rappe, K. (2010). Book review: *Partners in Thought: Working with Unformulated Experience, Dissociation and Enactment*. By Donnel B. Stern. New York: Routledge, 2009, xx + 229 pp. *Journal of the American Psychoanalytical Association, 58*: 797–804.

Angelino, L. (2005). Note sul dialogo tra Merleau-Ponty e Melanie Klein [Some notes concerning the dialogue between Merleau-Ponty and Melanie Klein]. *Chiasmi International, 6*: 369–381.

Aulagnier, P. (1975). *The Violence of Interpretation: From Pictogram to Statement.* (A. Sheridan. Trans.) Hove, England: Brunner-Routledge, 2001.

Bachelard, G. (1960). *The Poetics of Reverie: Childhood, Language, and the Cosmos.* Boston, MA: Beacon, 1971.

Barale, F. (2011). Postfazione [Afterword]. In: G. Civitarese, *La Violenza delle Emozioni. Bion e la Psicoanalisi Postbioniana* (pp. 185–198). Milan, Italy: Raffaello Cortina.

Barale, R. & Ferro, A. (1992). Negative therapeutic reactions and microfractures in analytic communication. In: L. Nissim Momigliano & A. Robutti (Eds.), *Shared Experience: the Psychoanalytic Dialogue* (pp. 143–165). London: Karnac.

Baranger, M. (2005). Field theory. In: S. Lewkowicz & S. Flechner (Eds.), *Truth, Reality and the Psychoanalyst: Latin American Contributions to Psychoanalysis* (pp. 49–71). London: International Psychoanalytical Association.

191

Baranger, M., & Baranger, W., & Mom, J. (1983). Process and non-process in analytic work. *International Journal Psychoanalysis, 64*: 1–15.

Baranger, W. (2008). The analytic situation as a dynamic field. *International Journal of Psychoanalysis, 89*: 795–826.

Baranger, W. & Baranger, M. (1961–1962). The analytic situation as a dynamic field. *International Journal of Psychoanalysis, 89*: 795–826 (2008).

Benjamin, J. (1999). A note on the dialectic: Commentary on paper by Bruce E. Reis. *Psychoanalytic Dialogues, 9*: 395–399.

Berger, J. (2001). *The Shape of a Pocket*. New York, NY: Pantheon.

Berger, J. (2004). *Modi di Vedere*. Turin, Italy: Bollati Boringhieri.

Berger, J. & Berger, K. (2010). *Lying Down to Sleep*. Mantua, Italy: Corraini Edizioni.

Bezoari, M. & Ferro, A. (1989). Listening, interpretations and transformative functions in the analytical dialogue. *Rivista di Psicoanalisi, 35*: 1014–1050.

Bezoari, M. & Ferro, A. (1991). From a play between "parts" to transformations in the couple. Psychoanalysis in a bipersonal field. In: L. Nissim Momigliano & A. Robutti (Eds.), *Shared Experience: The Psychoanalytic Dialogue* (pp. 43–65). London: Karnac, 1992.

Bezoari, M. & Ferro, A. (1992). El sueño dentro de una teoria del campo. Agregados funcionales y narraciones. *Rev Psicoanál, 49*: 957–977.

Bick, E. (1968). The experience of the skin in the early object-relations. *International Journal Psychoanalysis, 49*: 484–486.

Bion, W. R. (1948). *Experiences in Groups and Other Papers*. London: Tavistock, 1961.

Bion, W. R. (1956). Development of schizophrenic thought. In: *Second thoughts* (pp. 36–42). London: Heinemann, 1967.

Bion, W. R. (1961). *Experiences in Groups and Other Papers*. London: Tavistock.

Bion, W. R. (1962a). A theory of thinking. *International Journal of Psycho-Analysis, 43*: 306–310.

Bion, W. R. (1962b). *Learning from Experience*. London: Tavistock.

Bion, W. R. (1963). *Elements of Psycho-Analysis*. London: Karnac, 1984.

Bion, W. R. (1965). *Transformations: Change from Learning to Growth*. London: Heinemann.

Bion, W. R. (1967). *Second Thoughts. Selected Papers on Psycho-analysis*. London: Heinemann.

Bion, W. R. (1970). *Attention and Interpretation. A Scientific Approach to Insight in Psycho-Analysis and Groups*. London: Karnac, 1984.

Bion, W. R. (1977). *A Memoir of the Future. Book 2: The Past Presented*, London: Karnac.

Bion, W. R. (1978). *Four Discussions with W. R. Bion*. Perthshire: Clunie Press.

Bion, W. R. (1985). *The Italian Seminars*. (F. Bion (Ed.). London: Karnac, 2005.

Bion, W. R. (1987). *Clinical Seminars and Four Papers*. Abingdon: Fleetwood.

Bion, W. R. (1992). *Cogitations*. London: Karnac.

Bion, W. R. (1997). *Taming Wild Thoughts*. London: Karnac.

Bion, W. R. (2005a). *The Tavistock Seminars*. London: Karnac.

Bion, W. R. (2005b). *The Italian Seminars*. London: Karnac.

Bion, W. R. & Rickman, J. (1943). Intra-group tension in therapy—Their study as a task of the group. *The Lancet*, 27 November 1943.

Bleger, J. (1967). *Symbiosis and Ambiguity: The Psychoanalysis of Very Early Development*, (C. Trollope, (Ed,)). London: Free Association Books, 1990.

Butler, J. (1990). *Gender Trouble: Feminism and the Subversion of Identity*. New York, NY: Routledge.

Carbone, M. (2008). *Proust et les Idées Sensibles*. Paris: Vrin.

Churcher, J. (2008). Some notes on the English translation of *The Analytic Situation as a Dynamic Field* by Willy and Madeleine Baranger. *International Journal of Psychoanalysis, 89*: 785–793.

Civitarese, G. (2004). The symbiotic bond and the setting. In: *The Intimate Room: Theory and Technique of the Analytic Field* (pp. 22–49). London: The New Library of Psychoanalysis, Routledge, 2011.

Civitarese, G. (2006). Dreams that mirror the session. *International Journal of Psychoanalysis, 87*: 703–723.

Civitarese, G. (2007). Bion e a demanda da ambigu idade [Bion and the problem of ambiguity]. *Revista de Psicanalise, 14*: 57–76.

Civitarese, G. (2008a). *The Intimate Room: Theory and Technique of the Analytic Field*. London: Routledge, 2011.

Civitarese, G. (2008b). "Caesura" as Bion's discourse on method. *Internatioanl Journal of Psychoanalysis, 89*: 1123–1143.

Civitarese, G. (2011a). *The Violence of Emotions. Bion and Post-Bionian Psychoanalysis*. London: Routledge, 2012.

Civitarese, G. (2011b). The unconscious. What is your theory of unconscious processes? What are other theories that you would contrast with your conceptualization? *International Journal of Psychoanalysis, 92*: 277–280.

Civitarese, G. (2012). *Perdere la testa. abiezione, conflitto estetico e critica psicoanalitica [Losing One's Head: Abjection, Aesthetic Conflict and Psychoanalytic Criticism]*. Florence: Clinamen.

Civitarese, G. (2013a). The inaccessible unconscious and reverie as a path of figurability. In: H. Levine, D. Scarfone & G. Reed (Eds.), *Unrepresented States and the Construction of Meaning: Clinical and Theoretical Contributions* (pp. 220–239). London: Karnac.

Civitarese, G. (2013b). *The Necessary Dream: New Theories and Techniques of Interpretation in Psychoanalysis*. London: Karnac.

Civitarese, G. (2014). Transformations in hallucinosis and the receptivity of the analyst. *International Journal of Psychoanalysis*. Online edition, http://onlinelibrary.wiley.com/doi/10.1111/1745-8315.12242/abstract [last accessed 10 December 2014].

Conci, M. (2011). Bion and his first analyst, John Rickman (1891–1951)—A revisitation of their relationship in the light of Rickman's personality and scientific production and of Bion's letters to him (1939–1951). *International Forum of Psychoanalysis, 20*: 68–86.

de Beistegui, M. (2010). Per un'estetica della metafora. In: D. Ferrari & P. Godani (Eds.), *La Sartoria di Proust* (pp. 17–46). Pisa, Italy: Edizioni ETS.

Derrida, J. (1967). *Of Grammatology*. Baltimore, MA: John Hopkins University Press.

Derrida, J. (2008). The spatial arts: An interview with Jacques Derrida. In: P. Brunette & D. Wills (Eds.), *Deconstruction and the Visual Arts: Art, Media, Architecture*. Cambridge: Cambridge University Press.

Eco, U. (1984). *Semiotics and the Philosophy of Language*. Bloomington, IN: Indiana University Press, 1986.

Etchegoyen, H. (1991). *The Fundamentals of Psychoanalytic Technique*. London: Karnac.

Faimberg, H. (1989). Sans memoire et sans dsir: qui s'adressait Bion? *Revue Française de Psychanalyse, 53*: 1453–1461.

Ferro, A. (1991). From raging bull to Theseus: the long path of a transformation. *International Journal of Psychoanalysis, 72*: 417–425.

Ferro, A. (1992). *The Bi-Personal Field: Experiencing Child Analysis*. New York: Routledge, 1999.

Ferro, A. (1993). The impasse within a theory of the analytic field: possible vertices of observation. *International Journal of Psychoanalysis, 74*: 917–929.

Ferro, A. (1994). Il dialogo analitico: costituzione e trasformazione di mondi possibili. *Rivista di Psicoanalisi, 40*: 389–409.

Ferro, A. (1999). *Psychoanalysis as Therapy and Storytelling*. London and New York: Routledge, 2006.

Ferro, A. (2002a). Some implications of Bion's thought: The waking dream and narrative derivatives. *International Journal of Psychoanalysis, 83*: 597–607.

Ferro, A. (2002b). *Seeds of Illness, Seeds of Recovery: The Genesis of Suffering and the Role of Psychoanalysis*. London: Routledge, 2004.

Ferro, A. (2006). *Mind Works: Technique and Creativity in Psychoanalysis*. Hove: England: Routledge, 2008.

Ferro, A. (2007). *Avoiding Emotions, Living Emotions*. London: Routledge, 2011.

Ferro, A. (2009). Transformations in dreaming and characters in the psychoanalytic field. *International Journal of Psychoanalysis, 90*: 209–230.

Ferro, A. (2010). *Tormenti di Anime. Passioni, Sintomi, Sogni* [Soul Torments: Passions, Symptoms, and Dreams]. Milan: Raffaello Cortina.

Ferro, A. & Basile, R., (Eds.). (2009). *The Analytic Field. A Clinical Concept.* New York: Routledge.

Ferro, A., Civitarese, G., Collovà, M., Foresti, G., Molinari, E., Mazzacane, F. & Politi, P. (2007). *Sognare l'analisi. Sviluppi Clinici del Pensiero di Wilfred R Bion.* Turin: Boringhieri.

Ferro, N. (1996). *In the Analyst's Consulting Room.* London and New York, NY: Psychology Press, 2002.

Ferro, N. (2007). Review of *The Tavistock Seminars; The Italian Seminars* by W. R. Bion. *International Journal of Psychoanalysis, 88*: 551–555.

Fielding, H. A. (1999). Envisioning the other. Lacan and Merleau-Ponty on intersubjectivity. In: D. Olkowski & J. Morley (Eds.), *Merleau-Ponty, Interiority and Exteriority, Psychic Life and the World* (pp. 185–199). Albany, NY: State University of New York Press.

Fornaro, M. (1990). *Psicoanalisi tra Scienza e Mistica. L'opera di Wilfred R. Bion.* Rome: Edizioni Studium.

Freud, S. (1891). *On Aphasia: A Critical Study.* New York: International University Press, 1953.

Freud, S. (1912). Recommendations to physicians practising psychoanalysis. SE 12.

Freud, S. (1912–1913). *Totem and Taboo.* SE 13.

Freud, S. (1913). The claims of psycho-analysis to scientific interest. SE 13.

Freud, S. (1914). Remembering, repeating and working-through (Further recommendations on the technique of psycho-analysis, II. SE 12.

Freud, S. (1915). On Transience. SE, 14.

Freud, S. (1917). *Introductory Lectures on Psycho-Analysis.* SE 15–16.

Freud, S. (1921). Psycho-analysis and telepathy. SE 18.

Freud, S. (1938). Findings, ideas, problems. SE 23.

Freud, S. (1950 [1895]). *Project for a Scientific Psychology.* SE 1.

Freud, S. (1985). *The Complete Letters of Sigmund Freud to Wilhelm Fliess, 1887–1904.* (J. M. Masson, Ed. and Trans.). Cambridge, MA: Belknap Press of Harvard University Press.

Green, A. (1992). *The Work of the Negative.* London: Free Association, 1999.

Grinberg, L. (1957). Perturbaciones en la interpretación por la contraidentificación proyectiva. *Revista de Psicoanálise, 14*: 23–30.

Grotstein, J. S. (2005). Projective transidentification. *International Journal of Psychoanalysis, 86*: 1051–1069.

Grotstein, J. S. (2007). *A Beam of Intense Darkness: Wilfred Bion's Legacy to Psychoanalysis*. London: Karnac.

Hofstadter, D. (2007). *I Am a Strange Loop*. New York: Basic Books.

Isaacs, S. (1948). The nature and function of phantasy. *International Journal of Psychoanalysis, 29*: 73–97.

Joseph, B. (1985). Transference: the total situation. *International Journal of Psychoanalysis, 66*: 447–454.

Junkers, G. (Ed.) (2013). *The Empty Couch: The taboo of ageing and retirement in psychoanalysis*. London: Routledge.

Klein, M. (1923). The role of the school in the libidinal development of the child. In: *Contributions to Psycho-Analysis 1921–1945* (pp. 68–86). London: Hogarth, 1965.

Kojève, A. (1947). *Introduction to the Reading of Hegel*. New York: Basic Books, 1969.

Kristeva, J. (1974). *Revolution in Poetic Language*. New York: Columbia University Press, 1984.

Kristeva, J. (2000). *Melanie Klein*. New York: Columbia University Press, 2001.

Kuhn, T. S. (1962). *The Structure of Scientific Revolutions*. Chicago: University of Chicago Press.

Lacan, J. (1947). British psychiatry and war. *Psychoanalytical Notebooks of the London Circle, 4*, Spring 2000: 9–34.

Lakoff, G. & Johnson, M. (1980). *Metaphors We Live By*. Chicago: University of Chicago Press.

Langs, R. (1973–1974). *The Technique of Psychoanalytic Psychotherapy*, Vol. I-II. New York: Jason Aronson.

León de Bernardi, B. (2008). Introduction to the paper by Madeleine and Willy Baranger: "The analytic situation as a dynamic field". *International Journal of Psychoanalysis, 89*: 773–784.

Levenson, E. (2009). The enigma of the transference. *Contemporary Psychoanalysis, 45*: 163–178.

Levine, H. B. (2010). *Partners in Thought: Working with Unformulated Experience, Dissociation, and Enactment*. By Donnel B. Stern. New York/London: Routledge, 2010, 229 pp. *Psychoanalytic Quarterly, 79*: 1166–1177.

Limentani, A. (1972). The assessment of analysability: a major hazard in selection for psychoanalysis. *International Journal Psychoanalysis, 53*: 352–361.

López Corvo, R. E. (2002). *The Dictionary of the Work of W. R. Bion*. London: Karnac, 2003.

Lussana, A. (1993). Antonino Ferro. *La Tecnica in Psicoanalisi Infantile. Il Bambino e l'analista: dalla Relazione al Campo Emotivo*. Milan: Cortina, 1992, 221 pp. *Journal of Child Psychotherapy, 19*: 107–111.

Meltzer, D. (1978). *The Kleinian Development. Part III. The Clinical Significance of the Work of Bion*. Perthshire: Clunie Press.

Meltzer, D. (1986). *Studies in Extended Metapsychology: Clinical Applications of Bion's Ideas*. London: Karnac, 2008.

Meltzer, D. (1992). *The Claustrum*. London: The Roland Harris Educational Trust.

Merleau-Ponty, M. (1945). *Phenomenology of Perception*. (C. Smith, Trans.). New York: Humanities Press, 1962.

Merleau-Ponty, M. (1948). *The World of Perception*. Abingdon: Routledge, 2004.

Merleau-Ponty, M. (1951). The child's relations with others. In: T. Toadvine & L. Lawlor (Eds.), *The Merleau-Ponty Reader* (pp. 143–184). Evanston, IL: Northwestern University Press, 2007.

Merleau-Ponty, M. (1961). Eye and mind. In: T. Toadvine & L. Lawlor (Eds.), *The Merleau-Ponty Reader* (pp. 351–378). Evanston, IL: Northwestern University Press, 2007.

Merleau-Ponty, M. (1964). *The Visible and the Invisible*. Evanston, IL: Northwestern University Press, 1968.

Mortara Garavelli, B. (2010). *Il Parlar Figurato. Manualetto di Figure Retoriche*. Bari, Italy: Laterza.

Murphy, A. (2008). Feminism and race theory. In: R. Diprose & J. Reynolds (Eds.), *Merleau-Ponty: Key Concepts* (pp. 197–206). Stocksfield: Acumen.

Neri, C. & Selvaggi, L. (2006). Campo. In: R. Barale (Eds.), *Psiche. Dizionario storico di psicologia, psichiatria, psicoanalisi, neuroscienze.* (pp. 180–185). Turin, Italy: Einaudi.

Nissim Momigliano, L. (2001). *L'ascolto rispettoso. Scritti psicoanalitici*. Milan: Raffaello Cortina.

Ogden, T. H. (1979). On projective identification. *International Journal of Psychoanalysis, 60*: 357–373.

Ogden, T. H. (1992). The dialectically constituted/decentred subject of psychoanalysis. II. The contributions of Klein and Winnicott. *International Journal of Psychoanalysis, 73*: 613–626.

Ogden, T. H. (1994a). The analytic third: Working with intersubjective clinical facts. *International Journal of Psychoanalysis, 75*: 3–19.

Ogden, T. H. (1994b). *Subjects of Analysis*. Northvale, NJ: Aronson.

Ogden, T. H. (2004). The analytic third: Implications for psychoanalytic theory and technique. *Psychoanalytic Quarterly, 73*: 167–95.

Ogden, T. H. (2005). *This Art of Psychoanalysis: Dreaming Undreamt Dreams and Interrupted Cries*. London: Routledge.

Ogden, T. H. (2007). On talking as dreaming. *International Journal Psychoanalysis, 88*: 575–589.

Ogden, T. H. (2008). *Rediscovering Psychoanalysis. Thinking and Dreaming, Learning and Forgetting*. London and New York: Routledge.

Ogden, T. H. (2012). *Creative Readings: Essays on Seminal Analytic Works*. London: Routledge.

Orange, D. M. (2010). Maurice Merleau-Ponty: Embodied intersubjectivity. In: *Thinking for Clinicians: Philosophical Resources for Contemporary Psychoanalysis and the Humanistic Psychotherapies* (pp. 55–76). New York: Routledge.

O'Shaughnessy, E. (2005). Whose Bion? *International Journal of Psychoanalysis, 86*: 1523–1528.

Peltz, R. (2012). Ways of hearing: Getting inside psychoanalysis. *Psychoanalytic Dialogues, 22*: 279–290.

Pontalis, J. -B. (2007). Penser l'intermédiaire. In: F. Gantheret (Ed.), *Le Royaume Intermédiaire. Psychanalyse, Littérature, Autour de J. -B. Pontalis* (pp. 313–320). Paris: Gallimard.

Proust, M. (1931). *Time Regained* (S. Hudson, Trans.). http://gutenberg.net.au/ebooks03/0300691.txt Last accessed 24 July 2014.

Puget, J. & Wender, L. (1987). Aux limites de l'analysabilité. Tyranie corporelle et sociale. *Revue Française de Psychoanalyse, 51*: 869–885.

Reis, B. E. (1999). Thomas Ogden's phenomenological turn. *Psychoanalytic Dialogues, 9*: 371–393.

Reynolds, J. (2004). *Merleau-Ponty and Derrida: Intertwining Embodiment and Alterity*. Athens, OH: Ohio University Press.

Rimbaud, A. (2002). *Rimbaud Complete*. New York: Modern Library Inc. (First published 1871).

Rothko, M. (2002). *Scritti* [Writings]. Milan: Abscondita.

Sandler, P. C. (2005). *The language of Bion*. London: Karnac.

Segal, H. (1954). A note on schizoid mechanisms underlying phobia formation. *International Journal of Psychoanalysis, 35*: 238–241.

Smith, H. (2013). Personal communication.

Stawarska, B. (2008). Psychoanalysis. In: *R. Diprose & J. Reynolds (Eds.), Merleau-Ponty: Key Concepts* (pp. 57–69). Stocksfield: Acumen.

Stern, D. B. (1997). *Unformulated Experience. From Dissociation to Imagination in Psychoanalysis*. Hillsdale, NJ: The Analytic Press.

Stern, D. B. (2013). Field theory in psychoanalysis, part II: Bionian field theory and contemporary interpersonal/relational psychoanalysis, by Donnel B. Stern. *Psychoanalytic Dialogues, 23*: 630–645.

Tarantino, Q. (2003). *Kill Bill*. USA.

Vanzago, L. (2012). *Merleau-Ponty*. Rome: Carocci.

Westen, D. (1999). The scientific status of unconscious processes: Is Freud really dead? *Journal American Psychoanalysis Association, 47*: 1061–1106.

Winnicott, D. W. (1945). Primitive emotional development. In: *From Paediatrics to Psychoanalysis* (pp. 145–156). New York, NY: Brunner-Routledge, 2006.

Winnicott, D. W. (1949). Birth memories, birth trauma and anxiety. In: *From Paediatrics to Psychoanalysis* (pp. 174–193). New York, NY: Brunner-Routledge, 2006.

Winnicott, D. W. (1956). On transference. *International Journal of Psychoanalysis, 37*: 386–388.

Winnicott, D. W. (1970). On the basis for self in body. In: C. Winnicott., R. Shepherd & M. Davis (Eds.), *Psycho-Analytic Explorations* (pp. 261–283). London: Karnac, 1989.

Winnicott, D. W. (1974). Fear of breakdown. *International Journal of Psychoanalysis, 1*: 103–107.

INDEX